JUST GOOD READING
from the pages of
THE CRITIC

JUST GOOD READING
from the pages of
THE CRITIC

edited by
KRIS TUBERTY

85981

THE THOMAS MORE PRESS
Chicago, Illinois

"Four Unpublished Early Masterpieces" by Miles Kington and "My Life With Hilaire Belloc" by Sylvia Hayman first appeared in PUNCH and are reprinted by permission of Punch Publications Ltd.

"I, Said The Sparrow" and "I Put My Foot Upon The Chair" are copyrighted © 1964 and © 1970 by Arthur J. Roth and are reprinted by permission of Harold Ober Associates Inc.

"That Was No Albatross," copyright © 1969 by Nelson Algren is reprinted by permission of Donadio & Ashworth, Inc.

"The Highwayman and the Saint" by Brian Friel appeared in THE GOLD AND THE SEA published by Doubleday & Co, Copyright © 1966 by Brian Friel and reprinted by permission of Curtis Brown, Ltd.

Copyright©1990 by the Thomas More Association. All rights reserved. Printed in the United States of America. No part of this publication may be reproduced, stored in a retrieval system, or transmitted in any form or by any means, electronic, mechanical, photocopying, recording, or otherwise, without the written permission of the publisher, The Thomas More Association, 205 West Monroe Street, Chicago, IL 60606-5097.

ISBN 0-88347-258-9

CONTENTS

Introduction — Kris Tuberty, 7

The Highwayman and the Saint — Brian Friel, 11

Catholic Eating — Joel Wells, 25

Teilhard de Chardin: The New York Years —
　John Deedy, 29

A Recipe for Catholic Worker Soup —
　Michael Garvey, 52

Confession — Stuart Dybeck, 55

I, Said the Sparrow — Arthur J. Roth, 57

The First Papal Press Conference — Andrew Greeley, 75

Irish and Catholic in the 1920s — Charles Rice, 90

On the Grass, Alas — Dan Herr, 104

Everything I Need — Peter Turchi, 108

Take a Number, Caesar — Joel Wells, 137

Death Row, Michael Posey, 140

The Cloak of Fortunatus — Samuel Hazo, 147

Never Gamble With a Man Named Doc —
Joel Wells, 150

Rome Wasn't Floundered in a Day — William Herr, 157

I Put My Foot Upon the Chair — Arthur J. Roth, 163

Why I Live Where I Live — Margo Howard, 171

Wedding Night — Bridget Kennedy, 181

A Rememberance of Wine and Roses —
John Deedy, 187

Four Unpublished Early Masterpieces —
Miles Kington, 204

The Very, Very Last of the Old Breed —
Richard Shaw, 212

The Arrogance of Evelyn Waugh — David Lodge, 222

Seven Fables For Our Times — Daniel Berrigan, 241

For Whom the Novelist Writes — Edwin O'Connor, 253

Oh Baby — Anthony L. Moore, 269

That Was No Albatross — Nelson Algren, 273

My Life With Hilaire Belloc — Sylvia Hayman, 281

Thoughts on the Gospel — Abbie Jane Wells, 286

I Wish I'd Said That — Dan Herr, 294

INTRODUCTION

THIS is only the second anthology of writing from *The Critic* to be published. The first, which appeared in 1969, limited itself to humor, cartoons, parody and one or two short stories. Plowing back through forty-four years worth of issues I discovered enough good writing and good reading to make a dozen anthologies. So much so that the hardest part about putting this one together was deciding what to leave out.

The magazine which has been published in various formats by the not-for-profit Thomas More Association of Chicago since 1942, has had five editors: John Tully, Paul Cuneo, Joel Wells (who was responsible for its eminent reputation), Michael McCauley and now John Sprague. It is only one among many ways in which the Thomas More Association seeks to realize its goal of promoting Catholic reading, culture and education. I asked publisher Dan Herr, who has been around almost from the beginning to shed some light on the publication's genesis. Here's what he told me:

"*The Critic* had a curious beginning. Soon after John Tully founded the Association, he decided he must do his part to combat immoral books and to promote 'Catholic books,' which have always needed help. (The publication of Thomas Merton's *The Seven Storey*

Just Good Reading

Mountain in 1948 heralded the first public recognition of the genre.) Tully started a magazine and called it *Books on Trial;* if there was any doubt about his editorial approach, the courtroom logo on the cover made the focus clear. There were book reviews, but the publicized feature of *Books on Trial* was a chart which rated current books, mostly from a moral viewpoint. These charts were reprinted and distributed to parishes to enable Catholic readers to keep up with what amounted to a Legion of Decency for literature. Books were rated under such categories as: 'Unfavorable'; 'Offensive or Objectionable in Whole or Part'; 'Disapproved'; 'Doubtful Merit'; 'Why Bother Reading'; 'Somewhat Questionable.' *Dragonseed* by Pearl Buck was found both unfavorable and offensive; *The White Tower* by James Ramsey Ullman was termed offensive because of 'inexplicable and objectionable language'; both *The Wayward Bus* by John Steinbeck and *Joseph the Provider* by Thomas Mann were rated unfavorable and objectionable and were disapproved. Unfortunately, many of the books meriting approval were never heard from again.

"The morality charts proved troublesome and were soon dropped. Few readers, even then, seemed to care. We changed the title of the magazine to *The Critic* to announce our new approach, a move somewhat startling to older subscribers. *The Critic*, as readers of this anthology will discover, was a far cry from *Books on Trial*, but the earlier magazine made *The Critic* possible."

Thanks to Joel Wells, in its scope and variety of material *The Critic* was and is like no other Catholic magazine published. Certainly no Catholic magazine,

From the Pages of *The Critic*

and not many general ones, can match its illustrious roster of contributors which includes T. S. Eliot, Evelyn Waugh, Graham Greene, Francois Mauriac, Arthur Koestler, Arnold Toynbee, Thomas Merton, Lawrence Durrell, Honor Tracy, Agatha Christie, Sean O'Faolin, Flannery O'Connor, Edwin O'Connor, J. F. Powers, Brian Friel, John Courtney Murray, Anthony Burgess, Joyce Carol Oates, Tom Wolfe, Brooks Atkinson, Martin Luther King, Jr., Andrew Greeley, John Shea—and others almost equally celebrated, many who were being published for the first time, as well as representatives of the handful of literate high churchmen, such as the late Cardinal John Wright.

Not nearly all of these are included here. My aim, as stated in the title of this book, was to select a variety of 'just good reading'; I also wanted to avoid somewhat dated pieces—because of the subject matter or the approach. To this end, thirteen of the twenty-nine pieces included come from the now quarterly *Critic* of the most recent five-and-a-half years under the outstanding editorship of John Sprague.

I hope you enjoy the resulting book as much as I did putting it together.

Kris Tuberty

THE HIGHWAYMAN AND THE SAINT

by Brian Friel

I NEVER really hated Mrs. Wilson, Madge's mother. I just thought of her as a bloody nuisance. But Madge hated her. No sooner would we be settled down to a bit of courting on the couch in the living room (and even though we were both in our late thirties we were eager enough) than the hand-bell would ring, and Madge would utter 'The old bitch!' and pull away from me and dash up the stairs to see what the old woman wanted this time. She never wanted anything, of course—Is the fire safe? Was there a ring at the door? What time is it? She was just making damn sure that Madge and I weren't going to enjoy ourselves. For a time we thought it was the long silences that made her suspicious, so Madge got me to recite poetry while we courted; anything to make it seem we were just chatting. I would recite over and over again the only poem I learned at school, *The Highwayman* by a poet called Alfred Noyes, and now and again Madge would throw in something like, 'It's a small world, isn't it?' or 'Just imagine. Fancy that.' This worked fine as long as I concentrated on what I was doing and not on what I was saying: I could rattle through the whole seventeen verses without a stop. But now and again a line would sound peculiar, and I would pause to wonder had I got it right, and then

Just Good Reading

I would get stuck altogether, and before I would have time to go back to the beginning, *The wind was a torrent of darkness among the gusty trees*, the bell would go clang-clang-clang, and Madge would spit out a curse, and the session would be wrecked. I think, too, the old woman got cute to the poetry recitals because many a night, when I was rattling along at full steam, she would summon Madge. "We're like those Russian dogs that used to drivel!' Madge would say. It just goes to show that a man should never court a woman in her own house.

The trouble was that Mrs. Wilson was invalided with angina, and we couldn't very well go out and leave her alone. Cissy Cassidy, the next-door neighbour, kept an eye on her during the day, until Madge got home from the shirt factory at six. I came around about seven (I'm a joiner in the Acme Furniture Company) and stayed until bedtime. Apart from the bell ringing and Madge's tempers I suppose it wasn't a bad way to spend the nights. It meant that I could save my wages and put down a deposit on a house in Riverview for ourselves, and anyhow we wouldn't have been going to dances or films because the old man wasn't long dead. I had met him a few times. He was average height, about the same build as myself, and a quieter or more civil man never walked. He was a stoker in St. Patrick's Hospital, and the heat of the furnace must have dried him out because he was as yellow as a duck's foot. He had the longest chin you ever saw and he was so shy about it that he had it pulled away back into his throat. This meant that his cheeks and his mouth were always lined, as if he were smiling, and that he looked at you from under his

From the Pages of *The Critic*

forehead. Madge inherited her chin from him, but in those days hers was stuck out, aggressive, like an amateur boxer's, and it got red and shiny every time the bell rang. The old man worked night shifts, and the only times I met him were on Sunday afternoons. He would sit in the back garden with a big book about birds on his knees and binoculars up to his face and watch the hedge sparrows hopping about the wall at the end of the yard. I used to wonder what he needed the binoculars for because the wall was five yards from where he sat. Maybe he thought they hid him; or maybe he knew you don't like interrupting a man with binoculars. Anyhow, we never had any conversation beyond 'Good evening, Mr. Wilson' and 'Oh, hello, Andy.' He dropped dead in the basement of the hospital with a coal shovel in his hand, and when they laid him out his chin stuck up so far above the sides of the coffin that they had to open his mouth to get the lid on. When she saw him gaping savagely up at her—I can tell you I got a bit of a fright myself—Mrs. Wilson collapsed. She was ordered to bed and never, except on one occasion, got out of it again.

Her bedroom was a sight. The bedside table was covered with medicines, and the walls were covered with holy pictures, and beside her on the pillow where Mr. Wilson's head used to rest—Madge said he chose night shifts to avoid his wife—lay the big brass handbell. It had belonged to Mrs. Wilson's grandfather, Flames Flaherty, who used to run before the fire brigade in the old days, clearing the streets; or so Cissy Cassidy told me. But the most important thing in the room was the shrine. It was really a chest of drawers completely covered by a white sheet, and it looked like an altar in a

Just Good Reading

church. At the ends were two lit candles and at the front a vase of artificial flowers and in the center was the statue of Saint Philomena.

Saint Philomena was a blue and gold and white girl, with a long graceful frock that touched the top of her bare feet. Her hair fell to her waist, and her arms were folded across her chest, and she held her head to the side as if she were listening for something. Mrs. Wilson had a habit of punctuating her prayers with deep satisfied sighs, and every time she did this, the candles flickered, and whatever way the shadows shifted, you would imagine Saint Philomena lifted her face a little bit higher. As the Rosary rolled on and on, I used to think that she was Bess, the landlord's black-eyed daughter in my poem, waiting for the highwayman to come riding across the purple moor; or that she was Mrs. Wilson, listening for the creaking of the springs of the living room couch; or that she was Madge, cocking her ear for the handbell, although how I ever saw any resemblance between this good looking girl and Madge I can't imagine now. Anyhow, between Bess and Mrs. Wilson and Madge I didn't pray much.

The prayers began every night on the stroke of ten. As soon as the big bell would ring, Madge would shout up to the ceiling 'Coming!' and then fix her hair and her clothes, and we would go up together to the bedroom. Mrs. Wilson was such a wee fairy of a woman that you would scarcely notice her in the huge bed. The first thing you would see were the two big soft innocent eyes, then the round white face, then the tiny hands lying patiently on top of the counterpane. She never raised her voice above a whisper even though she opened her

From the Pages of *The Critic*

mouth as if she were eating a juicy pear. She always addressed me as Thomas (I was christened Thomas Andrew) although everybody in Omagh knows me as Andy.

'Good evening, Thomas,' she would whisper. 'Are you going to join in the family rosary?' As if I had come up to play poker!

'Yes, Mrs. Wilson.'

'Good boy. Good boy. Madge, fix my head so that I can see Saint Philomena.'

Madge, leading with her chin, would stuff the pillows behind her back as if she were punishing them.

'Lovely. Thank you,' the old woman would say. 'It's so nice for me to have you both kneeling at my bedside. As Father Peyton says, "The family that prays together stays together."'

'Get on with the Rosary!' Madge would snap.

'And Father Peyton's right, isn't he, Thomas?'

'Yes, Mrs. Wilson,' I would say, avoiding Madge's wild eyes.

'Indeed he is. I'm so lucky to have you both.' Then, to the statue, 'Thank you, Saint Philomena.'

I could see that she was as crafty as hell, playing Madge and me and Father Peyton and Saint Philomena against one another, but somehow I could never get angry with her. Maybe that was because Madge had enough anger for the two of us. But for no good reason at all I began to hate Father Peyton and Saint Philomena. I felt that they were responsible for all our troubles. Here I was, not as young as I might have been, with a house ready to step into and a woman ready to marry me; and there was Father Peyton and Saint Philo-

Just Good Reading

mena coming between me and a normal life—just because I was civil enough to join in the Rosary every night. As if things weren't awkward enough for us without making them permanently awkward by praying together! It amounted to this: every time I got down on my knees in that bedroom I cut my own throat.

After the Rosary, Madge and I would go down to the kitchen for supper. The prayers always seemed to knock any notion of courting out of our heads. We would sit there at the table and talk listlessly about our problem.

'We could take her with us to Riverview,' I would begin.

'Not bloody likely! Besides, she would never leave this house.'

'What about getting her into St. Patrick's?'

'She's not sick enough. They have no spare beds for cranks.'

'The Nazareth nuns would take her into their Home. If she sold this house and brought the money with her, they would be damn glad to welcome her.'

'She wouldn't go to them above all people.'

'Well, what are we going to do? She's your mother.'

'I don't know, Andy. Honest to God, I just don't know.'

'You don't expect me to come in here, do you?' I would say, thinking of Saint Philomena and Father Peyton and getting annoyed. 'I mean to say, leaping into the air every time you hear that bloody bell isn't my idea of married life! By God, you don't expect that of me, do you?'

Sometimes her eyes would flash with anger and she would say, 'The old bitch! I'll tell her tomorrow that

From the Pages of *The Critic*

we're going to clear out, and she can damn well forage for herself!' Sometimes she would just sit there and cry, her big chin quivering. And sometimes she would fling her arms around me and kiss my ears and my neck, and I would have to plunge into The Highwayman, in the excitement sometimes beginning at Part Two, *He did not come in the dawning; he did not come at noon.* Sudden courting like that was the sweetest of all. I would forget altogether the bloody mess we were in.

It was the Acme Furniture Company that finally pushed us into marriage. They landed a big contract to fit out a new hotel that was being built near Belfast airport, and all the unmarried carpenters in the firm were being sent off on the eighteen-month job. I explained the situation to Madge. It was now or never, I said. She didn't hesitate for a second.

'We'll get married next Wednesday!' she said.

'What about the old woman?'

'We'll worry about that afterwards.'

'And we'll live in Riverview?'

'Andy,' She said, smiling up at me, 'I love you that much I could eat you!'

We didn't get married that Wednesday because Cissy Cassidy had the flu and there would have been no one to look in on the old woman, but we got married the following Saturday. Immediately after the ceremony we came back to the house to see her. She cried her eyes out with happiness. So did Madge. They held on to one another and laughed and cried, and I stood there beside the altar, grinning, all stiff in my new suit, like a bloody fool. Mrs. Wilson's mouth kept opening wide but not even a whisper came. Her big innocent eyes were on

Just Good Reading

Saint Philomena, and I believe she was mouthing Thank you, Thank you. Then she signalled for Madge and me to get down on our knees beside her and she joined her hands and said some sort of a prayer over us, and Madge and she hugged one another again, and we were all so happy that I stepped forward like a man and kissed the old woman on the forehead. Maybe I cried, too; I don't remember. Anyhow, we got away eventually and took the bus to Portrush where we stayed in the Grand Hotel until Monday morning.

The biggest mistake I made was to go back to the house after the honeymoon, even for a week, until the painters were finished in Riverview. Because the week stretched into two, and then into a month, and then into three months, and then the old woman got a chill, and then it was Christmas, and finally Madge said one night that since furnished houses were fetching such high prices we should let Riverview.

'What the hell do you mean?' I said.

'It's pointless having it idle, isn't it?' she said, tilting up her chin.

'It shouldn't be idle,' I said. 'We should be in it.'

'And what about mother?' There wasn't so much of the 'old bitch' now.

'She's welcome to come with us. And well she knows it. And well you know it.'

'I'll tell you what, Andy. We'll leave here in the spring. The evenings will be longer, and it won't be so lonely for her. Just wait another two months.'

'You've given me time limits before.'

'I mean it. Honest to God, I do. The spring, and that's the end.'

From the Pages of *The Critic*

I think she really did mean it.

'Is that a promise, Madge?'

But then the hand-bell rang, and she said 'The old bitch!' the way she used to say it; only I got the notion she said it just to please me. Anyhow, she ran away upstairs without promising.

And that was the funny thing about the bell-ringing now. Before we were married the old woman always rang it when there was a silence downstairs. Now we might sit in the living room for a whole night without speaking a word to one another, and there would never be a tinkle from the bedroom. But as soon as we would start chatting the clang-clang-clang would waken the dead; you would swear the town was on fire. Another difference in our lives was that I stopped going up for prayers at night. Madge didn't speak to me for a week when I stalled first, and for the most of that time I didn't even know she wasn't speaking to me, not until she told me. But as I explained to her, why should I pray together when staying together was the last thing in the world I wanted? She accused me then of flying in the face of providence, and I pointed out that it wasn't providence I was up in arms against but Father Peyton and Saint Philomena, the Terrible Twins, as I called them. Only for them, I said, the old woman wouldn't have a leg to stand on. I can tell you that brought the colour to her chin!

It's funny, too, how things turn out. If Madge hadn't forgotten to put my lunchbox in my coat pocket that day, I wouldn't have gone to the works canteen; and if I hadn't gone to the canteen I might never have known of the Vatican announcement. Anyhow, there I was, sit-

Just Good Reading

ting beside George Williamson, eating my lunch, and not thinking about anything in particular. All I knew about Williamson was that he was a French polisher in the finishing department and a bitter black Protestant.

'D'you see this?' he said, reaching over the paper he was reading.

'What that?' I said.

'It would appear,' he said, smirking, 'that the Pope isn't infallible after all. Now, isn't that a terrible shock?'

'I don't know what you're talking about, mate,' I said.

'It's in the paper here,' he said. 'Look, man. Read it for yourself. "The Saint That Never Was. Saint Philomena Is Pushed From Her Pedestal."'

At the mention of Saint Philomena I snatched the paper from his hands and read through the news item. My God, he was telling the truth! Official Vatican sources today announce, the paper said, that the devotion of all Roman Catholics to Saint Philomena must be discontinued because there is little or no evidence that this person ever existed. I didn't trouble to read any more. All that mattered was that Saint Philomena was no more a saint than my granny was. And with her out of the way Father Peyton was a pushover!

'Williamson,' I said, slapping him across the back, 'may you never know want or discomfort, and may all your dreams come true!' And ignoring his calls to me to give him back his paper I skipped out of the canteen like a ten-year-old. I think that was the happiest moment of my life.

I shouldn't have got drunk after work. That's what spoiled everything. I should have nursed my news and gloated over it and chuckled privately about it. But I

From the Pages of *The Critic*

went and got plastered and then, singing 'God Save Ireland,' I marched to the house and straight up to the old woman's bedroom. I threw the paper at the old woman and said, 'There's something for you to read.' But I was more interested in Saint Philomena than in the old woman. I caught the statue and held it above my head and went waltzing around the room, reciting the fifteenth verse of The Highwayman at the top of my voice: *Back he spurred like a madman shrieking a curse to the sky,/with the white road smoking behind him, and his rapier brandished high/!Blood-red were his spurs i' the golden noon, wine-red was his velvet coat,/ When they shot him down on the highway,/Down like a dog on the highway,/And he lay in his blood on the highway, with a bunch of lace at his throat.*

Then, all hell broke loose: the old woman screaming and ringing the bell; Madge roaring at me and trying to console her mother at the same time; Cissy Cassidy pounding on the front door to know what was wrong. Still reciting, I went down and opened the door for her. She gave me a quick look and shot past me. I swaggered into the kitchen and put on a kettle for tea and went back out to the foot of the stairs and shouted up, 'Yo-ho! Yo-ho! The family that thinks together drinks together!'—or some silly nonsense like that. I went into the living room and bounced up and down on the couch until the springs hummed. 'Listen!' I called up to the ceiling. 'Do you hear? Can you hear me, Philomena?' Then, I went back to the kitchen and set the table for myself and sang hymns and ate a bloody big tea. My God, I felt like a king! I must have fallen asleep after that because the next thing I remember is waking up at 1:00 a.m. and

Just Good Reading

trying to piece together what had happened. I had a very sore head.

The house was as still as a graveyard. I tiptoed upstairs and looked into our bedroom. Madge wasn't there. I went into the old woman's bedroom. The bed was empty! The bell was there on the pillow, and the candles were lit on the altar, but the old woman and the statue were gone. Holy God, had I killed the old woman! I can tell you the sweat broke on me then. I dashed downstairs and just as I got to the bottom the front door opened.

Cissy Cassidy came in first. So that was where they were—next door. Then came Mrs. Wilson. She was wearing a coat over her nightdress, and her face was white and sad and holy looking. Madge was last, her arm around the old woman in support. None of them said a word. The three of them just walked past me and up the stairs, as if I weren't there. I tried, to look into Madge's face, but she kept her eyes on the ground, and her chin, I noticed, looked as if it were polished. I went into the living room and sat on the edge of a seat, like in the old days when I was waiting for Madge. But now I was the one that was doing the listening, trying to pick up any sound from the bedroom above. I could hear nothing.

In the end I could stick the silence no longer. I had to go up. As soon as I entered, they began the Rosary. The old woman was in the bed, propped up with pillows, facing the altar. Madge was kneeling beside the bed, Cissy near the door. I knelt down beside Cissy. Madge and her mother prayed with their eyes closed. They did a lot of sighing.

From the Pages of *The Critic*

'God forgive you for this night's work,' Cissy hissed to me.

'Shut up!' I hissed back.

'Depriving the poor woman of the saint of her life.'

'Don't blame me. Blame the Pope.'

'But you'll not steal the next one from her. Because you'll never be told who she is. And we've decided not even to have a statue.'

'What are you talking about?'

'She has fixed on another saint—in place of Saint Philomena.'

'Who?'

'That's something you'll never know. Never!'

'What d'you mean?'

'Wild horses wouldn't drag that information out of us. You'll never know who you're praying to. You'll do no more damage.' Madge heard us whispering. She glanced across at us. And as she did, I noticed that her chin was no longer thrust out aggressively but was withdrawn into her neck so that her cheeks and her mouth were lined in a fixed sad smile. Then, her eyes glided back to the altar, and from under her forehead she stared dreamily at the space between the two lit candles.

I have a good tenant in Riverview. He pays me regularly on the first Saturday of every month. Occasionally I walk over there and take a look at the outside of the house: he has rose trees in the front and a vegetable plot in the back. It looks very cosy. But by the time you get home from work and get washed you don't feel like going out much. So, if the weather is good, I usually sit out in the back garden and watch the hedge sparrows through the old man's binoculars. Then, when the bell

Just Good Reading

rings, I go up to the old woman's bedroom for the Rosary. Madge sleeps there now, ever since that night, just in case the old woman might get an attack. Not that that's likely; the doctor says she'll outlive us all. And her mind's as clear as ever. When I go into the room she whispers, 'Good evening, Thomas. Are you going to join in the family Rosary?' and then she smiles over at the candles and the artificial flowers, and you can see her lips saying Thank you, Thank you. Of course, she never drops even a hint of who her new saint is. Indeed, she has got so crafty she doesn't even mention Father Peyton's name. All she says is, 'It's nice for me to have you both kneeling at my bedside. As a certain American priest says, "The family that prays together stays together."' By God, you've got to admire the old bitch! She could handle a regiment.

CATHOLIC EATING

by Joel Wells

ALLOW me to present myself. I am Carlo Mascacholli, ristorante and food critic for *L'Osservatore Romano* for seventeen years. Your editore invite me to tell some of my experiences and knowledge with you readers. My English is not large but I will try to do this if you scuzzi my—how you say?—hazhappened way.

****

People are asking me. "What does Il Papa eat?" "Where does he eat?" "Have you ever ate with him?" and many such like things.

I answer Il Papa is not a big eater, but he is liking many different sorts of ethnic foods. The Vatican kitchen does room service for him and the cook there tells me private that he hates when Il Papa goes off on another journey.

He comes back from Mexico wanting tamales and refried beans at two in the morning. He comes back from Africa wanting poached zebra liver and itsa very hard to find a zebra in Roma, even on the Via Veneto.

Most times Il Papa eats in his private chambers alone or with an advisor. But he has asked people from papal audiences to join him in his small private dining room not so often. This "knocks their socks off, you bet" (I

Just Good Reading

get these words from my *Julia Child Cookbook*), to have lamb stew and paschal dumplings with Il Papa.

Me personal have only ate with him one time. It was breakfast and we had Tasmanian-style omelet, which is not a big love of mine because I think maybe the eggs are not coming from chickens but from some kind of lizard. I could not swear to it, but some little things were maybe moving around in it. And Il Papa put big piles of sun dried tomatoes on his, which did not help my interest.

Il Papa was not pleased.

"This wounds us sorely," he said. "Thousands around the world go hungry and you do not even clean up your plate. It is perhaps that our simple fare is not fit for a gourmand such as you?"

I feared greatly for my employment.

****

Now I will tell you two truths about Catholic eating.

Uno is, never eat at a monastery if you can at all help it. Monks are not big on washing up in the kitchen. There are no women—not even mamas—to make them honest so there is some dirty pots and plates. Many times I have bowed my head for the benediction and see a fork with no proper space between the tines because last night's beans are still there.

The bread and cheese the monks make can be ate with little peril but there has been feathers in the chicken soup and bristles on my bacon. Also they read bloody stories from the lives of the martyr saints all through meals. It helps not much that monks do not indulge in the luxury of hot baths for their own bodies so that the smells of

From the Pages of *The Critic*

the kitchen mix badly with what St. Benedict called, if I am not wrong, "the odor of sanctity."

It is another truth of Catholic eating not to do it near any great shrine or place of pilgrimage. With so many hungry people at their doors, the food kiosks and cafes can serve what swill they want and charge like they have three stars from the Guide Michelin. I have often put it to myself why I see no cats or dogs near these places. I mean no disrespect to Our Lady of Fatima or of Lourdes, but the greatest miracles at their shrines is that thousands do not perish from the ptomaine, the botulism and the dysentery.

****

The patron saint of Catholic eating is St. Thomas of Aquino. In his little known "Summa Appetitus" he admits that he grew to love food in "excessio inordinato." At first he used the pleasure of eating to dull the effect of the carnal temptations which his family threw in his face to get him out of his tower of ivory and sanctity. But he fell into the habit of eating whole capons and roast hares, also puddings and pasta, so that his belly grew to such a size that a bow had to be cut into the table to make room for it. It did not assist him that he sat long hours writing or that what you call aerobics and jogging had not yet been discovered. Food got so much with him that it even found voice in some of his writing and hymns.

****

You must not conjure that my job is not intellectual. Gourmet bishops and lay people of all sexes ask me,

Just Good Reading

"What is the greatest Catholic ristorante in the world?" I do not like to give answer cheaply from my whole life's work so I confuse them with theology of my own making. "What makes a ristorante Catholic? Is it one that is owned by Catholics? Is it one in which the chef is Catholic? Is it one in which Catholics eat? Is it one that gives out only Catholic food? What then is Catholic food? If it is true as St. Paul wrote, 'We are what we eat,' then how can one be a Catholic without knowing what is Catholic food?"

"Go and ponder these questions," I tell these people, "and when you have the answers return to me and I will tell you what is the greatest Catholic ristorante in the world."

Their faces fall in, these people, and they go away.

Of course I know the answer. I know the place. I have a regular table there. I am revered by the owners. I can make reservations for you. All you must do is send to me a return envelope with proper postage and an international money order for Lire 100,000.

Ciao.

TEILHARD DE CHARDIN
THE NEW YORK YEARS

by John Deedy

FROM Grant's Tomb on Morningside Heights, to the plaques commemorating tree plantings along 42nd Street, New York is a city of landmarks and monuments to its famous. It is inevitable that a few worthies have been overlooked. But not many. New Yorkers have been as conscientious about remembering their notables, as innkeepers about chronicling the beds in which George Washington slept. They've missed few . . . and given the benefit of the doubt to many. There are people commemorated around New York that it would take a day's hunt in the Public Library to identify.

Marie Joseph Pierre Teilhard de Chardin—geologist, paleontologist, philosopher, evolutionist, Jesuit priest—is among the overlooked. The New York Public Library card file on Teilhard is almost three inches thick, but the traces of him along the streets outside are as scarce as the fossils he tracked across several continents in search of the links between man and ape: a few cultists; a shrinking number of old associates; a few enduring enemies; and the American Teilhard de Chardin Association, a small but purposeful organization dedicated to extending knowledge and understanding of his thought—still sadly twisted, be it said. Last year one right-wing group petitioned the New York Archdiocese to declare Teil-

Just Good Reading

hard a "heretic" and correct the "unfortunate error by which he was given a Catholic burial."

Jesuit Father Pierre Teilhard de Chardin lived his last years in New York, and died there on an Easter Sunday afternoon some thirty-five years ago. In New York he endured his last anguishes, a paradox to the end: genius and obedient servant; man of science and of belief; honored in the world, but still an enigma in the church he served more loyally and trustingly than it served him.

Teilhard lived in New York from 1951–1955—a celebrity, of course, but not so celebrated as to be spared his tiny rectory room when the Jesuit community at 83rd Street needed the space. Nor so celebrated that after his death people rushed about erecting memorials to his memory or renaming halls in his honor. Some have spoken of him in the same breath as Aristotle and Aquinas; very many regard him as a giant of the twentieth century. But around New York there are no public Teilhard reminders; no Bloomsday-like walks to the scenes of his activities; no Teilhard trails; no annual pilgrimages to the Jesuit cemetery upstate, where he is buried. Teilhard de Chardin lived and died an outsider, and he remains a stranger. When the *New York Times* noted the 75th anniversary of St. Ignatius Loyola Church, its story recalled the rich and distinguished who had worshipped there: McDonnells, Murrays, Cuddihys, Graces, Farleys, Roskobs, Bouviers, Wagners. No one thought to tell *Times*woman Laurie Johnston: "Teilhard de Chardin also lived here, prayed here, helped out occasionally with a parish Mass."

Yet this may be as it should be. Teilhard did not em-

From the Pages of *The Critic*

brace New York any more fervently than New York embraced him. He liked the city, including the heavy snows and crisp winter days; they reminded him of Peking. He was even hopeful that New York could be his "second Peking." "In 1925 Peking was the chance of my life." Teilhard wrote just before Christmas, 1952. But the enthusiasm was quickly tempered by the reflection: "I'm no longer 40 years old."

In fact, Teilhard was past 70 when he settled in New York, and the city was in some respects more a place of exile than it was a spot which Teilhard, given his background, would seek out for its great personal challenges. He came to New York to assume the post of research associate at the Wenner-Gren Foundation for Anthropological Research in up-town Manhattan, and to research the fossil collections of New York's Museum of Natural History. As events developed, he also came to wind down a life that had begun inauspiciously in Auvergne in 1881, and built to controversial summits, particularly among churchmen, as, out of his findings, Teilhard spun an evolutionary philosophy about God and man . . . in a complex and often mystifying new vocabulary, featuring words like Christogenesis, complexification, noosphere and anthropocentrism, and concepts like Hominization and Omega Point. Teilhard's thought hardly conformed to Jesuit or Roman orthodoxy, and he had long since been forbidden to teach and to publish.

When Teilhard made his decision to come to New York, his standing with church authorities was at a low ebb. Ostensibly that decision was Teilhard's own. However, subtle ecclesiastical pressures were also at work, including Pius XII's 1950 encyclical *Humani Generis*, a

Just Good Reading

document which Teilhard, with reason, suspected was aimed at his theories. Teilhard concluded that he had become "an embarrassment" to ecclesiastical officialdom, and decided that a "shelter out of France" might be best for all concerned. And where was a sensitive septuagenarian with a serious heart condition to take himself to be out of the way? To the scenes of happy memories and large triumphs of earlier years? Not when these are in the remote parts of China, central Asia, the East Indies, Burma, Java and the sub-Sahara. Teilhard opted for New York.

Many European friends resented his New York "assignment." They figured Teilhard was being hustled, and felt that it was hypocritical for his superiors to allow him to go to New York, "on the pretext that this would best forward his scientific work" when at the same time they were holding a blanket of censorship over the results of most of that work. (Shortly before, a German translation of some Teilhard articles in *Etudes*, a Jesuit monthly, had been barred from publication by church officials, and there was no guarantee that his writings in the United States would fare any better.) Before departing from Paris, Teilhard heeded the advice of friends and established a private agency for the preservation of his letters and manuscripts. A canonist was consulted on whether a person who had taken the vow of poverty was free to dispose of his own papers, and he found ecclesiastical law of two views on the matter. With some friendly clerical nudging. Teilhard chose the more favorable of the interpretations, and appointed his devoted secretary Mlle. Jeanne Mortier as his literary executrix. That wisdom was to insure the eventual pub-

From the Pages of *The Critic*

lication of the immense body of Teilhard's work. His bibliography grew to some 500 titles within a decade or so after his death.

Whatever ideas Teilhard managed about the purity of the New York "permission" faded as an expected one year in the city grew to several, then were wiped out in summer, 1954, after Teilhard had returned to France to lecture and for some sentimental journeying. It was not a successful trip. The publicity was extravagant and upset his essentially modest nature. He was visibly tired and under considerable strain. The principal lecture of his itinerary—a talk on Africa and the origins of man—did not go well, and when Teilhard went to superiors to ask permission to respond to a critic, they seized the opportunity to order him back to New York. Ironically, the order reached him on the feast day of St. Ignatius, his Order's patron, July 31. Five days later, Teilhard left Paris for London. After another five days, he sailed for New York. It was to be his last sea voyage. A depression set in, of the type that had once impelled him to say to a Canadian friend: "Pray for me, that I may not die embittered."

Teilhard had every reason to die embittered. Rome had kept a wary eye on him since 1922, when some speculations of his on possible new interpretations of Original Sin had sent orthodoxies fluttering. The Jesuits provided some protection (possibly out of the practical consideration, as Martin Jarrett-Kerr has argued, that any condemnation of Teilhard would also have constituted a condemnation of the Society). But the protection was not foolproof. By and large, Teilhard's life as a religious

Just Good Reading

was a constant struggle with censorship and repression. The substance of his work—including *The Phenomenon of Man*, completed in the early 1940s—was of course not published until after his death; he was forbidden to participate in major intellectual conferences, including one in New York in 1940 involving Albert Einstein and Jacques Maritain; when a professorship became open at the Sorbonne in 1948, a post that he dearly wanted, he was prohibited from standing for it. Church officials admired his spirituality and, of course, were gratified by his respect for authority, remarkable even for a day of great clerical deference to officialdom. But obviously they preferred him away from the center of things—off in China somewhere, or in New York. Teilhard sensed as much and was given to "fits of weeping" and states of near-despair. "What distresses me," he once commented, "is not that I am shackled by Christianity, but that Christianity should at the moment be shackled by those who are its official guardians: The same problem that Jesus had to face 2,000 years ago." Nor did Teilhard find bliss in New York. "My life is running along more or less smoothly," he wrote a friend in January, 1952, "with just a slight undertone of disquiet from not feeling completely at home here in my Order. Everyone is as kind as possible to me, but even so I can't help appearing rather a bird of passage, or something of a parasite."

Except for passing complaints in his correspondence, Teilhard's feelings over the way he was handled by the church were extraordinarily controlled. (A fellow Jesuit once remarked: "If you met the devil, I expect you'd say, 'You know, he's not as bad as all that.'") Biogra-

34

pher Claude Cuénot has written that Teilhard "was no reformer in the sense of the sixteenth century reformers," and he was correct, of course. There was never a strong possibility of a breach between Teilhard and his Order, though Teilhard often discussed "in the abstract" the idea of leaving the Society of Jesus and was encouraged to make the break by several of his associates; reportedly he was held back by "an instinct of military honor" and "respect for the *grande dame.*" Still less was there a possibility of a break with Rome, in spite of very real grievances. Teilhard was able even to live with censorship and the *Index of Prohibited Books*, though he found them revolting and absurd and was penalized mightily by the rationale that infused both.

When it was nearly all over, Teilhard would look back on the occasion of his golden jubilee as a Jesuit and comment that he would do the same thing again, if he were able to turn the clock back. He would say something of the same four months before he died to Father Joseph Donceel, S.J., of the Fordham faculty, when Donceel inquired whether he was not sorry he had become a Jesuit because so many of his ideas had been suppressed. "But if I had not been a Jesuit I would not have had these ideas," Teilhard responded. "I picked them up in the Society."

"He was the most marvelously benevolent man I've ever known." Teilhard's good friend Roger W. Straus, Jr., president of the New York publishing house of Farrar, Straus & Giroux, commented recently. "He took the long view, and felt that his ideas would be accepted in time."

Teilhard settled in New York on November 26, 1951,

Just Good Reading

securing "billet" (his word) in St. Ignatius rectory, "thanks to the good offices of Father [John] LaFarge," then of *America* magazine. Teilhard had hoped to move in with the editors of *America* at their residence on 108th Street—a hope apparently entertained also by Father LaFarge. The arrangement adopted, however, was a fourth-floor room in the rectory at 980 Park Avenue, near 83rd Street. The space was tight but the neighborhood suited Teilhard fine. It reminded him of Paris' rue de Grenelle, and had the advantage, Teilhard wrote, of putting him "in the center of the city, a quarter of an hour from the Natural History Museum, and, more important still, from the Wenner-Gren Foundation."

Then, as now, St. Ignatius was a composite religious community, made up of the teachers at Regis High School, the fathers of St. Ignatius Loyola parish, the staff of the Jesuit Seminary and Mission Bureau, and several Jesuits assigned to individual apostolates. The community numbered about 70, overall, many of them lodged in a series of brownstone flats running along 83rd Street. Later, (early March, 1954), when it was decided to raze these flats and erect a new residence, bedrooms became scarce, and "guests" or "extras" in the community—about seven in all—were required to find rooms elsewhere. Out went Teilhard. In characteristic good grace, he sympathized with the person who had to give the order.

He moved in briefly at the Lotus Club, courtesy of Roger Straus, and finally into a small bedroom-sitting room of the Fourteen Hotel on East 60th Street. This he shared with Father Emmanuel de Breuvery, S.J., an economic specialist at the United Nations also displaced by

From the Pages of *The Critic*

the construction at St. Ignatius. In his new location, Teilhard shifted to saying Mass at the Dominican church of St. Vincent Ferrer on Lexington Avenue at 66th.

Meanwhile, Teilhard's room at St. Ignatius was assigned to a young Jesuit just out of tertianship teaching at Regis High, Martin J. Neylon. Neylon, now Bishop of the Caroline and Marshall Islands, recalled its dimensions in a letter last January from the American trust territory: "The room was very narrow, with one window—chest high, almost neck high for a tall man. [The window] looked down on Park Avenue and a small market, Florence Market, sandwiched between two large apartment houses. Behind the door, there was a single straight-backed chair, a washstand, in that order, from door to window. I kept the room just as Father Teilhard had it. Being so narrow, you could do nothing else with it." (During Teilhard's occupancy, a visitor remarked that the room no doubt had been designed as a servant's bedroom—which Teilhard jestfully agreed was an anachronism proving the fact of social progress.)

One Sunday morning, while correcting papers, a knock came to Father Neylon's door. It was Teilhard looking for an umbrella that he had left behind. Teilhard sat down on the edge of the bed, and for two hours they chatted away. The conversation is lost to posterity. "I do not remember now what we talked about," Bishop Neylon wrote.

Other memories are stronger. Father Robert I. Gannon, late of Fordham and Teilhard's New York superior as rector at St. Ignatius, lauds him as an exemplary

Just Good Reading

Jesuit, "amiable, gracious and humble," a man who "never missed the customary monthly chat with the superior." Father Charles E. F. Hoefner, who arrived at St. Ignatius in 1929 and is now its perfect, remembers him as "most gentle and very easy to get along with—never moody or sad." For Father William R. Walsh, S.J., parish priest at St. Ignatius and librarian for the community, Teilhard was an "unassuming, modest, pleasant" man. Father Walsh occasionally served Teilhard's daily Mass, in the community tradition of one priest serving the priest who followed him to the altar. He recalls Teilhard's Mass as "devout, simple, correct—rubrical in the old-fashioned way." (Years earlier Mme. Charles Arsène-Henry, wife of the French ambassador to Japan, had said: "Whoever has not seen Teilhard say Mass has seen nothing.")

Yet, though respect was obviously present in the relationship between Teilhard and his New York confreres, there seems to have been a marked formality about it. Mrs. Rachel H. Nichols of the Wenner-Gren Foundation has recorded how Teilhard would help with the dishes after Foundation parties, "gaily" wiping glasses while she washed, and how "he was as delighted as a child" when she took him to see "the bright lights of Broadway." No kindred warmth brightens recollections at St. Ignatius. Teilhard is remembered as an alert man and one who was always welcome at recreation because of "his sense of humor" and his "cultivated and charming" ways. However, to the disappointment of some, he "did not talk shop" and, most disappointingly, he "was not a raconteur." Nor would the cerebral Teilhard plop down in a chair to enjoy that new novelty gadget, the televi-

From the Pages of *The Critic*

sion. "He was a good companion," one Jesuit sums up, "but not striking in any way." (Which is not to say that Teilhard was aloof. Father Donald R. Campion, S.J., editor of *America*, cites young Jesuits of his day meeting Teilhard in Washington and finding him "very direct, very democratic and very much fraternally interested in their own scientific inclinations.")

The Jesuit in New York who probably encountered Teilhard's ideas most immediately was his superior, Father Gannon. Twenty years after Teilhard's death, Father Gannon, now retired, carries the theological misgivings that imbued ecclesiastical authorities of the 1950s. "The general impression he made . . . was that of a poet and a scientist who did not worry too much about the implications of Catholic theology," Father Gannon said last December. "It did not seem to bother him that some of his poetic ideas created difficulties with regard to Original Sin, Grace and the Redemption. When such matters came up in conversation, he would laugh and change the subject. He was dreaming up interesting theories, not denying his faith."

In New York Teilhard enjoyed a special renown. He neither gloried in it, nor used it to gain favor for himself. He went about his affairs quietly and inauspiciously, making no special requests and expecting no more than the next person. He felt, as Claude Cuénot notes, that he had a prophetic gift. But that feeling he carefully modulated. "His modesty was such that he never seemed to realize the genius he possessed, thinking that he was no better, or more important than anyone else."

Teilhard gave the bulk of his New York time to

Just Good Reading

Wenner-Gren, though he came and went on his own terms and was not involved in general hours and procedures of the foundation, except to advise the late director, Dr. Paul Fejos from time to time. He was pleased when the foundation agreed to sponsor a return field trip for him to Africa in 1953, enabling him to set down on paper some last thoughts on the origins of man. He would also write about being "preoccupied . . . with the urgency of bringing about a reform of anthropology." Between January 30, 1951 and January 14, 1955, Wenner-Gren provided grants-in-aid totaling $22,500 to Teilhard to do research on human evolution and to help finance the African trip. Yet the fact is that he appears to have been occupationally dissatisfied much of the time in New York. "I find plenty to do from day to day," he commented in May, 1952, "but I do wish that some main objective would present itself." Four months before his death, he complained in a letter: "Time goes by, and for six months there has been nothing of real importance in my existence." For a person who had been a physical and intellectual dynamo all his life, no complaint could be more significant.

With considerable time on his hands, Teilhard read a lot (Greene to Dostoievski; Blondel to Spengler); played the tourist (Central Park, the Bronx Zoo); called on friends (Childs Frick, the wealthy amateur palaeontologist, in Roslyn, Long Island). He especially welcomed opportunities to be with French people and old associates, and here New York was generous. Romain Gary, the novelist-diplomat, was at the United Nations. André Malraux occasionally passed through town. So, too, Georges Salles of the Louvre. Claire Taschdjian, his

From the Pages of *The Critic*

secretary at Peking Union Medical College in the early 1940s, was over in Brooklyn with her husband Edgar. (Teilhard had married them in Peking.) Jacques Maritain was nearby at Princeton University. He seldom lacked for company.

A born traveller, Teilhard frequently got away from New York to discover the wider United States. By train and bus, he visited Montana, New Mexico, California, the Mid-West, Maine—being thoroughly impressed with the natural wonders of the country, but puzzled why phenomena like "the granitization of America" had never been probed. The wonder of his American odyssey seems to have been the cyclotrons at Berkeley. Teilhard viewed these as one of the "extraordinary products of the 'noosphere'"—his word for the collective memory and intelligence, the milieu in which individuals think, love, create and feel together as integral members of one organism, Humanity.

The 1950s were Eisenhower years, and though Teilhard "shed a tear" for Adlai Stevenson, he came to find Ike "more and more likeable." The appointment of John Foster Dulles as Secretary of State disappointed him, however, as he saw this translating into a hard line with Moscow. Eisenhower's choice for the Vice President likewise caused distress, and set Teilhard thinking about the anomalies of the American political system, particularly that by which "a second-rate stop-gap . . . may at a moment's notice" be raised by some accident to the highest office in the land.

Such opinions notwithstanding, Teilhard was essentially an apolitical person. Nor were the politics of

Just Good Reading

religion his. On occasion he was offended by political American Catholicism, but he maintained a strict discretion—even when he showed up at Boston College to receive an honorary degree only to be told the award had been withdrawn. Apparently Boston's William Cardinal O'Connell had given the Jesuit institution a choice between His Eminence's presence on stage and that of Teilhard's. Boston College caved in. Teilhard quietly took a place in the commencement crowd.

The immaturity of American Catholicism frequently amazed Teilhard, and he was once especially struck by some comments of Redemptorist Father Francis J. Connell, late dean of Catholic University's School of Sacred Theology, on the possibilities of flying saucers and of inhabited worlds other than earth. *Time's* issue of August 18, 1952, had Father Connell speculating that "if these supposed rational beings should possess the immortality of body once enjoyed by Adam and Eve, it would be foolish for our superjet or rocket pilots to try to shoot them. They would be unkillable." One can imagine Teilhard's further bemusement when he read Father Connell's listing of the four principal classes into which outerspace dwellers might fall: (1) they might have received, like earth men, a supernatural destiny from God . . . might even have lost it and been redeemed; (2) God could have created them with a natural but eternal destiny . . . i.e., like infants who die unbaptized they could live a life of natural happiness after death, without beholding God face to face; (3) they might be rational beings who sinned against God but were never given the chance to regain grace, like evil angels of the Fall; (4) they might have received supernatural gifts and

From the Pages of *The Critic*

kept them, leading the paradisaical existence of Adam and Eve before they ate the forbidden fruit.

Inanities notwithstanding, Teilhard was flattered to be honored by American Catholicism—although honors became noticeably less official after he received the Gregor Mendel Medal from Villanova University in 1937 and startled traditionalists with some "dangerously Darwinian" propositions. In Philadelphia, Teilhard also addressed the Academy of National Sciences and gave press interviews which had him affirming a conviction that "man was born from the animal kingdom," and speculating that the "missing link" would one day be found in a lower stratum from the one in which Peking Man was found, in 1925. (Later he came to regard South Africa as a better possibility.) His comments were widely reported, and when Teilhard sought to correct certain misrepresentations, the results were "only slightly less sensational." Catholic authorities took note—most immediately, it seems, in Boston; it was the Philadelphia incident that most likely led to the rescinding of the degree at Boston College.

Institutional nervousness over Teilhard's orthodoxy quickened with the years, so that after he settled in New York in 1952, any honoring of him took on, if not clandestine, then certainly uncharacteristic features: A cocktail party at Catholic University; dinner with the priest-editors of *America;* a closed meeting at Fordham. Sometimes these events assumed exaggerated significance with biographers. The Fordham meeting, for instance, is depicted by Robert Speight as a "symposium," and by Cuénot as "an officially organized discussion." In fact, nothing official appears to have taken place at Fordham

Just Good Reading

until well into the 1960s, when Teilhard was dead and Vatican Council II had made it possible to sponsor on Catholic campuses events that would have been proscribed in the 1950s. Father Donceel recalls a private Fordham gathering in the early '50s, at which four or five carefully chosen persons were invited to discuss evolution and scientific theories with Teilhard. However, Father Laurence J. McGinley, S.J., Fordham president at the time, has no recollection of it—a detail which would make any gathering that might have taken place very unofficial, indeed. Fordham's official Teilhardian events took place mainly between 1965-69, when Father Christopher F. Mooney, S.J., was head of the theology department and organizing an annual Teilhardian seminar. (The world was beginning to change. When Mooney was working on his doctorate between 1961 and 1964 at the Institut Catholique in Paris, he guarded his topic, lest he be yanked off it by superiors. The doctorate: *Teilhard de Chardin and the Mystery of Christ*, subsequently published by Harper & Row and in Doubleday's Image series.)

Death came to Teilhard swiftly and mercifully—and on the day he had frequently prayed to be "delivered"—Easter Sunday. He appears to have been ready—even anxious—for his "escape." The last months had been marred by the deaths of several close friends; by news of the suppression of the priest-worker movement in France; and by the exposure of Piltdown Man as a forgery. (The last was the hypothetical early man whose existence had been inferred from skull fragments found at Piltdown, England, in 1912. The "discoverer," Charles

From the Pages of *The Critic*

Dawson, had been a friend of Teilhard's, and Teilhard himself seems to have been set up to "find" an eyetooth of the specimen.) Teilhard had his suspicions about Piltdown Man, however, and so was not overly unsettled by the news. He was less prepared for the suppression of the priest-worker movement, an experiment he had followed with considerable interest. The suppression made him virtually despair of Rome. "The sin of Rome (for all its casual benedictions on technique and science) is not to believe in a future, and an achievement (for heaven) upon earth," Teilhard commented. "I know because I have been stifled for fifty years in this sub-human atmosphere." At the time he wrote those words Teilhard was speaking more and more of death, confiding to many, including his diplomat-cousin Jean de Legarde, that he would like "to die on the day of the Resurrection." On Saturday, April 9, he went to confession to Father de Breuvery.

Easter morning—April 10, 1955—Teilhard rose early and celebrated Mass as usual. Originally he had planned to have dinner with Roger Straus at Straus' country home in Purchase, but in a telephone conversation that morning Teilhard called the date off, saying he "felt a little tired." Reorganizing his Easter, Teilhard headed for St. Patrick's Cathedral and the Pontifical High Mass. Teilhard, as Speight notes, was "no lover of ecclesiastical pomp, but it seemed as if he could not have enough of the Resurrection." In the afternoon, Teilhard strolled through Central Park, then enjoyed a twin production of *Pagliacci* and *Cavalleria Rusticanna* by the New York City Opera. Afterwards he stopped for tea at the apartment of Mrs. R. Hoff de Terra at 39 East 72nd Street.

Just Good Reading

It had been an exceedingly pleasant day, in spite of the tiredness, and what better way to cap it than with a visit to a friend from the exhilarating field days when each new fossil discovery might unlock some mystery? Teilhard had known the de Terra family from expeditions to the East Indies (1935), Burma (1937-38) and Java (1938), and the bond was close; he and Helmut de Terra "understand each other like a couple of brothers," Teilhard once wrote.

Teilhard was in excellent spirits, and was congratulating himself on this "magnificent day," when suddenly everything came apart. Teilhard placed a paper on the window-sill and was about to take a cup of tea, when he toppled full length on the floor "like a stricken tree." Father Pierre Leroy, Teilhard's friend from his second Peking period, recorded that "it was thought at first that he had fainted and a cushion was placed under his head." After a few minutes Teilhard opened his eyes and said, "Where am I? What's happened?"

"You're with us, don't you recognize me?" said his hostess.

"Yes, but what's happened?"

"You've had a heart attack," he was told.

"I can't remember anything," remarked Teilhard. "This time I feel it's terrible." Teilhard had actually suffered a rupture of the coronary artery.

Teilhard's doctor was called; he was out; another was summoned. His advice was to send for a priest. Father de Breuvery was phoned; he too was out. A call then went to St. Ignatius. Father Gannon took the news and rang on the inter-com the priest on door-duty, Father Martin T. Geraghty, now in retirement at Seven

From the Pages of *The Critic*

Springs, a Jesuit house in Monroe, N.Y. "Father de Chardin has just died," Father Gannon said. "Please go and anoint him." It was about 4 or 4:30 in the afternoon, according to Geraghty, 6 o'clock, according to another source. Father Geraghty continues the narrative:

"He gave me the address . . . I dressed quickly in my street clothes, took the Holy Oils, hailed a cab, and arrived at the town-house, while thinking all the time since having received the call about Father de Chardin's death: What a beautiful day to die . . . Easter Sunday, the day of Christ's glorious victory over sin and death, the day when Christ made death no longer a transition from the land of the living to the land of the dead, but a passing from the land of the dying to the land of the living.

"The town-house had been converted into apartments. On either the second or third floor (I think it was probably the second) was the apartment that I wanted. At the door two middle-aged ladies met me, and led me into the kitchen, which was the first room one entered. I had never met Father de Chardin in life. Thus, my first meeting was to encounter him lying still in death just beyond the doorway that led from the kitchen to the livingroom that fronted on the north side of the street. In death he had dignity. He was dressed in his clerical street-clothes, but his Roman-collar and rabat had been removed in an attempt to help him breathe. His body was lying in an east-west position, with his feet facing the east and his head facing west, the direction where the sun goes down, where a luminary like Father de Chardin subsides. It was an ascetic, aristocratic head,

Just Good Reading

looking very calm and peaceful, even joyous, in death. 'O death, where is thy victory? O death, where is thy sting?' It was Easter Sunday—Christ had conquered death. With Him, we are more than conquerors. That is what the serene expression on Father de Chardin's face silently said.

"Near Father de Chardin's body, on the floor, was a foot-wide, shallow bowl of water that was tinged with blood. Apparently, in falling, Father had hit his head on the floor, and the two ladies had tenderly wiped away the blood from the bruise on his head. The blood and water, intermingled, remind one in retrospect of divinity and humanity, of the blood and water from the dead Christ's own side, of the red richness of grace and the pale weakness of human nature. All of these were Father de Chardin's life-long concern, his very life; it is fitting that a little bowl filled with blood and water, stark symbols, should have been present at this death.

"I anointed him, with the short form first, having first given conditional absolution. Then I supplied the longer form, anointing the five senses, remembering to anoint the hands on the back, since the palms had been anointed at his Ordination with the holy oils of the Priesthood, marking golden stigmata on his hands that make him forever a priest according to the order of Melchisedech, the mysterious, shadowy, sublime High Priest who emerges so briefly in the Old Testament. Then I read the prescribed ritual prayers over him. He was a fellow Jesuit, I never knew him; yet we were united by common bonds.

"Having ministered to Father de Chardin, I extended the words of sympathy and consolation to his friends.

From the Pages of *The Critic*

The coroner had been notified; he had three other deaths to certify, before he was able to come. We lit a candle and placed it on the floor next to Father's body, in a chiaroscuro of light and darkness, the warmth of the flame next to the marble cold of his body. This, too, was fitting. Father de Chardin had brought the light of his intellect and the warmth of his life to humanity. His brilliant mind had illuminated the dark mysteries of a cosmos; his human kindness had warmed all who met him. The Jesuits who had known him in life, and had lived with him, said that he was a saint.

"I returned to the rectory, and noted his death in the deathbook. Although he was a world-famous anthropologist and I knew how to spell his name as well as I can spell my own, I think I may have inadvertently, subconsciously, written: 'Father de Jardin, S.J..' Perhaps I wrote 'jardin,' the French word for 'garden,' because it was a flowering Easter Sunday, and because the impact on me, in giving him the Last Rites, was rather one of glad joy for him than of sadness." (In fact, the name is correctly recorded in the death register. It may be that Father Geraghty incorrectly spelled the name for the person who kept the register—all the entries at the time being in the one printed hand—who then caught the mistake in making the entry.)

Teilhard's death had no shattering impact on the Catholic community. By and large, the diocesan press passed it by for weightier stuff, like the theatrical debut at Loras College of Ronald Ameche, Don's boy, in "Finian's Rainbow." *Commonweal* took no notice. Nor did Donald McDonald in the syndicated column that was

Just Good Reading

the liberal Catholic press' touchstone of respectability. *America* handled the death in one cautiously worded paragraph in a column of notices.

The *New York Times* caught up with Teilhard's death in its Tuesday editions, printing a nine-paragraph obituary focusing on Teilhard's co-discovery of "Peking Man" and his belief in evolution. The *Times* reached back to the controversial 1937 press interview in Philadelphia, in which Teilhard held that man had evolved from lower orders of the animal kingdom, and quoted Teilhard's conviction that such a belief is not irreconcilable with religion. "I find absolutely no barriers and no hurdles between my beliefs as a scientist and as a priest," the *Times'* obit continued. "The two are parallel. As a scientist I must admit the evidence that man was born from the animal kingdom. But he was not an animal. The great, the tremendous, the significant fact about man is the coming of thought with and through him."

The obituary appeared on the day of Teilhard's funeral in St. Ignatius church. It did nothing for the house. Only a handful of people were present; a few close friends; the French Ambassador, M. Hoppenot; Dr. Fejos from Wenner-Gren; and "about eight or ten Jesuits" from the St. Ignatius community. Most were said to have been away due to the Easter holidays. Father de Breuvery celebrated the Requiem—a low Mass, with no singing, no *In Paradisium*. Private Masses continued, assembly-line fashion, at side altars, with people coming and going. Outside it was a dismal, rainy day. The only flowers, says Cuénot, were a floral cross sent by Malvina Hoffman, the sculptress, Rodin's pupil, the

From the Pages of *The Critic*

dear friend who did the bust of Teilhard for the Paris Museum of Modern Art.

Father Leroy and the Father Minister of the St. Ignatius community accompanied the body to its burial place: the cemetery at the Jesuit novitiate of St. Andrew-on-Hudson, 60 miles north of the city. The fates followed. First the ground was too hard to be opened up, so the coffin had to be placed in a temporary vault to await the Spring thaw. When the final interment took place, neither friend nor minister was present, only the gravediggers.

Then it was discovered that the headstone had been incorrectly carved. It read: "P. Pierre Teilhard, S.J." The embarrassment was corrected, and Teilhard got his full name and exact Latinization: "P. Petrus Teilhard de Chardin, S.J." But not before word got around.

Bedevilment continued. In 1962, Rome slapped a *monitum*, or warning, on Teilhard's philosophical and theological writings—an edict more honored now in the breach than in the observance, but nevertheless one that has never been formally withdrawn. Finally, a radically evolved world of religion left the departed Teilhard further isolated in the church he had hung with. St. Andrew's was closed down, and the buildings sold to the Culinary Institute of America. The cemetery remains, but the odors that waft over it are not those of sanctity but of food. Old St. Andrew's is now a cooking school and *tres cher* restaurant.

A RECIPE FOR CATHOLIC WORKER SOUP

by Michael Garvey

ONE OF the by-products of involvement with the Catholic Worker movement is a deeper enjoyment of soup. It would not be reckless to say that the soupline at noon on Fifth Street has introduced many hungry people to a culinary experience that would make Julia Child, the Galloping Gourmet, the kitchen staffs of Luchows and Le Pavillon all hang their heads in shame. There is no secret recipe for Catholic Worker Soup; the unstructured and arbitrary methods by which it is produced have, at times, resulted in disappointments, but are more often striking examples of the poetry engendered when the undisciplined imagination confronts kitchen hardware and barren icebox.

The hardware problem is easy; a large pot, a long spoon, and a sharp knife. That elegantly simple trinity, if your goal is good, honest soup, is all you need.

Some things to be kept in mind:

1. In the early days of the Catholic Worker, Peter Maurin and Dorothy Day thought that it would be a good idea to keep a soup pot simmering at all times. This could be continually replenished by whatever vegetables the people of the house could acquire. It was a brilliant idea for a symbol of communal sharing, cer-

From the Pages of *The Critic*

tainly. But, even more certainly, it was responsible for delicious soup. The longer soup simmers, obviously, the better it tastes, and the vegetables and flavors that do not become compatible, even complementary, after four hours companionship in a boiling pot are rare.

2. Far too many modern problems (our fascination with violence, our racism, our waste of resources, our fragmentation as people) are grounded in unnecessary fears. One minor, but definitely unnecessary fear is the fear of making too much soup. Soup that has been reheated after forty-eight hours in the refrigerator tastes much better than the soup you made this morning, and serves as an excellent theme for even better soup. I like to think that in the soup I had at noon today, there may have been a few dim atoms of the soup served on the day our house here opened. Good soup is one way we can preserve the treasures of the past, and demonstrates that tradition is never a dead thing, but always a fresh and enriching perspective on the present. Good soup has, in common with great art, and the Gospel itself, the characteristic of eternal freshness and beauty.

3. The phrase "too much garlic" is meaningless.

4. So is the phrase "too many onions."

5. The idea may be unorthodox, but sometimes, by concentration on visual aesthetics, to the exclusion of the more vulgar urgings of the palate, one can stumble into higher realms of soup-making and soup-eating pleasure. About a month ago, I emptied an annoying can of

Just Good Reading

catsup (it had wasted space in our icebox for too long and its moment had come) into what had previously been an uninteresting liquid of drab, brown appearance. I stirred in the catsup hesitantly, watching deep red clouds from the bottom of the soup kettle merge gently with the brown. Soon the pot was simmering again, this time with a wine-dark surface. It smelled wonderful, but tasted strangely sweet. Onion salt, gradually added, brought the taste of the soup from sweet to rich. More space in the icebox. Better looking soup. Better tasting soup (the men in the house nearly all came back for seconds) and a proud and happy soupmaker. All of this as a result of inclusion rather than exclusion.

A person of longer association with the Catholic Worker could make other suggestions, and in the interests of space conservation this should be cut short. It wouldn't hurt to remember that soup is best as a shared food; that all food becomes better when shared. That is what the miracle of loaves and fishes teaches us. This is what the child's story "Nail Broth" celebrates. Most people on the North American continent have at this moment, in their refrigerators, ingredients which, when added to a quart or so of boiling water, could delight and enrich them. Especially if they used too much of everything, and invited too many to eat with them. The reason that such an idea is preposterous to us is our own unnecessary fear.

CONFESSION

by Stuart Dybek

FATHER BOGUSLAW was the priest
I waited for,
the one whose breath,
through the thin partition
of the confessional,
reminded me of the ventilator
behind Vic's Tap.

He huffed and smacked
as if in response to my dull litany
of sins, and I pictured him
slouched in his cubicle,
draped in vestments,
the way he sat slumped
in the back entrance to the sacristy
before saying morning mass—
hungover, sucking an unlit Pall Mall,
exhaling smoke.

Once, his head thudded
against the wooden box.
Father, I whispered, Father,
but he was out, snoring.
I knelt, wondering what to do,

Just Good Reading

until he finally groaned
and hacked himself awake.

As always, I'd saved the deadly sins for last:
the lies and copied homework,
snitched drinks, ditching school,
hitch-hiking, which I'd been convinced
was an offense against the Fifth Commandment
which prohibited suicide.

Before I reached the dirty snapshots
of Korean girls, stolen from the dresser
of my war hero Uncle Al,
and still unrepentantly cached
behind the oil shed,
he knocked
and said I was forgiven.

As for Penance:
Go in peace, my son,
I'm suffering enough today
for both of us.

I, SAID THE SPARROW

by Arthur Roth

BEFORE I start this story of how a boyhood friend lost his eye, I have to tell you about "convoys." When I recently went home to Ireland, after an eighteen year absence, I was sure that the "convoy"—like thruppenny chunks of Yellow Man candy, the big Turkey Market in November, and the Sunday pitch-and-toss school behind the ball alley—had been long ago unceremoniously banished among the quaint rituals of social history by the members of a younger generation that, not content with just *embracing* the twentieth-century, had it already half digested and were reaching for whatever tidbits they could glimpse of the twenty-first. The young crowd now, true Europeans to a man, thought nothing of hiking through France or Italy on their holidays, or even setting off on a two week boat, rail and plane tour of Lapland; whereas in *my* time vacation had been a three-hour crawling train journey to Bundoran in County Donegal, all of forty miles away, to confront what seemed to us to be the greatest natural wonder in the world: a grey and brawling Atlantic that periodically took a chest-heaving breath and sent its cavalry charging into the cliffs—great sullen brutes of waves that looked as if they'd leap Donegal itself and land far back in County Tyrone. Watching the breakers explode

Just Good Reading

into fifty-foot columns of spray, it was easy then to believe in Saint Patrick's dying wish: that Ireland be immersed beneath the seas a year before the rest of the world went up in flames, a legend that was supposed to be comforting, though I don't know why, remembering those waves.

But getting back to convoys, they'd been a regular thing in the past. Even in 1945, the year I left, you still heard of one every now and again. They were widely held back in the last century, when every Irish railway station had its convoy morning, and again in the decade after World War I, when another big wave of emigrants went over.

A convoy was simply a party for someone who was emigrating, a party that started in the late evening and went on all night and into the morning, with singing and dancing and relays in the kitchen of "a little cup of tay and a bite in your hand." When morning came the hardiest souls, along with the emigrant and his family, would troop to the railway station to wave a red-eyed exile off on the nine-fifteen to Derry City. There he caught the tender out of Moville and transferred to the Cunard liner anchored at the mouth of Lough Foyle. Back in the twenties Friday had been convoy day in my town and it was common then to find a dozen emigrants at the railway station, surrounded by their families and late revellers. But times have changed. The transatlantic liners no longer call at Derry City, and emigrants now leave from Shannon Airport on great silvery jets that bear the exotic shields of a score of different nations.

Convoys used to be charged with the same sort of gay melancholy that infuses a good wake, which in effect

From the Pages of *The Critic*

they really were, as in times gone past most of the emigrants never returned. I suppose it's this business of returning that holds the key to the gradual disappearance of convoys. It's hard to get all worked up over a fellow who's liable to pop back in the summer on a twenty-one day jet excursion fare.

Anyway, I had been home almost a month when one evening my twenty-one-year-old cousin Sean, the milking all done, came into the kitchen, rubbed his hands together and asked me how I'd like to go to a convoy that evening. Teezie Devlin, of the Mullinaslin Devlins, was emigrating to Philadelphia.

A couple of hours later I found myself, along with Sean and his sister Bella, squeezed into the front of Sean's Austin van, bouncing along a sunken lane that cut through a patch of rough mountain pasturage. Whin bushes, crowned with tiny yellow blossoms, towered on either side of us and only when we came rising over a hump was it possible to see the surrounding land. Although it was ten-thirty there was still plenty of light. It was mid-July and in our part of Ireland—which is roughly the same latitude as Northern Labrador—we get those long, almost arctic, twilights. With the bouncing of the van it was impossible to make conversation and we braced our jiggling bodies as best we could while Sean, with a casual one-handed expertise that was largely for the benefit of his "poor wee cousin from Yankeeland," guided the vehicle along until we breasted through Mullinaslin Gap and went flying down a long straight hill. At the bottom Sean spun the wheel in a sharp right turn and we headed straight for a pair of large stone pillars. I grabbed the door handle. We shot

Just Good Reading

through the open space with all of an inch to spare and came to a wheel-locking stop in the middle of a large farmyard.

Already half a dozen assorted cars and vans were parked in the yard, plus three motorcycles, a scooter, and a few bikes. In my time it would have been all bicycles, twenty or thirty of them, with maybe a pony and trap or two.

We entered the kitchen to be introduced around, whereupon I was immediately captured by old Mrs. Devlin, the only one to be wearing a shawl, I noticed, and in no time at all she had Teezie and I off in a corner and for the next half-hour, a bottle of stout in my hand, I held forth on the assorted pitfalls and promises of Philadelphia, a city I had visited only once, for twenty minutes or so, driving through on my way to Washington. At one point I was about to make my escape when Mrs. Devlin heard from Sean that I was a high school teacher, a fact that set her off on another round of exclamations. She stepped back and eyed me with a new respect. "Did you hear that, Teezie? A high school teacher!" She clapped her hands, everybody seemed to be clapping their hands at me that evening, and exclaimed. "Ah God love him, hadn't he got on well? And sure when he left here he was just a wee lad running around with his stockings at half-mast and a drop at the end of his nose that would drown a kitten." Which wasn't the image I had of myself at all. In retrospect, it seems to me that I had been one hell of a man with the women and all thunder and lightning on the football field. Be that as it may, I finally got out of the kitchen, and went out to the yard where I stood for a moment, nostalgia weighing me

From the Pages of *The Critic*

down as I looked around at the familiar shapes of my childhood; the byre, the creamery cans, the big square doughal, even the pointed twin white pillars that marked the entrance to every farmyard in the North of Ireland.

Of course the pillars had long since lost their innocence; a college professor having taught me to recognize *those* particular shapes as phallic symbols, hangover from a Celtic past, erected (forgive the pun) to propitiate the goddess of fertility or some similar esoteric prompting. Yet looking at them, I suddenly realize that they had been built round and smooth like that to eliminate any sharp edges that might catch the side of a cow and cause harm. There's a sort of Murphy's Law for cattle also: if two cows can get jammed in a gap they will. The reason for the dunce cap hoods that crowned each pillar was equally plain and practical. Internal moisture was the great enemy of anything built with lime-mortar, and what better shape for shedding rain and snow than a cone? For a moment I was twelve years back in the past, taking a course entitled "Primitive Peoples of Western Europe," listening to Professor Burckhardt explain the significance of those particular shapes. I saw myself rise to my feet and softly state, I beg to take issue with you on that point Professor, but it so happens that those pillars are constructed in such a fashion because . . .," and on to jamming cows and lime-mortar. Yield Burckhardt, I've got your number. How I would have relished that moment; I had a natural hatred of anyone who could possibly consider the Irish a primitive people, not to mention the Scots, the Welsh, the Bretons and the Basques.

Leaving Burckhardt vanquished there in the dust of

Just Good Reading

the farmyard, I turned away and began to track the sound of an accordion; followed it up an outside flight of stone steps, ducked my head to clear the low lintel beam of the doorway, and entered a noisy and crowded hayloft. Making my way along the wall, I sat down on one of the benches and looked around. The stone walls had been newly whitewashed and, considering that the place was actually a barn, the floor was in pretty decent shape, having been specially made smooth for the night's dancing by the liberal application of Lux soap flakes, little drifts of which could be seen in the corners and along the walls, swept there in the drafts kicked up by trouser cuffs and belling skirts. Up through the open rafters overhead I could see resting a horse's complete harness—collar, hames, britchings and bridle—and I wondered at the equipment being stored in such an awkward place merely to clear the loft for a one-night dance. Then I noticed the coating of dust on the leather and remembered the yellow Fordson tractor, parked in the little orchard behind the house.

There must have been thirty couples on the floor, doing a set, and the exuberant way they went about it caused the planks beneath my feet to set up their own creaking rhythm. I glanced over at the band; there were four musicians, sweat glistening their foreheads as one bellowsed the accordion, two sawed away on fiddles and the fourth punished his drum. With a queer little start I noticed that one of the fiddlers was Poke McAleer. There was a time when Poke and I were inseparable.

The dance ended and Sean came over and sank down beside me, half panting still from the strenuous demands of the six-hand-reel. "Are you not dancing?" he finally asked.

From the Pages of *The Critic*

"I just came in."

"I see your old friend Jimmy Grimes is here."

"Oh, yes?" I looked around and sure enough there he was in a corner, surrounded by half a dozen younger fellows.

"Blathering away as usual," Sean said, trying to get a rise out of me.

"Right enough, Jimmy was always a great one for talk."

"Aye, and other things," Sean said darkly.

The little group shifted and I had a good look at Jimmy. The passage of time had worn some fairly deep ruts. Though still only thirty-seven, he had the face of a man in his late forties; that great square jaw of his had grown wattles; his upper cheeks wore the permanent flush of a heavy drinker, while the lower jaws curved in, revealing all too plainly that most of his back teeth had fallen by the wayside. The eyes looked the same, though I knew if I got a bit closer they'd likely be bloodshot from the succession of wee nips he'd undoubtedly downed earlier in the evening. Then once more I looked over at the band, at Poke McAleer running a cube of rosin up and down one of the fiddle strings. Even with the collapsed eyelid Poke looked ten years younger, the face still sharp and unseamed, the forehead smooth. Yet all three of us were the same age. This was my first look at Poke since I'd been back, though I'd caught a glimpse of Jimmy before, from a distance, sloping into McCarran's entry after hours one evening, on the prowl for another thirsty diehard like himself.

As luck would have it, Jimmy noticed me at that moment and came up the hall, a big smile on his face.

Just Good Reading

Watching him, you'd swear the man was stone sober but I knew my Jimmy of old.

"So you're back?"

"I am indeed, Jimmy."

"By God," he exclaimed in that boisterous way of his, "you're looking well. The States must agree with you."

"You're not much changed yourself, Jimmy."

"I'm not, that's a fact. I'm still at the dances every week." He leaned closer, bathing me in whisky fumes as he whispered, "but sure the women are a lot smarter nowdays."

Which meant, I knew, that he didn't have his pick and choice anymore.

He pinched my arm. "Listen, I've a bottle in the car below, you'll give me a hand with it?"

"I'd rather not, Jimmy," I lied easily. "I had a few early on and they didn't sit too well."

He was mountainously offended. "What do you mean? Hell to your soul, wasn't it *me* that taught you to drink?"

Couples were moving out to the floor to take their places for a set and I glanced around for someone I could say I had promised the dance to. Most of the girls were unknown to me and Bella already had a partner.

"We'll just slip out for a minute," Jimmy urged, pulling at my arm.

I let myself be persuaded and we edged through the forming groups of dancers, went out the door and clattered down the stairs. I followed him across the cobblestoned yard to his car, an old Morris Eight with the back cut away to form a cargo bed. He clambered in front,

From the Pages of *The Critic*

shouting instructions, "Go you around and get in the other side. Mind the door, it's a bit balky."

I got in and closed—as best I could—the badly sprung door.

Face turned sideways and head resting against the steering wheel, one hand down between his thighs, Jimmy was rummaging away in the interior of the front seat. He closed his eyes and I wondered if he had fallen asleep, but a final shoulder-wrenching squirm and he pulled out a half-full bottle of Old Bushmills.

"Have to hide it," he grunted. "There's a bunch of wee snots running around to the dances now that'd steal you blind."

He offered the bottle and I pulled out the cork and took a token swallow.

"America must have ruined your thirst," he said, noticing how little I'd had. "Go on man, have a decent drink. Sure I'm not charging for it."

I swallowed another mouthful and handed the bottle back. He rested it on the steering wheel and stared out through the windshield at the gable of the house. "Did you see him?"

"I did."

"He can play the fiddle, can't he?"

"He plays well."

"I'm not codding you, he's a genius with the bloody thing." He lifted his arm and began worrying the neck of the bottle.

"You're not married yet, Jimmy," I said, trying to change the subject.

"No more than yourself."

Just Good Reading

"Sure we've plenty of time yet."

He wiped his mouth with the back of his hand and said bitterly, "Ach, I should have left this bleeding kip when you did. You're well out of it."

"It's not a bad wee spot all the same, I've often been homesick for it."

With a drunken change of mood, he brought one hand down on my shoulder and gave me an affectionate squeeze. "God be with the old days. We had some smashing times, didn't we?"

"That we did, Jimmy."

"Will you ever forget the night the three of us took off for a dance in Altmore with the one bicycle, and us blind to the gills."

I fell in with his mood. "With me on the bar and you pedaling and Poke trotting alongside."

"It was like a bloody dance so it was, the three of us changing partners every turn of the road."

"When we weren't pulling the bicycle out of the ditch."

"The three must-get-theirs, we were a holy terror weren't we?"

"We were I suppose."

"Have you talked to him at all?"

"Not yet."

"He's changed a lot."

I said nothing and like an old recurring nightmare the scene came back to me, Poke on his knees in the snow, his hands covering his face and screaming in a voice that made both Jimmy and I want to take to our heels.

Up till then we'd been bosom buddies, the three of us. Jimmy had been the ringleader and both Poke and I

From the Pages of *The Critic*

would have followed him anywhere. That was the sort of personality Jimmy had. There wasn't an ounce of fear in his body, he was a natural football player, and a charmer with women; three qualities that Poke and I admired extravagantly. We closed our eyes to the touch of tyrant in him and like two flatterers fought for his favor. And Jimmy took advantage of it, he was forever setting one of us against the other, although never to the point where we three broke up. He was good at pouring oil when it suited him. I suppose that sort of adolescent friendship with its fanatic, almost feminine, underground of passion and intrigue had to fade away eventually. Indeed, it was probably fading already that winter of the blizzard but the accident finished everything.

That winter is still called in Dungarvan the year of the big snow. In fact the town had been completely cut off for three days, that being part of the whole misfortune too, for the accident happened the first afternoon of the snow. Earlier, Jimmy and I had been fooling around on the Square, kicking at the quarter-inch of snow that had already accumulated. With a bit of scraping, there was just enough to pack into a snowball and we fired an experimental few at the hanging sign that marked the northwest corner of the Square, "C. Lagan, Licensed to Sell Beer, Wine and Spirits to be Consumed on or off the Premises." We decided the snow wasn't deep enough yet for really effective work, so we went over to Foyle's and talked to Old Hughey for a while. Half an hour later we checked the snow again, pronounced it in fine shape, and went to look for Poke to see what mischief the three of us could invoke. As luck would have it, we turned

Just Good Reading

the corner of the Square and there, about twenty yards ahead, in the middle of the road and with his back to us, stood the bold Poke, looking up at Brophy's second story window. Breege had the curtains half parted and was staring down at him. I don't know but Poke might have been considering the idea of letting fly with a snowball to throw a bit of a fright into Breege, not too much of a fright because we all knew that Jimmy was a bit taken with her. You might say she was his current girl friend, although current usually meant a month at the most with Jimmy. Naturally Poke and I hated her.

Anyway, we stood there for a moment, the four of us, Jimmy and I with a snowball apiece in our hands; Poke, his back to us, staring up at the face framed between the two curtain halves; and Breege looking over Poke's head and down to where we stood, a few yards behind him. This whole scene has to be visualized through a veil of drifting snow, fine white powdery granules, a pointillist effect you might say.

Then Jimmy said something like, "I'll shout at him and when he turns around we'll both let fly." Just then Breege motioned to Poke with her hand, stabbing her forefinger back and forth as though to say, "There, behind you see?," either in an attempt to warn him of our intentions, or in the hope that he would turn around and present a more enticing target for her boyfriend to aim at. To this day I don't know what made him turn, Breege's warning, or Jimmy's shout, or some sixth sense of his own, but turn he did and caught a snowball between the eyes and one on the chest. He fell to his knees in the middle of the road and I, for one, naturally assumed he did so in order to retaliate, to get closer to the

From the Pages of *The Critic*

ammunition. But, his hands up and covering his face, he began to scream, rocking himself back and forth.

There'd been a piece of sharp gravel in one of the snowballs and it had pierced his left eye. I ran down for Doctor Fitzgerald while Jimmy stayed behind, but the Doctor was out on a call. I left a message with the housekeeper and then went to Sheehy's. Mrs. Sheehy had been a nurse before she married Tom. I told her what had happened and she threw on a coat and came hurrying up the street. I meant to go back and see how Poke was, but the memory of him screaming, rocking his body back and forth in the snow, was too terrifying to face so I sneaked in the back way of our place and hid in my room.

It almost seems as though Poke was fated to lose that eye. Doctor Fitzgerald didn't get back until eight that night—he'd run into trouble with the state of the roads. By then over a foot of snow had fallen, a fine, dry and powdery snow that was drifting as high as three and four feet in places. Doctor Fitzgerald did what he could but it snowed all that night and half the next day and it was yet another day before the roads were clear again. By the time they got Poke to a hospital there was no hope anymore of saving the eye.

Later we made it up, Jimmy and I, to say that we didn't know whose snowball it was that hit Poke in the face. Actually mine hadn't; I'm sure I would have felt the stone when I was making the snowball, but maybe Jimmy thought the same.

Psychologists claim we tend to repress unhappy memories but it hasn't worked out that way for me. Periodically now for eighteen years I have seen two snowballs

Just Good Reading

winging through the flake-filled air, one a little above and a little behind the other, both of them converging on the dark blur of a head in motion. For eighteen years I've willed both snowballs to collide and break into harmless fragments, but for eighteen years they've missed each other and continued true to their target. I see one of them hit Poke in the face and sense the other breaking on his chest. It isn't that I see the one that did the damage more clearly because I am following the flight of my *own* snowball, it's simply that the one that struck him in the face had the more dramatic impact. It hit the bridge of his nose, clung there for a second, then slowly broke apart and fell in two halves.

In my countless re-creations of the scene I must admit that—when we turn the corner and see Poke staring up at Breege—I have often detected a violent flush of jealousy on Jimmy's face as he bent to knead the snow. But it wasn't like that at all. Jimmy's suggestion that we snowball Poke seemed the most natural thing in the world; the same thought had crossed my own mind. At other times I have even, illogical as it sounds, somehow succeeded in summoning an ambulance, an American one oddly enough, which I send forth on a journey down through the years to emerge on our street and make its way, slowly but doggedly, rear wheels spinning, up to where the consoling Jimmy and wounded Poke are kneeling in the snow. Sometimes I am sitting beside the driver, urging him on, while other times I am behind the vehicle, pushing. But in all my re-shufflings of that scene, I cannot make those two snowballs collide and fall harmlessly to the ground; no matter how I bend

From the Pages of *The Critic*

their trajectories, one always whispers past the other to strike home.

So there you are, I can't help feeling that a quarter-inch piece of gravel changed all our lives. I emigrated about a year after Poke lost his eye and though I had a dozen good reasons for leaving Dungarvan, I often wonder if the sight of that sunken, somehow accusing, eyelid wasn't the real cause of my flight. I can remember all too clearly my irritation at Poke for not wearing the glass eye that the hospital had furnished. As for Jimmy, he never prospered after that. The youthful drinking sprees grew longer and longer, became inspired less by spontaneous acts of joy and more by the grimly predictable and ordinary happenings of everyday life. He's let the old Grimes farm go to rack and ruin, blackberry bushes all over the fields, gaps in all the hedges. It's only a matter of time before he loses the place.

And Poke? Surely he would never have taken up music and fishing, those two somehow solitary pasttimes that became such a part of his life after losing the eye. I *hate* that phrase. It sounds as though he absent-mindedly misplaced his eye, set it for a moment in an old can of screws and nails out in the barn and then forgot where he put it. Anyway, before the accident, I don't think Poke had ever had a fiddle in his hands, although he did go, like the rest of us, to Lough Bracken every once in a while to try for a pike.

Before I tell you what happened to Breege let me finish with the convoy. I finally managed to get away from Jimmy and make my way back to the dance. As it turned out the band was having a break. It's usually the custom

Just Good Reading

to leave behind one man to play for the crowd until the rest of the band comes back, an accordionist or fiddler who runs through a medley of old tried and true numbers with every now and then a modern hit thrown in. I remember, for example, how incongruous "Oh Mein Papa" sounded that night, its typically teary and German sentimentality completely out of place among the lilting drives of jig, reel and hornpipe.

I went up and joined the crowd that had formed around the makeshift platform where Poke, the stay-behind man, was playing one of those old Irish airs on his fiddle, "The Rakes of Mallow" or "The Sweets of May." He was really making the instrument sing, throwing back his head and lifting the fiddle as he reached for a high note, then bending low to croon at the bridge. I noticed, of course, that he stood sideways, presenting his good profile, but as I watched the oblivious ecstasy on his face and in his movements, I thought that of all of us he had come out of the incident the best. I sensed, with a sort of sad, tumbling-into-middle-age feeling, that never would I get out of teaching, or Jimmy get out of the bottle, what Poke got out of his fiddle. But then again, maybe that's what I *wanted* to think.

With a quivering, sawing-down movement of the bow he brought the piece to an end. A round of clapping broke out; he had carried all of us with him, and he lifted his sweat-drenched face in pleasant surprise, his one eye travelling around the circle of onlookers.

"I heard you were back."

"Back for a visit."

"You'll have to drop over some evening."

"I will surely, Poke," I said, though I had no intention

From the Pages of *The Critic*

of doing so. I was trying to think of a way to frame a compliment on his playing when the other three musicians came back, dragging on the butt ends of the cigarettes. From the sheepish satisfaction on their faces I knew that they'd been asked down to the kitchen for a few bottles of stout, "to take the edge off their thirst." That's part of the custom too. I took advantage of their return to move away from the platform, ostensibly looking for Sean or Bella. They were both involved with companions and I didn't feel like breaking in on either of them, so I walked outside and went down the steps, intending to see if I could scrounge another bottle of porter in the kitchen. As I crossed the yard I passed Jimmy's odd-looking wagon and noticed him slumped inside, his folded arms laid over the steering wheel, his head down and fast asleep. I was tempted to wake him, changed my mind and headed for the front door of the farmhouse. Just before I entered I heard the band start up again.

And that's all that happened at the convoy, which brings me now to Breege and here I have to be careful. You see the trouble is that I've told this story before, many times. Once, for example, to a charming old lady I met at a teacher's convention and for *her* I omitted any reference to myself. There's only Poke, Jimmy and Breege, and to give the story a nice pleasant ending Breege marries Poke and they eventually become the proud parents of four bouncing baby boys. On another occasion, trying to illustrate the Irish sense of guilt for a school psychiatrist friend of mine, I've hewed much closer to the truth and had Breege—in this version a very beautiful girl—enter a convent where she takes the

Just Good Reading

name of Sister Santa Lucia after the patron saint of the blind. Actually Breege today *is* in a convent, just outside Liverpool, only her name isn't Sister Lucia, it's Sister Mary Anunciata. Nothing there. Still, I can't help wondering sometimes if, in the small hours of the morning, there in her cell with its lone candlestick, its prayerbook on top of the small plain bedside table, with a moonbeam slat falling across the heavy wooden crucifix above the head of her bed (I know it's a romantic picture but it's very difficult to imagine a nun's bedroom), she doesn't sometimes wake up and stare at the ceiling as *she* too re-creates the scene, tries to take back her warning gesture, or wills the two flying objects to pass wide of the mark. I can see her, vaguely troubled, reaching for her Rosary to say a few prayers for herself, or to pray for Poke, or for Jimmy, or even me.

But perhaps she never thinks of the accident at all, perhaps even if those snowballs had never been thrown, we would today all be exactly as we are. There's always *that* possibility, too.

THE FIRST PAPAL PRESS CONFERENCE

by Andrew Greeley

KEVIN CARDINAL ORSINI was elected Pope by "inspiration" on the forty-third day of the conclave; ninety-six-year-old Cardinal Antonelli leaped from his throne in the Sistine chapel and shouted in his feeble voice, "Orsini Papa!" With varying degrees of weariness, surprise, dismay and joy, all the other cardinals echoed the shout—"Orsini Papa!" It was then pointed out by several of those present that this was indeed a legitimate and definitive way of selecting a pope, even though it was one that apparently had not been used in the history of the Papacy. Almost without realizing it, the cardinals had selected their youngest member, the forty-six-year-old Orsini, as the new pope. There were some, later on, who claimed that Antonelli had been sound asleep and in his sleep had a nightmare of Orsini becoming pope. His cry of "Orsini Papa!" it was alleged, was not an inspiration from the Holy Spirit, but the result of a bad dream. In any case, Orsini's supporters had seized the opportunity to proclaim their man the victor, and after forty-three days of a conclave in which nine cardinals had already died, no one was prepared to dispute his claim to the Papacy.

In his first act as pope, Orsini, now known as Kevin the First, giving the traditional blessing, *Urbi et Orbi*, in

Just Good Reading

a black business suit and tie, had announced that, while he had deep respect for the College of Cardinals, and had every intention of continuing it as an important arm of the Church, he thought it would be inappropriate, under the circumstances of the modern world, to continue the College as the Papal electoral body. He announced that henceforth the Pope would be elected by all the archbishops of the world. "Unless," he added, "my colleagues in the Synod can come up with a better idea."

The day after his election, Orsini announced the first English language Papal press conference. Before the Pontiff arrived in the banquet room of the Rome Hilton, where the conference was to take place, members of the Vatican press corps compared notes on the very strange background of Kevin the First. His father was Prince Raphael Orsini, now a member of the Italian Senate, and Princess Annie (nee O'Brien) Orsini, a Dublin actress whom Prince Raphael had wooed and wed while he was the third secretary of the Italian mission to Dublin. Their son had been raised in the Flatbush area of Brooklyn while Prince Raphael was on the staff of the United Nations, and he had attended Fordham University and the Harvard Graduate School of Business before beginning his theological studies at the Pontifical Gregorian University. His rise in the Papal diplomatic service had been meteoric, but his reputation for pragmatism, liberalism and a somewhat off-beat sense of humor, as well as the fact that he spoke both Italian and English with a Brooklyn accent, had made him an unlikely candidate for the Papacy.

From the Pages of *The Critic*

Kevin the First, attired in a gray Seville Row suit, light blue shirt and paisley tie, finally arrived at the Monte Mario for his press conference, a transcript of which appeared the following day in the *New York Times*.

Q. (Times of London) *Your Holiness, the whole world is wondering—*
A. Please don't call me Your Holiness. I don't know that I'm all that holy and it's sort of an old-fashioned name. You can call me Pope and Mr. Pope, but please don't call me Your Holiness.
Q. *Well, yes, Sir. The whole world is wondering what your position will be on the birth control issue.*
A. I think it's a very complex issue and one that I certainly wouldn't want to address myself to in any specific detail this morning. We have really messed up this sex business in the Church for a long time and I don't think we're going to be able to make any coherent Christian statement on family planning until we do a lot of thinking and talking about the whole question of sexual personalism. I'm going to summon the Synod of Bishops into session the week after next, and certainly one of the top items on my agenda will be to ask my colleagues if they will set up a commission to consider a statement on the meaning of sex in the Christian tradition.
Q. (Chicago Sun-Times) *Do we understand, then, Mr. Pope, that you intend to convene the Synod of Bishops at once?*
A. Why yes, of course I do. This is an extremely difficult job I've been saddled with and I certainly don't

Just Good Reading

intend to try and do it all myself. What's the point of having all these bishops throughout the world unless they're going to bear some of the responsibility? I'm going to have them in session for a couple of months every year for the rest of my administration, and they may as well resign themselves to buying commuter tickets to Rome.

Q. (Times of London) *But, Sir, if I understand you correctly, there is going to be some considerable delay before you address yourself to the birth control issue. In the meantime, aren't you afraid that most Catholic couples will continue to consider artificial contraception a mortal sin?*

A. No, I don't think so. If they do think it's a mortal sin, they are, in my judgment, wrong, but I'm certainly not going to try and impose my views on their consciences—at least not until I have been advised by my colleague bishops.

Q. (St. Louis Post-Dispatch) *There has been considerable talk of restoring the practice of popular election of bishops to the Catholic Church. Would you care to comment on this possibility?*

A. Oh, I'd be happy to comment. Two of my predecessors of happy memory—I can't quite remember what their names were, but they were back in the sixth century—said that it was sinful to choose a bishop by any other method besides popular election. Being at heart a very conservative fellow, I agree with them, so I'm going to do everything in my power to sell the Synod of Bishops on restoring popular election as soon as we can. It may take a bit

From the Pages of *The Critic*

of selling, but when they see how tough their job is going to be in my administration, I think a lot of them are going to be only too happy to have a successor in four or five years.

Q. (St. Louis Post-Dispatch) *Then am I to understand, Sir, that you are in favor of limited terms for bishops and perhaps even for the pope?*

A. Well, if you think I'm going to stay in this office until I die, you're sadly mistaken. This may be a fine job for five or ten years, but after that I'm going to want to retire someplace where it's peaceful and quiet. It doesn't seem to me to be fair to ask anybody to hold a major leadership position for more than five or ten years at the most. I assume that when the Synod of Bishops ponders this matter at some length, they will agree with me.

Q. (New York Times) *Have you made any decisions about the selection of a Papal cabinet?*

A. That's a very good question, Scotty, and I'm not sure that I can give a complete answer, but at least I have some ideas. Sister Mary Luke is going to be made Secretary of the Congregation of the Religious, and Barbara Ward, Secretary of the Congregation of the Laity. I also am going to ask Bishop Butler if he'll head up a new office combining all our relationships with other religions, and I think Cardinal Suenens will make a great Secretary of State, if I can ever persuade him to leave Belgium. Beyond that, I am consulting with some of my closest advisors to find out what other talent is available that we might be able to recruit to serve in the cabinet.

Just Good Reading

I hope to have more specific announcements in a week or two, but you've got to realize that this whole thing has taken me somewhat by surprise.

Q. (Wall Street Journal) *Are we to take it, Sir, that you are going to make public the financial status of the Vatican?*

A. Well, I'm going to try to do it as soon as I can figure out what the financial status is. As far as I can understand, nobody but God exactly understands the finances of the Vatican, and unfortunately he's not about to make a private revelation on the subject.

Q. (Triumph) *Most Holy Father—*

A. I'm not Holy, and I'm certainly not Most Holy, and I'm also certainly not your father or anybody else's, so call me Pope, or Mr. Pope, or Bishop, and drop the rest of that nonsense.

Q. (Triumph, *again*) *You will, of course, maintain the Papal diplomatic service?*

A. I will most certainly do no such thing. The only reason we ever had diplomatic service in the first place was that communications weren't very good and they had to have somebody on the scene who could make decisions in the name of the Papacy. Given the kind of communication we have now, the diplomatic service is obsolescent. So it seems to me that the first thing we do is to transfer all the powers of the nuncios or the apostolic delegates to the National Conference of Bishops. Then they should send representatives to Rome to deal with the central offices here. There's no point in running the Church as though the jet airplane and the radio-telephone hadn't been invented.

From the Pages of *The Critic*

Q. (National Catholic Reporter) *What contribution, if any, do you think the lay people have to make to the life of the Church?*

A. What contribution, if any? Well that's kind of a silly question; they don't have any *contribution* to make —they *are* the Church. Without them we might just as well fold up our tents and steal away into the hills, if only because without them nobody is going to pay to keep the organization going. As a matter of fact, given the way we've treated the lay people for so long, I am surprised that they have paid as much as they have to keep us going. We shouldn't make any major decisions, it seems to me, until the implications of these decisions have been kicked around at the grass roots and we've got the reaction of the rank-and-file membership to what's going on. So we've got to have an assembly of the lay people of the parish and of the diocese and of the national Churches, and then finally, of the international Church. As soon as we can possibly get this sort of thing set up, we're going to do it. The trouble is that we can't do it overnight, so we're going to have to limp along for a while without having the advantage of grass roots participation. But one of the first things I intend to toss into the laps of my colleagues when I get together with the Synod is the problem of how we can most quickly get an international network of lay senates established. If we don't have them, we are certainly going to make the Holy Spirit work overtime.

Q. (Los Angeles Times) *Do you expect, Sir, that there is going to be much change in canon law in the near future?*

Just Good Reading

A. You better believe there's going to be changes. I have the highest respect for the code of canon law; it is one of the greatest legal masterpieces of all time, and that's why I think we must let it be a *living* masterpiece and evolve into something that's even more perfect than itself. Of course its evolution is going to be rather dramatic, I think, in years to come, because very clearly what we need is some sort of international constitution which sets down general principles and, particularly, general rights and freedoms, and then lets the local hierarchies worry about legislating to meet their own problems.

Q. (St. Louis Post-Dispatch) *Do you expect to separate the legislative and judicial functions of the Church?*

A. Oh, you almost have to do that if you're going to keep everybody honest. It seems to me that we ought to turn the Roman Rota into a kind of supreme court of the Church to which people can appeal when they feel that their rights have been violated by the lower courts; and the exact shape of the lower courts should be determined by each national hierarchy. Given the complexity of the world today, it would be a terrible burden on the Roman judges to expect them to understand the problems that come in from every country. So they really should only have to hear the most important kind of appellate cases.

Q. (Detroit Free Press) *Does that mean, Sir, that you intend to have a reform of marriage legislation?*

A. I almost wish you hadn't asked that, because it is one of the most fouled-up problems that we have to face. I've already got some of my staff working on temporary changes that are going to improve the

From the Pages of *The Critic*

methods we're already using. I certainly hope that somebody in the Synod of Bishops has a brilliant idea on how we can straighten the mess out permanently, but I, for one, am at a loss as to how to do it. Nevertheless, I think we ought to get out of the divorce trial business. It just seems to me that the Church would have been better off long ago if all the people we've trained to be canon lawyers had been trained to be counseling psychologists instead.

Q. (Le Figaro *of Paris*) *Do you plan, Sir, to make any Papal trips?*

A. Well, I like to travel as much as the next man, and maybe even a little more. But it seems to me that traveling is more of a vacation than anything else, and I don't expect to learn much on my trips. If the national hierarchies elect good leaders, I presume they'll be the ones who will keep me informed on what's going on. It seems to me that the Papal trip really is pretty much a waste of time. Just the same, let me assure you I'm not going to spend the rest of my term in Rome.

Q. (The Guardian, *Manchester, England*) *What do you intend to do about* L'Osservatore Romano?

A. I wish to heaven I knew what to do about it—would you like to be editor of it?

Q. *No, Sir, I wouldn't.*

A. Yeah, that's what they all say. Next question, please.

Q. (New Orleans Times Picayune) *What is your position on the celibacy question?*

A. Well, it's pretty clear we've got to do something about it, though I don't want to be stampeded into it

Just Good Reading

until we give the Synod and the various priest and lay senates around the world the time to talk about it. I think we ought to make it easy for people to get out of the priesthood when they want to, with the promise that, if we do decide to have a married priesthood, we'll give them the option of getting back in—although I think we're going to want to take the option of not letting them back in under some circumstances. You know, every once in a while I'm inclined to think we should let anybody leave the priesthood who wants to, just so long as they and the women they're going to marry are ready to undergo a year of psychotherapy. But I don't suppose you could impose that anymore—that might be too autocratic. Just the same, it might be nice if we made the therapy available for them; we would also probably run out of psychiatrists.

Q. (Frankfurter Allegemeine Zeitung) *Do you expect there to be any heresy trials in your administration?*

A. Good God, no!

Q. (Frankfurter Allegemeine Zeitung) *But what is your opinion of heresy?*

A. Well, I don't know that I can find much trace in the Bible of the idea that there was such a thing as heresy—it seems to me to be an idea that came along much later on, and I wonder if we might not be well-advised to put it aside. I think there may be some theologians who speak a little bit beyond what the consciousness of the Church's own message would be able to permit, at the present time; but I'd much prefer to handle this by having a board of theologians sit down and discuss the matter with the theo-

From the Pages of *The Critic*

logian who seems to have gone beyond the consciousness and see whether it can be worked out —see whether he really can say the things he says and still, at least at the present time, be part of us. But the idea of excommunicating people and labeling them heretics seems to me to be terribly old-fashioned.

Q. (Frankfurter Allgemeine Zeitung) *But what do you think of the case of Reverend Dr. Hans Küng?*

A. You mean do I think Hans is a heretic? Why, don't be silly. Hans is basically a conservative. I never could understand why people thought he was dangerous or a radical. How in the world can anybody who owns a Mercedes-Benz be a radical?

Q. (Il Messaggero *of Rome*) *What, your Holiness—I mean, Pope—what is your opinion on the forthcoming Italian elections?*

A. I hope everybody votes in them.

Q. (Il Messaggero) *But what party are you supporting?*

A. We've got a secret ballot in this country just like most other countries and whom I vote for is my secret.

Q. (Il Messaggero) *But are you going to take a stand in Italian politics?*

A. What's the matter? Do you think I'm crazy?

Q. (Il Messaggero) *Does this mean, then, that the Vatican is assuming a policy of non-intervention in Italian politics?*

A. You bet your life it is.

Q. (Milwaukee Sentinel) *Do you intend, Sir, to continue the practice of censorship of books that are written by Catholics?*

Just Good Reading

A. I think it would be a good idea to take every imprimatur in the world and throw it in the furnace, and we ought to throw half of the book censors in the furnace too. The basic thing to say about censorship is that it didn't work, it doesn't work, and it's never going to work, and the quicker we forget about it, the better off we're all going to be.

Q. (Washington Post) *From all you've said so far, Sir, it would seem that you are really anticipating a very notable decline in Papal authority. I wonder if you could tell us whether you think that this is a drastic change in Church doctrine?*

A. Well, I don't know where you got that idea; I must say, as a matter of fact, I think what I'm talking about is a rather notable increase in Papal authority. A pope who is informed by his colleagues in the Synod and by the lay people of the world and a network of lay associations, who has had for his advisors the best theologians and scholars in the world, who makes informed decisions and can rely on cooperation with these decisions, isn't exactly a weak leader. On the contrary, I think he's a pretty strong one. It's not my intention to weaken the powers of the Papacy at all, but to strengthen the powers of the Papacy; and the reforms that I've discussed are designed to do just that. I might also say that it's probably going to increase the work of the Papacy and that's why I don't intend to spend much more than five or ten years in the office. You know it's kind of easy to make unilateral decisions, but it's awfully hard to gain consensus.

Q. (Philadelphia Inquirer) *Do you mean, then, that you*

From the Pages of *The Critic*

view the Papacy as being essentially a role of one who presides over a consensus?

A. Well, it depends on what you mean by presides. If you mean do I just sit back and wait until everybody's ideas come in and then coordinate them, I can assure you that's not how I intend to play the part. Nor do I see myself as providing the answers to questions. It seems to me that the most important job of a man in my position is not to answer questions, but to ask them; not to supply people with answers, but to challenge them to find out what the answers are. That's certain to be a pretty tough job and I'm going to have to gather some of the best minds in the world around me if I'm going to be able to pull it off.

Q. (NBC News) *Do you think, Sir, that your job as Sovereign Pontiff is going to be a difficult one?*

A. Sovereign Pontiff! The trouble with you, Chet, is that you've been reading *L'Osservatore Romano* too much. Sure, it's going to be a difficult job. Any top level administrative job is difficult, but if you surround yourself with a good staff and make sure the channels of communication are open, it's not an impossible job. As I say, I think ten years is plenty in it, but I'm rather looking forward to it.

Q. (Le Monde) *What do you think about the conflict between science and religion?*

A. I don't think there is one, and if there has been one, we'll now put a stop to it.

Q. (CBS News) *Do you have any opinion, Sir, on the question of the emerging nations?*

A. Well, I'm certainly going to support the encyclicals

Just Good Reading

on the subject written by my predecessors, though I don't think I'm going to issue any new encyclicals—as a matter of fact, I think we probably ought to declare a moratorium on encyclical writing. I'm going to wait until we get the Synod together and see what my colleagues from these nations think would be the best policy for the Church to assume in the matter. Given the immense number of people that we have in many of these nations, it seems to me that we ought to be doing a much better job than we are. I have a hunch that there might be something wrong with the leadership the Church is providing in the new nations and, if there is, you can believe that there's going to be a real shakeup.

Q. (Miami Herald) *Do you think the religious life of the priests and brothers and sisters is going to survive?*

A. It's not going to survive unless a lot of religious communities get a move on and take themselves out of the Middle Ages. Those who are willing to modernize, democratize, and treat the members like human beings, I think have a great future ahead of them. This is a day when everybody is crying for community, and a good religious order should be able to provide more community than anything else. But my personal opinion is that a lot of them are so bad that they simply are beyond redemption. That's one of the problems that my colleagues in the Synod are going to have to work out, too.

You know, there's something I'd like to say to you fellows. These questions have all been pretty good, but they're mostly on the internal problems of the Church. I suppose I can understand why you'd ask

From the Pages of *The Critic*

them, because most of the news the Church has made in the last couple hundred years has had to do with internal problems. We were bogged down for so long in ancient morbid structures that I guess the modernization of these structures was news. But I think I can tell you that by a year from now, or two years at the most, we're going to be so modernized that all you'll be able to ask me will be substantive questions, like What has the Church got to say about the meaning of human love? or What does it have to say about the quest for freedom? or What does it have to say about life and death? What does it have to say about getting old? or about leisure? or about the mass media? I'm kind of glad you're not asking me those questions now, because I haven't the faintest idea what the answers are. I can't even promise that I'll have very good answers a year from now, but they're going to be better than the present ones. Any more questions?

Q. (Seventeen) *Do you have anything to say to young people?*

A. Well, I'd say to the young to be patient with us older people because we're going to try to learn how to listen to you, and that we'll try, in our turn, to be patient with you while you try to learn how to listen to us. I don't think there's much wrong with young people that a little bit of experience won't cure—and there's not much wrong with older people that sharing the enthusiasm of the young won't cure.

Q. (New York Times) *Thank you, Mr. Pope.*

A. You're quite welcome, Scotty.

IRISH AND CATHOLIC IN THE 1920S

by Charles O. Rice

HOW did it start? Well, my father was a buyer for P. H. Butler Co., a Pittsburgh grocery chain, when I was brought back to the USA in 1920. How an ex-Irish Christian Brother became a chain store executive and how I happened to spend seven years in Ireland are stories that, if you are good and I am diligent, will be related in due time.

A salesman for Red Seal Lye, Ed Volk by name, "called" on my father, the buyer. We were also neighbors. The Rices lived on Bailey Ave., a reasonably posh address—the house cost $10,000 in 1920. Papa probably paid too much, at least he bought at the top of the market. The house, still standing, is worth more now. Volk lived behind us on Kambach St., not so posh. We overlooked the city from a height and were the first Irish Catholics on our block.

Our immediate Protestant neighbors at first were not overjoyed at the arrival of us Irish Catholics, but we got along. They were not Kluxers, although my mother would mutter the word after an argument over religion. Volk was no ordinary neighbor, being a Marxist and an all-around intellectual rebel. On the Russian Revolution he looked kindly and that had some influence on me over the years, here and there. Ed was an atheist, sort

From the Pages of *The Critic*

of. There must have been a tacit understanding between him and Papa because he never dropped any atheistic propaganda on me or Pat, my brother.

From Volk I got an admiration for Clarence Darrow and H. L. Mencken, accepting their version of the Scopes trial as I do to this day. That was an exciting trial. The verdict was not important, but the trial itself was, as Darrow sparred with Williams Jennings Bryan, who, as you know, had been a Democratic candidate for President more than once, and was a flat-out, corn-fed fundamentalist. Catholic Democrats were always a bit uneasy with Bryan. Darrow whipped him, but the Tennessee jury favored Bryan and voted that Scopes was guilty. The climax was the sudden death of Bryan who had grown enormously fat. If Darrow had died suddenly, the fundamentalists would have taken that as a sign from the Lord. Volk and our whole family followed the thing as if it were an athletic contest. Can you imagine what TV would have done with that?

We Rices were caught up in the Irish struggle for independence and Volk agreed with us. Natural Democrats, we were uncomfortable with Woodrow Wilson and his Puritan outlook, but what caused the family to vote for the Republican Party in 1920 was Wilson's hard-nosed stand against Irish freedom. In his Fourteen Points, he demanded freedom for small nations, but excepted Ireland. In 1924, Papa voted for Robert Marion La Follette, the Progressive Senator from Wisconsin, but 1928 found us back in the Democratic fold because of Al Smith. Could we have been a bit bigoted ourselves?

Ed Volk was an early radio buff and provided us with a crystal set, cat whiskers and all. We had a long aerial

Just Good Reading

reaching from our backyard fence to the third floor. Later we got hold of a loose coupler. I am not sure whether or not that thing was battery-operated. If it was, we used a dry cell which was rather bulky. Then we assembled a radio with vacuum tubes and a regular storage battery. It was a while before they worked out how to operate a radio from house current. However it was on one of our primitive radios that we listened to the Dempsey-Firpo fight. Graham MacNamee's announcing of that fight is still a vivid memory. You could actually see Dempsey being knocked out of the ring and coming back in to wallop the big Argentinian. Jack Dempsey was a Mormon, but to us he was an Irishman. Our neighbors did not like him, claiming that he was a slacker in WWI, but in our impartial Irish way, we ignored that. Dempsey was very unpopular in that day, believe it or not, as he blasted all before him. He did not join the Services during the War, being too busy in the ring, but a picture was published of him in overalls working in a shipyard. Unfortunately, a pair of expensive patent leather shoes peeped out from beneath the overalls. How different from the noble Ronald Reagan, who acquired no opprobrium from putting on a military uniform so that he could make war movies, causing him sometimes to fantasize publicly that he saw action.

Volk was also a photographer and had me taking and developing my own pictures. Fortunately I turned out to have an allergy to the developing fluids, or I might have wasted tons of time on that activity.

With all that background there should have been no surprise that I, as a young priest, bourgeois background not withstanding, was an ardent supporter of Franklin

From the Pages of *The Critic*

Delano Roosevelt and his New Deal and the burgeoning labor movement, especially the CIO when it came along in 1936.

My father was born in Ireland in 1873, the third of nine children, seven boys and two girls. The place was the townland of Bellurgan, which has an Upper and Lower Point. We were on the Upper, directly on the Bay. When the tide was in, it came up virtually to the front door. On a couple of occasions, it crossed the road and came right in the front door. The family was poor and farmed eleven acres. My grandfather was primarily a farmer, but he would supplement the family diet with fish and shellfish, caught or gathered by him and his sons. It helped that my grandmother was a good cook.

The way out of poverty was teaching. Papa was into it as a monitor in the local national school when he was recruited by the Irish Christian Brothers in his early teens. I am not sure of the date because I wrote none of this down when he was alive, but he was professed and spent ten years in India. Why the Christian Brothers pushed him out was a mystery to him. Possibly it had something to do with his health, which was very bad, after bouts with yellow fever and smallpox.

In India he taught school in Calcutta and Darjeeling, and had many stories to tell.

His pupils were the children of the Irish members of the British garrison, which garrison was mostly Irish.

In characteristic Irish fashion, the Christian Brother connection was kept from Pat and me. I think I learned of it toward the end of my college days. Bellurgan was a small close-knit community when I was growing up there between 1913 and 1920. While visiting Ireland

Just Good Reading

recently I had a discussion with a first cousin of mine, and I wondered why Papa's religious profession wasn't "thrown up" to us. All sorts of other things were in the course of the occasional bitter quarrels we had with our peers. "Ye were too young," she said. There were ground rules evidently, but I find it amazing, in retrospect, that this ground rule was observed.

When I was a sophomore in high school back in the States, a brother came around recruiting for the Brothers of the Holy Cross, the Notre Dame crew. I came home and announced that I was going to join up. An explosion came which I couldn't understand but accepted. For poor Papa, it was *deja vu.* Later on, I learned that it was not only his own bad experience with brotherly life that swayed him, but the conviction that young men and boys were entirely too vulnerable to be thrust into a situation where religious superiors had control over their lives. Never did he waver in his Catholic faith, nor in his respect for priests, brothers and nuns. He just didn't want me to go through what he did.

Around 1900, he was sent back to Ireland from India, on the P & O line. Never one to complain, he said that he spent his non-posh voyage in the cabin sewing buttons and patches on his clothes. (Posh is an expression that is said to come from the P & O Line's voyages to the Orient. If you were wealthy your cabin was Port on the way Out; Starboard on the way Home.) For years he harbored bitterness against the order and its members. But in 1947, shortly before he died, I took him back to Ireland, and we visited the Christian Brothers at their Dublin headquarters where he encountered some of his

From the Pages of *The Critic*

old contemporaries. He was at peace as they swapped reminiscences.

After he got back to Ireland around 1900, he spent a year recovering his health. For a while, he clerked in a grocery store in Dundalk. Then off to America.

His mother had some parting words: "Michael, if you are going to be good, you will often be lonesome." She also told him that she understood there were Irish policemen in New York (a resounding understatement), and when he got off the boat, he should ask one of them if he knew where there was a job for a young Irishman. It worked exactly as she predicted. There was an Irish policeman, a large, friendly one, who, when asked did he know where there was a job, said: "That I do, my boy. Go over there to that building that says James Butler, and since you are a tall, fine-looking Irish lad, they will hire you." He did, and they did.

The joke in Irish circles used to be that James Butler hired them off the boat, which is what happened.

Butler, an Irish immigrant himself, owned a racetrack, amassed tons of money, put up the money to start a religious order (of which his sister was foundress and Mother Superior), was a power in New York, a most prominent Catholic Irishman, and withal, a hard-hearted, tyrannical sonofabitch, Lord rest his soul.

In 1915 Papa left him for the A&P and was sent to Pittsburgh. Shortly he left the A&P for an executive position in a local grocery chain, and eventually retrieved us in 1920.

We had been sent to Ireland upon the death of my mother in 1913 and had seven formative years being

Just Good Reading

raised by my grandmother and some aunts and uncles. That time, which has a golden hue about it in my memory, will have to wait.

Back we came to America, April 1920. A long, horrible ocean voyage. Although Papa had paid for second-class passage on the Celtic, we came steerage. During most of the long ten-day voyage, we were buffeted by storms and seasick.

Pittsburgh in 1920 was gritty and smoky. Some bright, winter days at noon you couldn't see a hundred yards ahead of you, but Pittsburgh was prosperous. Prosperous and Republican. There was a small Democratic opposition, mostly Irish, and Papa and Uncle Joe used to argue with them at wakes over Irish and American politics.

I had retained no useful memories of America, and started from scratch. The heat of the summer was awful. The strange accents and customs were puzzling. Ice cream cones were a delightful discovery. I missed going barefoot in the summer, the pavements were too hot.

School was totally different and I had trouble adjusting, partly because I had become terribly nearsighted and it was six months before they figured out that I needed glasses. For Pat, things went swimmingly. His quiet personality endeared him to his schoolmates and he was both bright and studious. Interestingly enough, in everything but Latin, of which we learned nothing in the Irish National School, he was ahead of his American contemporaries.

Pity my poor stepmother, my mother's older sister, the eldest of six. Not so pretty as Anna, my mother. As Protestants from County Clare, they were better off

From the Pages of *The Critic*

than the Rices but not rich by any means. Forty acres is better than eleven, however. Their mother died young and Aunt Jennie helped to raise the rest; she was a workhorse and didn't like it a bit. She was the first of the family to emigrate. She got hold of the passage money by raising her own pig and selling it for five pounds, which paid her way.

Neither she nor my father ever discussed their actual voyages from Ireland to the United States. Was it grim or just uneventful?

About four years after the death of Anna, Papa married Jennie. If I ever knew the actual dates, I have forgotten them.

Papa remarried to make a home for us but he was an affectionate husband, and quite demonstrative for an Irishman, as he was demonstrative of his love for us two boys. No children to the second marriage.

Jennie was jealous, although she tried not to show it, of her younger and more pampered sister, and of the aunts and uncles who raised us and whom we, especially I, missed openly and terribly. I was so lonesome for everything about Ireland in those early years in Pittsburgh!

In addition, I was a skinny, restless, rather outspoken and tactless kid. Clumsy, also. I would not shape up. Jennie would be furious with me, and I don't blame her.

The nuns in school had their problems with me. Not at all studious, I read everything I could get my hands on other than the required school books. In school, fidgety and talkative, I always brought home a poor report card. There was one mark called deportment, on that I generally got sixty, and my handwriting was as

Just Good Reading

bad as the deportment. Writing was important because that was the day of the Palmer Method when all school children, especially those in Catholic schools, were expected to write uniformly. You were to practice the various strokes and swirls and eventually receive a diploma—I never did.

School in America was miserable for me in those early days of my re-Americanization. Our own parish had no school so we went off a mile-and-a-half to St. Mary on the Mount, a huge parochial school in a lovely big parish that was an Irish Catholic ghetto sprinkled with Germans and having an Italian fringe. There were WASPs in the neighborhood, a distinct minority with a touch of minority psychosis.

At the start, I got along better with the mostly Protestant kids around Bailey Avenue than my schoolmates, and now I know why. School makes kids aggressive. Being put in with scads of other kids stirs you up. A child, especially a male child, will be meaner and more hostile in a school playground than he will be in his neighborhood. Same things for girls, *mutatis mutandis.*

Those sisters. All Irish, it seemed, more than forty of them stuffed into a convent too small, dealing with fifty kids in a classroom, some of the kids being rather tough. The nuns had to be strong, and they were. The parish knew what they were putting up with and revered them.

They were a special group, most of whom came from Scranton and they wanted you to learn, behave, and be a believing Catholic. On the last, I gave them no trouble, but I would not study, would not be quiet and could not sit still. Not great for paying attention, I would occasionally realize what was going on and I

From the Pages of *The Critic*

would ask an impudent question. They were always telling me how much nicer my brother was, which was true, and wondering why I couldn't be like him. That raised no resentment in me, nor did it cause me to do better.

The nuns would say, "He could do better if he tried," but one sweet nun said, "Poor fellow, he is doing the best he can." I was mortified and put on a spurt to show her I had the potential, then I slackened off and went back into my dream world.

In the beginning, especially since I had undiagnosed myopia and couldn't read the blackboard, I was a bit withdrawn and docile. After I got glasses, life got better and I changed.

Although the Master in Bellurgan had been stern and demanding, and occasionally caned us, I was used to him. For all sorts of reasons, at first, the teaching nuns scared the hell out of me. In Ireland I had had nothing to do with nuns, saw them only from afar, and had a reverential awe toward them. Meeting them face to face and witnessing them cope with their impossible teaching situations overpowered me.

In Bellurgan our male teacher was dealing with only 25 or 30 of us in 4 grades and I hadn't many contemporaries, so mass parochial education took getting used to.

We were taught our religion in Ireland and taught very well. It was a totally Catholic environment, a different learning and teaching atmosphere.

It used to be said that American teaching in general was women-dominated, and that was in all the schools. Certainly at St. Mary of the Mount that was so. The priests would come in with some regularity, and I saw more of them on a formal and informal plane than I had

Just Good Reading

seen of the priests in Ireland. The American priests were likeable. The Irish priests of my day were distant figures whom a child just did not get to know, even an altar boy.

I was taught how to be an altar boy the way Mickey Rice, a neighbor and no relative, told me he trained his hunting dogs. "The auld dog trains the young dog." No urban spit and polish. We charged around the altar and shouted our Latin responses. Tommy Rice, again no relation, just slightly older, but much bigger, was the "auld dog" bullying us and even threatening to make the younger lads go to confession to him. Being an altar boy in America was a more genteel experience.

The regimentation of a large American parochial school was another thing that took getting used to, since my Irish school had been more informal, although quite effective. I was familiar with Macbeth and other classics because the Master taught them to the upper form and did it magnificently, scattering insight and relishing the poetry while I listened instead of doing whatever I was supposed to do. Study, I think.

I have to say another word about the sisters. They were great women, and while they had to be severe, no injustice rankles me and I have no horror stories. I feel so bad about the old nuns who are living out their days in a certain insecurity, while many authors boost sales by taking cheap shots at the way they used to teach and discipline. Unsung and uncomplaining heroines they, to quote Yeats, "weighed so lightly what they gave."

There was a bit of Puritanism, however, but it was not unhealthy. Most of us were made very strong Cath-

From the Pages of *The Critic*

olics. The fear of hell and mortal sin was instilled later on by priests, givers of missions, and retreat masters in the seminary.

We were taught Pius X-type Catholicism with which I was comfortable at the time. In high school we got *The Catechism of Perseverance* by De Herb, a translation from the French with strictures against modernism and a bad word about so many good Frenchmen like Voltaire and Rousseau. That took a while to shake off.

All in all, my years at St. Mary of the Mount strengthened me in every way. I am glad that I had been part of the hurrah just before the last hurrah of a system and a way of life that well served God, country and people.

On a less solemn note, I had to get glasses for my myopia, which was bad and progressive, but that brought its own woes. Spectacles were expensive and fragile. Real tortoise shell, which a lively kid like me often broke to the disgust of my rather tolerant father who had to pay. Probably because the things were so expensive, not many kids wore them. One who did was a sport and was often referred to as "four eyes," as in "you four-eyed so-and-so." The language of the rougher parochial school children could be quite undenominational. Strong glasses were an affliction because you were nearly blind when you took them off and you had trouble with sports and fighting. Particularly in the early days, you had to remove your glasses for most violent activities and you were helpless and hopeless without them. Swimming was fine, but not diving.

I had another affliction. I was skinny, and my ears stuck out, oddly enough they no longer do. Some large

Just Good Reading

tougher kids were unkind enough to speak of bird-kite ears and note a resemblance to a taxi cab coming down the street with both rear doors open.

Scrawny kids have special problems if they insist on winning verbal arguments, especially if they are afflicted with myopia and a combative disposition. At least I did. For some reason or other, I am reminded of Billy Conn, the great light heavyweight who almost beat Joe Louis. Rich men occasionally would pay Billy to teach their kids how to fight, something that some kids cannot learn. When he would tell a father that nobody could teach his kid how to fight, the father would say, "Then what will I do?" Billy's classic response was, "Teach him how to apologize." I wasn't all that good at either.

Before I leave the '20s, I have to talk about our automobile. In '23 Papa bought a Willy's-Knight touring car; black canvas top, isinglass curtains, lovely wooden wheels, four cylinders, sleeve valve. Sleeve valve meant no pistons and no power. We burned a lot of oil, and left a trail of blue smoke. Before the invention of Duco enamel, cars were hell to wash. You polished with a chamois and spent hours on the process.

Soon we got into Buicks which had their own problems, since Buick was stubborn and late getting into four-wheel brakes.

In that day many people simply put the car up for the winter. We didn't.

A salesman once came around to sell Papa a used car. I was impressed when he said, "This car was owned by an old-maid school teacher who never drove more than 20 miles an hour." Papa was not. After all, Papa was a professional buyer.

From the Pages of *The Critic*

I really should have said more about him in this memoir, his influence and the family's influence. In his generation the members of the family were all strong characters. With few exceptions they were passionately interested in politics. With no exception they opposed toadying and respected not the successful but the principled. That was true of papa, of my priest uncle, Father Peter, and of my late beloved, elder and only brother. Pat was a priest, earned a J.C.D. at Catholic University, was a pastor and a Monsignor when he died in 1971 leaving a hole in my life.

ON THE GRASS, ALAS

by Dan Herr

SURELY the most persecuted of minorities in the animal world—or the bird world if you want to be more precise—is the pigeon. With the exception of Charles Darwin and me, noboby ever has a good word to say for that poor creature. He (or she, as the case may be) does not harm anyone, minds his or her own business, does not attack other birds, does not disturb peace and quiet with song, has simple food wants, is sleek and shapely, does not despoil flora.

If you did not know better, you would think the pigeon would be the most prized and beloved of birds, even ahead of the canary whose mouthings can quickly pall on a listener. But instead, the pigeon is universally despised and too often the butt of organized campaigns of hatred and violence. Even Shakespeare was not above pigeon-baiting—he makes Hamlet confess to being "pigeon-liver'd."

The Bible isn't much better. Most of the relatively few references are to offerings for sacrifice—a rather dismal approach, I suggest. In the Douay version there is a reference to "pigeon dung," but biblical scholars claim this is a translation error.

Which brings up a question that must be answered before we proceed further into this engrossing subject:

From the Pages of *The Critic*

"Why has the pigeon become the schlimazel of the bird world?"

I will tell you why, even though the more squeamish among you may find the subject offensive. Our antipathy toward pigeons is directly traceable to the disposal, or rather lack of disposal, of their fecal matter. Pigeons are not furnished litter boxes like those lavished on cats, nor do they have masters and mistresses to follow them around with pooper-scoopers as do dogs. Since there are a hell of a lot of pigeons and they tend to congregate, I will admit they sometimes seem to be a slight nuisance. But, as a kind soul recently pointed out, if the automobile and the bus had not made the horse obsolete, the pigeon defecation problem would seem minor by comparison. (It is estimated that an adult horse "produces eight and a half tons of manure a year.") You might say, therefore, that the pigeon is another victim of progress.

Having settled that matter—to your satisfaction, I trust—we can now talk more positively on the pigeon and his pomps.

Let us begin our discourse with another question: in the words of Justice Shallow (*Henry V, Part Two*), "Are there no young pigeons?" Both you and I will admit, I think, that we have never seen one. Then you might logically ask, "Where do pigeons hide their young?" I regret I cannot offer an answer. Nor, if the results of my scientifically conducted survey of fellow pigeon-fanciers truly indicate the state of the question, can anyone else. Unfortunately, my standbys in all such matters, the *Encyclopedia Britannica* and the *Columbia Encyclopedia*, are unhelpful.

The reference books, however, do have useful infor-

Just Good Reading

mation about our pigeon friends. Depending on which encyclopedia you put your faith in, there are 289 or "about" 250 species, but both books agree that "all members of the family suck liquids, rather than sip and swallow as do other birds, and all pigeon parents feed their young 'pigeon's milk,' the sloughed-off lining of the crop, the production of which is stimulated by the hormone prolactin. The nestling obtains this 'milk' by poking its bill down the parent's throat." (A disgusting exhibition, I suspect, so it may be just as well the young and their peculiar eating habits are hidden from our view.)

The "typical or true" pigeons are of the species Columbinae and are reputed to be the first bird that man tamed. The more stalwart of the breed can live for 35 years No small achievement in this turbulent world. Their diet is mostly fruits and seeds. More provocative is the revelation by the *Columbia Encyclopedia* that pigeons are "monogamous and amorous" and "are known for their soft, cooing calls." That insight should make them more appealing.

At this point I should discuss the sex life of pigeons, but for some reason my reference guides do not seem interested in that bound-to-be fascinating subject. I am not even sure how one can distinguish the female from the male by sight, although an informant from Texas—through an Alaskan intermediary—assures me that the sex of the bird can be determined by its feet. As yet that is all the information I have been able to unearth, but my colleagues and I are engaged in a serious study of the sex life of pigeons and plan to publish a monograph when it is completed.

From the Pages of *The Critic*

Speaking of feet, tradition has it—and who are we to defy tradition—that the pigeon's characteristic red feet go way back to Noah. According to the story, which differs somewhat from the account in Genesis, when Noah suspected the deluge had come to an end he despatched a pair of pigeons to check if the waters were receding. They returned triumphantly with their feet covered with red clay, proving that land was clear again. To commemorate that moment, God decreed that henceforth and forever pigeons would sport red feet.

It is interesting to note that doves, from the same family as pigeons, are much beloved while pigeons are generally despised. Doves sure as hell have had better public relations. There is, of course, a similar situation with rats and squirrels—proving there is no more equality among animals and birds than among humans.

Except for the fact that homing pigeons are believed to navigate by the sun (if true, don't expect them home at night) and that the long-extinct dodo was from the pigeon family, that's all you really need to know about pigeons.

EVERYTHING I NEED

by Peter Turchi

THE kid behind the counter was talking like a duck.

That was why the old guy on the end was half laughing, half shaking his head. You're the cartoon, the old guy said. Mickey Mouse.

Something like that. Cory could see the M's coming off his lips.

The kid scowled. Donald Duck, he told the old guy, pretending to be annoyed. He was just jerking around.

Yeah, the old guy said, sort of revolving on his stool, a little this way, a little that. That's it. Donald Duck. He was smiling one of those big gummy smiles. He paused, trying to think of something to say. Not that he had anything in particular to say, but it was a conversation.

Cory was listening to the radio on his headphones, sitting in the first booth inside the door of the Casa Loco, a Mexican place just off Michigan Avenue. The restaurant was about the size of a two-car-garage, pale green with lights bright enough to show the dirt. Booths went around two sides, looking out on the street corner; the counter and the kitchen took up the rest of the space. Room for two cars, Cory thought. Two cars and a riding lawnmower, tops. He came here because it was small, because it was never busy, and because the customers were all kinds: black, white, Mexican. The juke-

From the Pages of *The Critic*

box was filled with hand-lettered slips of paper. Cory couldn't read Spanish, but he recognized words like *El* and *La*, *Señor* and *Casa*. When he felt the vibrations of the heavy bass through the floor he imagined a Spanish woman singing about a lost lover; when customers came in he played a game, filling in the words to their conversations.

The kid came over to get the order but Cory didn't take off his headphones. The kid knew him by now.

Dos burritos, Cory said, imagining he heard himself saying it in a flat Spanish accent. He was listening to an ad for a travel agency.

The kid gave him a look like, What?

Cory said, Two. Two burritos. The kid took the menu, a yellow card covered in old plastic, and went back behind the counter.

Cory propped his feet up on the seat across the booth. Steven Michaels had the noon show on the radio; he said it was 12:06, then cued the farm report. Twenty-four minutes. If he ate fast he'd have time for a phone call before getting back to the line.

If someone had told Cory six years ago, when he was still in high school in Arizona, that he would be listening to talk radio, he would have laughed. Maybe in sixty years, he would have said. Maybe in six hundred. Before his father died he had driven Cory to school every morning, Muzak on the radio. "Eleanor Rigby" played by seventy thousand violinists on morphine. You know what this stuff is? he had asked his dad. This is for people with dead ears. His father had shrugged and said, So I've got dead ears. He wasn't being funny, and he didn't say anything else. Cory's father had been a quiet man.

Just Good Reading

But here he was, listening to talk radio. Back then, when he was still in Benson, a skeleton of a town in the middle of the desert, he would have said talk radio was the same as Muzak, even worse. Now he knew there was a difference. The station his father managed to pull in from Tucson boasted that it played more music than the competition, there were fewer interruptions; but even then Cory had yearned for the interruptions, had sat on the hot, cracked vinyl car seat and waited for the sound of a voice, a sign that someone was out there.

When he moved to Chicago it took a long time to find one station he could pick up everywhere—at work, on the drive in, at home—and that he could stand to listen to all day. He had tried tapes, but they were expensive, he hated carrying them around, and he couldn't stop to flip them over when he was on the line. Besides, no matter how well produced they were, tapes always sounded flat, dead. Radio was alive.

The old guy left, the kid swept up the change, and a hand from the kitchen put the burritos on the ledge between the kitchen and the counter. The kid brought the burritos over, whistling, looking out the window.

The headphones only came off when he was in the shower, or getting a haircut, or when he had to change the tiny watch battery. He wore them at work, in the car, while he ate. He even wore them to bed, the volume low, friendly voices murmuring softly about the mayoral election and spring training and books about life on other planets. It was illegal in Illinois to wear headphones in the car, so he had bought the smallest set he could find. The radio dial was in the right earpiece, volume on the left. In the car he swung them down

From the Pages of *The Critic*

under his chin, the brown plastic hidden in his beard. From a little distance—from the far side of his bedroom, looking in the mirror—you couldn't tell he had them on. It had been uncomfortable to wear them at night, at first—he slept on his side, and the earpiece pressed into his head—but he had adjusted, finding true comfort in the voices talking through the night.

Steven Michaels came back on after the farm report to take a call on a missing truck driver.

The night before, a man had called the radio station from Texas. He said he was the dispatcher at a trucking company, that one of their drivers had been scheduled to make a delivery in Chicago two days ago, and that the delivery wasn't made, the truck had disappeared. The driver had worked for the company for twenty years, he had always been reliable; there was no reason to think he would have just driven off. Even more than that, the man said, the reason the company was worried was that the driver had called his sister in St. Louis from a pay phone and told her his arm was numb, his chest hurt.

Lloyd Peters, the evening disc jockey, told the man that he would spread the word. This was the kind of thing the station was good at: getting information, making pleas. When Cory moved to Chicago to help his grandmother, the city had seemed enormous, filled with mobs of people struggling through a tangle of streets and train lines, the suburbs scattered like cards exploded from a bad shuffle. The radio sorted everything out.

The man on the phone with Steven Michaels now said he was a trucker. We're all looking for him, the man

Just Good Reading

said. I personally, myself, have been to six truck stops, and I've talked to truckers all over the state. I just wanted to clear up some confusion. The rig is blue and white, with a white trailer. Some people said they had heard brown and white.

Blue and white rig with a white trailer, Steven Michaels said. Got it.

That's right, the man said. He repeated the Texas license plate number and the trucking company's name. He said, if we can get everyone to cooperate, we ought to be able to find this man today. There are only so many places to park eighteen wheels.

Thanks very much for your help, Steven Michaels said. I'm sure that if anyone can find him, the brotherhood of truckers can. He repeated the information about the truck once more, then did a spot for vacuum cleaners.

A tall man crossed the street from the hotel, walking fast. Expensive warm coat, three-piece suit probably, under it. Lawyer, Cory thought. A jogger. Maybe a racquetball player.

The lawyer walked right to the corner and pushed through the door. The kid behind the counter looked up—this tall guy wasn't a typical Casa Loco customer. The guy, who was about six seven, walked up to the counter, stepped between two stools, and leaned toward the kid. Cory could tell he was used to having his own way. The kid was trapped behind the counter, looking nervous. Cory felt sorry for him.

What've you got I can eat fast? the guy said. Whatever it was, he said it in one shot. Cory watched him,

From the Pages of *The Critic*

listening to hog prices, cattle, November wheat. Wall Street was up ten points in moderate trading.

The kid's English wasn't so good; he shrugged. The tall guy reached toward a rack of packaged pastries right behind the kid, next to the soft drink machine. What are those? the guy said, leaning so far that he nearly touched them. He'd be great in court, Cory thought—intimidating as well. The kid held up one of the pastries like a piece of evidence. Exhibit A: Yellow Cupcakes.

The tall guy shook his head, annoyed—he had figured this would be easy—and pointed to the refrigerated case near the end of the counter. He was so tall he could have bent over and opened the door himself, Cory thought. The guy pointed to a slice of pie and asked for a glass of milk. The kid set him up. Watch me, the lawyer said, handing the kid a bill. I'm going to eat this faster than you've ever seen anybody eat in your life.

That wasn't right. He wouldn't really say that.

The lawyer choked down the pie, drained the milk in two chugs, and left two coins on the counter. He was almost to the door when he seemed to remember something, turned back, picked up the coins and hurried out. Cory thought, One day he'll be playing racquetball and his heart will explode. He had just watched a man committing suicide.

The first time Cory heard the station, he had been thrown off. Some who called were like the people you always heard on call-in shows—people trying to lose weight or quit drinking, people with intricate plans for what to do about the Russians and, late at night, people with desperation in their voices: people whose bad luck

Just Good Reading

had caught up and was running over them making one last attempt to explain themselves, to get somebody to listen. But most of the people called just to be part of the show.

We've got Barbara on the line from Wheaton, Bill Charles had said. Barbara said, Hi Bill. I just wanted to let you know that there's a bad accident out here and Roosevelt is backed up for two miles. She went on for a minute, then Bill thanked her and said hello to a woman who had information for someone who had called earlier: a couple was going to London and wanted to know where they could get good steaks.

At first Cory thought Bill Charles really knew those people he called by name, that they were guests on the show; then he realized that they *were* the show. There were other things, too—interviews with doctors and authors and actors and athletes, the news and sports and weather, even some music—but most of the time people called in to ask questions, others called in to answer.

That's why Cory had started listening. Because he liked the conversation, the sound of people helping each other. But after a while, even on this station, in the middle of the day, he realized that a lot of the callers sounded the same: older men with cigarette rasps, hesitant older women, a few cheery housewives. Occasionally there would be a new voice, but Cory came to understand that there were certain kinds of people who called radio stations, people whose common characteristic was clear even in the sounds of their voices. The people who called didn't think of the radio as something that played in the background; the radio was part of their lives. Cory tried to imagine them, people who

From the Pages of *The Critic*

would stop what they were doing to pick up the phone, dial the station's number, wait on hold—during the popular shows, for as long as half an hour—all just to say three sentences to a radio personality.

There were people who called, Cory thought, and there were people who listened. More and more he saw other people with headphones, in restaurants, on the streets, riding buses. Some of them were listening to tapes, some of them were listening to other radio stations, but some of them, he knew, must have been listening to his station. He liked to think of all those people tuned to the same frequency, laughing at the same corny jokes, shaking their heads at the same bad news. He liked to imagine everyone in the city wearing headphones, cranking up the volume for the Beatles singing "Twist and Shout." He imagined everyone on the lookout for the lost truck driver from Texas.

Cory was starting on his second burrito when a black guy in a Cubs warm-up jacket came in off the street. This guy looked bad. The jacket might have been nice when it was new, but it was chewed up now. There were black streaks of grease across the front, one arm was nearly falling off. The guy had pulled it out of the trash somewhere. It was too cold out for a baseball jacket.

Hey my man, the black guy said. The kid knew him—Cory could tell—but he didn't look up. I'm hungry, the guy said. The kid sighed. Cory had seen this before—not this guy, but this scene. Look, the black guy said, spreading his hands like Jesus at the Last Supper, just until tomorrow. I'll get it back to you. The kid didn't answer and the guy's arms collapsed onto the counter. He

Just Good Reading

looked like a big molting bird, his long arms out, his jacket eaten away.

How much you got? the kid asked. Cory could see his mouth; it looked like, How much you got? The black guy had his back to Cory, facing the kid. Three cents, the guy said. Something like that, something pitiful. He wasn't looking at the kid now. I had a dollar this morning, he said. The kid banged the cash register with one hand and said, shit. The kid looked like a teenager, twenty tops, and he was kind of short; the black guy was taller, wider across the shoulders, hungrier. Cory imagined the fight: the black guy reaching over the counter and grabbing the kid. But no, there's the cook. Somebody in back, in the kitchen. Cory had never seen the cook, but somebody handed up the food. When business was slow the kid turned and talked through the little window behind the counter. Now Cory realized there would be no fight: if this guy was that desperate, he would have robbed somebody. You don't beat up a counter boy to get lunch.

No one did anything. The black guy kept looking at the kid, trying to break him down. To the black guy, the kid was the answer, the man with food. But the kid was thinking about that lawyer who had just stiffed him on the tip. Cory watched them as he reached into his back pocket for his wallet. His grandmother's twenty, a five, and two ones. The kid and the black guy had run out of lines. Cory waited for something to happen, but the two of them kept their places, like a chair balanced on its back legs that freezes in position before tipping. Cory had intended only to pay his bill, but he felt he had to make something clear; he wanted to disassociate himself

From the Pages of *The Critic*

from that lawyer. Before he knew what he was doing he said, hey.

The kid looked over. Cory pointed at the black guy. The kid said something, the guy turned around. The Cubs emblem drooped from his jacket.

Here, Cory said, holding out the ones. In his ears people were singing about mufflers. He gave the black guy the two pieces of paper, their eyes didn't meet, and the black guy turned away. No thanks, nothing.

The scene regained its balance; it was as if the chair had been nailed to the floor after all. Cory sat there in his booth, feeling himself growing angry. He had never given anyone a handout before, and he felt the loss immediately. His grandmother's money and his five felt lonely in his wallet. People would say anything to get what they wanted, what they needed, but when they took your money they had nothing to say. It was as if helping them was the final insult.

The kid turned to the kitchen and called back an order for the black guy, who was sitting quietly. Cory stood up, paid for his food, said thank you. The kid looked at the headphones, nodded.

The sun was out but there was a chill in the air. Cory had never gotten used to the cold. Steven Michaels said today's high would be forty-four, but there was a steady breeze from the northwest at ten miles an hour. Flying Officer Kavanaugh reported slow-moving traffic on the Stevenson, an overturned delivery van on the outbound Eisenhower.

Cory hit the bar across the back door to the plant at 12:24; six minutes. He headed for the pay phone near the restrooms, dialed ten numbers, deposited fifty cents,

Just Good Reading

and slipped back the left earpiece, a warm spot the size of a nickel pressing behind his ear. There was a brush of static and for a moment Cory thought of the lost trucker, far from home, arm numb, dialing his sister in St. Louis. Millions of people in Chicago and he called St. Louis. Cory got a report on government support for farmers in his right ear, a recording about safe sex practices in his left. The message from the phone ended and another voice cut in, high-pitched and happy. Ooh, baby, the girl's voice said. I've been waiting for you. Did you have a hard day? I bet you need to relax. Cory heard the sound of a zipper, the smack of lips, the girl's voice saying, let me slip you out of those clothes.

Gramma? Cory said, rapping on her front door. It's me, Cory. The television would be on full blast. Gramma? He was shouting so loud he could nearly hear himself.

The door opened slowly and Cory's grandmother peered out, ready to slam it shut and throw the bolt against an intruder. She lived in a good neighborhood, but she was certain that one day she would be robbed. Cory knew that anyone could knock her over, empty the house; that was one of the reasons he had moved near her.

Cory honey, she said, reaching up to peck him on the cheek, her lips as hard as a peach pit. She moved to the huge old black and white set and pushed a button. As the picture shrank into a tiny square of blue light and dissolved she said, I always turn off the television when you get here.

I know, Cory said. He set the bags on the kitchen table. Here's your list, he told her, handing over the

From the Pages of *The Critic*

envelope covered with shaky, looping handwriting. Eighteen seventy-five, he said. They were out of the big bottle of vitamins, so I had to get the small one. Here's the coupon.

He put away the groceries as he talked, stepping around his grandmother. She was in her late seventies, short and stooped and carrying extra weight like sandbags hanging over the sides of the basket of a hot-air balloon. She made motions to help him, then sat on one of the kitchen chairs so yellow they depressed him. When he finished he folded the brown grocery bag and put it in the pantry in a box filled with folded bags. Then he sat across the table from his grandmother and reached into the small white bag.

Here you go, he said. A fish fillet, french fries, and a strawberry milkshake.

Oh, she said, opening the styrofoam container carefully, thank you, honey, but I can't eat all this.

Cory took a bite from his hamburger. It was the same thing she ate every Monday. Cory tried to get his grandmother to eat other food, something that would be better for her, but for as long as he had been in Chicago she had been following the same pattern: a fish fillet from McDonalds on Monday, Taco Bell on Tuesday, Wendy's on Wednesday, a cold cut sub from Hogie Heaven on Thursday, Kentucky Fried Chicken—the two-piece dinner box, all white meat, original recipe—on Friday. On the weekends she used her microwave, a present from Cory's mother, and ate by herself: frozen dinners and frozen pizza.

Cory slipped back the left earpiece in order to hear his grandmother, even though he knew what she had to

Just Good Reading

say. He wasn't sure she even knew what the headphones were, but he didn't have it in him to ignore her completely, to shut her out.

This is delicious, she said, taking a bite the size of a fingernail from her sandwich. Cory ate with her every weeknight—on Saturday he helped out at his aunt and uncle's in Joliet; Sunday was his own—and she had become expert at stretching out the meal. You couldn't make something this good yourself, she said. She paused, forgetting her lines, and he almost said them for her.

She said, I never learned to cook, and this is no time to start. When your grandfather was here we had a woman who came in to cook and clean during the week, a nigger girl. He took over on the weekends. I wanted to help—Lord knows I told him so—but he'd say, Rosemary, you just set right there. And I'd set here and talk to him while he cooked. Wouldn't let me do so much as break an egg. The skin around her eyes wrinkled when she laughed.

Cory felt something against his leg: Marilyn, his grandmother's dog. His grandfather had brought the dog home from the pound a year before he died. He had named it Marilyn Monroe, but Cory knew his grandfather must have thought of the name before he had the dog: it was a dachshund, short and silly looking, brown with black feet and a tiny, pointed face. His grandmother overfed it terribly: Marilyn was so amazingly fat that Cory was afraid to touch her, afraid she would explode.

Marilyn is too fat, he told his grandmother. You shouldn't feed her so much.

From the Pages of *The Critic*

His grandmother set her sandwich on the table and reached for her milkshake. She only eats one meal a day, she told him. If I fed her any less the neighbors would have the SPCA in here.

Every Monday's groceries included seven pot pies, four chicken and three beef. Each morning his grandmother used the oven to heat one, broke the crust, and covered it with cold applesauce. That was Marilyn's one meal. The rest of the day she snacked from the twenty-pound bag of dog biscuits lying on its side next to the washing machine. Every week or so Cory made a point of standing the bag on its end, the opening out of Marilyn's reach, and setting five dog biscuits on the table. The next night he'd find the bag back on its side, Marilyn crunching away on the living room rug.

Suddenly, with an agility that contradicted her inflated body, Marilyn jumped up onto a stool by the window and from there onto a carpet remnant on the window ledge.

Look, Cory's grandmother said in a stage whisper. Marilyn's looking for the squirrel.

Cory heard Jim Frey say that the Cubs couldn't afford any more free agents no matter how good they were.

When Marilyn was just a puppy, his grandmother said, when your grandfather was still here, she used to set on that ledge to watch a squirrel that liked to climb that tree. It would start to climb, then it would look over and see Marilyn and stop. Set so still you would've thought it was a picture. Granddad would say, Get the squirrel! Go get it! But Marilyn would just set there and scratch at the window, waving to it. It was the cutest thing you could ever want to see.

Just Good Reading

I don't see any squirrel now, Cory said. It was too dark to see the tree clearly.

Oh honey, I haven't seen a squirrel on that tree for years. Marilyn hops up and looks ten times a day. It just breaks my heart to see her waiting there.

Cory was only half listening. The squirrel story always reminded him of something he had seen downtown. When he first got the job on the assembly line, dropping bottles of makeup and perfume into their places in plastic trays, he had worked the night shift. Early one morning he left the building and was walking to his car when he saw a black man, drunk, heading toward him on the sidewalk. He was scared at first, but when the man actually staggered, just like a drunk in the movies, he knew there was no danger. The man stopped by a garbage can, pulled out a handful of trash, and sifted it through his fingers. He stopped, looked down at something that had fallen, and picked it up: a strip of negatives. The drunk held them up to the streetlight, studying them.

Cory had remembered that, but he didn't know why. And he didn't know why it reminded him of Marilyn watching for the squirrel—or was it his grandmother watching Marilyn? He knew there was no explaining anything a homeless drunk did at four in the morning, but still he wondered what thought had been in the man's mind, what he had been looking for as he stared at the negatives of someone else's photographs.

Lloyd? a voice in Cory's ear said.

Yes Martin, Lloyd Peters said.

I've got some news for you on that lost truck driver.

From the Pages of *The Critic*

Where are you calling from? Lloyd asked.

Out on I-5, Martin said. Out near the western end of the tollway. There's a rest area a ways off the road by here, and that's where they found him.

And? Lloyd asked.

He was in the cab of his truck, Martin said. He was dead. Of a heart attack. The paramedics said they think he probably died sometime Friday.

Damn, Cory thought.

We're all certainly very sorry to hear that, Lloyd said.

It's been quite a scene, Martin said. The police said that, outside of them, with all the truckers and people with CB's and all the other people who had heard about it on the radio, they estimate something like five hundred people were actually going out of their way to find this man. They said they were getting hundreds of phone calls.

It's too bad it had to end like this, Lloyd said.

I agree with you, Martin said. It's real sad.

That's for sure, Lloyd Peters said.

But I've been thinking, Martin said. I don't mean any disrespect or anything, but maybe there's something good to come out of all this. I mean, I think we'd all like to think that, if it was us stuck somewhere, lost or sick or something, people would care enough to do something. They'd stop what they were doing and try to help.

You're right about that, Lloyd Peters said. There was a short pause and then he said, thanks for your call.

Cory took a sip of his soft drink, but when it reached his stomach it made him feel queasy; he was thinking of the man from Texas, far from home, dying in the cab of

Just Good Reading

his truck. It was hard to imagine an eighteen-wheel truck with someone in it being lost for four days and within one hundred miles of Chicago. Then Cory had an awful thought: if his grandmother died on a Friday night, he wouldn't find her until Monday.

Gramma, Cory said, Maybe I'll come by this weekend.

She was looking at the blank television. Cory knew she wanted it on, and he knew she'd never turn it on as long as he was there.

He said, I was thinking you might like to go out for a drive on Saturday. To go see Uncle Leo and Aunt Jane.

Leo, she said. I've got nothing to say to him.

Cory let it drop. He knew that Uncle Leo didn't want to see her either. He sighed and said, Sunday then. I'll take you for a drive Sunday.

Drive? his grandmother said. Drive? As if he had just invented the word. She looked at him, most of her fish sandwich still in her hand, and said, Where would we drive?

Anywhere you want, Cory told her. We could go out, or you could come to my apartment. . . .

I'd like to see your apartment, she said. It sounds darling, honey. She had been saying that for three years.

Or, he said, we could do something else. Go out for dinner. What would you like?

I don't need to go out for dinner, she said. What can they cook that I can't fix right here in my own kitchen?

Marilyn jumped down from the window ledge and left the room.

Well, then come over to my apartment, he said.

From the Pages of *The Critic*

She said, I don't need to go anywhere. I've got everything I need right here.

For a moment Cory thought she meant him.

I've got my puppy and my TV, she said. That's all I need. She took another absurdly delicate bite from her sandwich.

Gramma, Cory said. What would you do if something happened to me?

She chewed slowly. There was no sign that she was ignoring him, no sign that she had heard him.

Gramma, he said again, louder. What would you do? What would happen if I broke my leg, if I couldn't drive?

I turn off the television whenever you're here, she said. She put her hand out as if to cover his but stopped short. She said, I wouldn't want anyone else to run my errands for me.

From the time that her husband died until the time Cory moved to Chicago, his grandmother had depended on the kindness of neighbors, grocery stores that delivered, teenaged boys willing to mow lawns for pocket money. But those boys had grown up; the neighbors had moved away; delivery services were expensive, and intolerant of an old woman's short-circuited memory.

It's not just errands, Cory said. I buy the groceries, I go to the bank, I pay your bills, I take Marilyn to the vet, I fix the drains—you can't get anyone else to do all that.

His grandmother ate three french fries and smiled. I've got everything I need, she said again. My puppy and my TV.

Just Good Reading

The doorbell rang. Marilyn raced to the door, barking. I'll get it, Cory said. He dropped his empty cup into the trash, then looked through the peephole that he had cut into his grandmother's front door. On the other side of the glass, looking small and distant, was Reverend Crawford. Cory thought, this is how she sees me.

Hi, Cory said, opening the door.

Reverend Crawford stomped his feet on the welcome mat and came in smiling, saying hello to Cory and petting Marilyn. He could only stay a minute, he hoped he wasn't interrupting anything.

Hello, Rosemary, the Reverend said. He leaned down and hugged her, then stepped back to lean against the sink. He said, Don't let me interrupt your dinner. I was just walking by and thought I'd stop in to say hello.

Reverend Crawford's church was only two blocks away from Cory's grandmother's house. Long ago, even before Cory's grandfather had died, they had stopped going to Sunday services, but the Reverend didn't seem to mind. He stopped by nearly once a month, and he didn't nag her to come to mass, he never asked for money. Cory wasn't sure why he came, but he liked to think the Reverend was simply a good man. He was tall and had a big face, full red cheeks; in his black winter coat he seemed to fill the kitchen, making it warmer, a better place to be.

Marilyn curled up at Reverend Crawford's feet.

Look at that, the Reverend said. The world's fattest dog.

She only eats one meal a day, Cory's grandmother said, smiling as if the Reverend had come to take her on a date. She's on a diet.

From the Pages of *The Critic*

Right, the Reverend said. The All You Can Eat diet.

Cory's grandmother looked at Marilyn as if she had just noticed her for the first time. I only feed her one meal a day, she said. Then Cory comes and gives her cookies.

At first he thought he had misheard; his grandmother wasn't joking. What reason did she have to blame him? He turned to tell the Reverend the truth.

I don't believe that for a minute, the Reverend said, smiling at Cory. I know better. If we had our way we'd have this dog on a real diet.

Cory had only seen the Reverend a dozen times in the years he had been helping his grandmother, but there was always a sense of conspiracy; the Reverend always seemed to be saying, we're in this one together. The truth was that he and Cory had never talked, never discussed any detailed plans to help Cory's grandmother. Even so, even though he was doing all the work, Cory enjoyed the implication that he and the Reverend were, somehow, a team.

Reverend Crawford said, the reason I came was to invite you to our Wednesday seniors' meetings.

Oh, Cory's grandmother said, beaming, what a kind man.

I have to come this way to pick up Mrs. Phillips, the Reverend said. I'll be happy to get you. Wednesday afternoons at one o'clock.

Mrs. Phillips, she said. Now there's a sad story. Doesn't have any family here, doesn't have anything to do. I call her when there's a good show on and she won't even turn on the TV.

Just Good Reading

She enjoys our meetings, Reverend Crawford said. You would too.

Try it, Gramma, Cory said. Just try it once.

No obligation, the Reverend said. No salesman will call. Except me, of course.

Cory's grandmother had lost her smile. Oh no, she said, taking a bite out of the fish fillet it seemed she would never finish. I'm busy on Wednesdays. I have too much to do.

Cory and the Reverend shared a look, agreeing not to challenge the lie.

Make room in your schedule, the Reverend said. He smiled at Cory again, a real smile. It was as if he were telling Cory that he understood what he was going through, that he was there to help, to let him know that he was doing the right thing. As he thought that, Cory was aware of the voice in his ear updating the weather forecast. He wondered if the Reverend saw the headphones, if he thought that Cory wore them only when he visited his grandmother, to block her out. He wanted to explain, but then Cory thought of the phone number he dialed almost every day at the end of his lunch break, the things those women said, his quick trips into the restroom. For all his smiles, the Reverend didn't know him; neither, Cory realized, did his grandmother. It was impossible to explain.

He heard someone reviewing a new show at the Chicago Theatre.

Reverend Crawford was serious now. Why don't you come with us on Wednesday? he said. I'll come by and pick you up at quarter of one.

A look passed over Cory's grandmother's face that he

From the Pages of *The Critic*

knew meant she had been confronted on an issue she would not discuss. Cory wasn't convinced that she was that scheming, that she was devious enough to consciously ignore others; he believed it had become automatic, involuntary: she was no longer able to discuss certain things.

The next moment she smiled and said, I never learned to cook. Why should I, when I can get a sandwich like this? She took a sip of her milkshake and for a moment a bright pink bubble held to her lips.

The Reverend tried again. Cory listened to the news headlines and patted Marilyn, who had come over to sit by his feet. He was sure dogs had emotions, that they could be happy or sad, just like people; he wondered if Marilyn wished she could be with other dogs, if she ate all of those dog biscuits because she was depressed. It was the kind of question he could imagine someone asking on the radio.

Well, Reverend Crawford said, buttoning his coat, I'll call you Wednesday morning. I have to drive right by here to get Mrs. Phillips, and we'd love to have you come with us.

Oh, Cory's grandmother said with no conviction at all, maybe I'll just do that. Maybe I'll get a ride over with you.

Just think what people will say if they see me driving along with two pretty women in my car, the Reverend said. Cory's grandmother laughed and waved her hand.

Cory opened the door and said goodnight. The Reverend said, if there's anything I can do for your grandmother—or for you—just let me know.

Let's get her in your car Wednesday, Cory said. Then,

Just Good Reading

as an afterthought, with cheerfulness and confidence he didn't really feel, I'm fine, thanks.

His grandmother put both hands on the table and pushed herself up. Excuse me, she said. I have to powder my nose.

Before he could say goodbye she was in the bathroom.

He looked at the clock over the sink; he had been there over an hour. He was tired, he wanted to go home, and now he remembered that he had forgotten to buy toilet paper for the apartment. He had to go back to the store.

On the kitchen table was the last bite of his grandmother's fish. He imagined throwing it in the trash and leaving, telling her the next night that she had finished and he had said goodbye, she had forgotten. He stared at the tiny fleck of white between two small pieces of bread. His grandmother was too busy to leave the house, but she took an hour and a half to eat a piece of fish.

Marilyn was back on her perch on the window ledge. Suddenly she sat up and scratched at the window.

Cory looked where Marilyn was looking, but it was dark out, he could only see reflections: himself, ghost thin in the glass, the kitchen cabinets, the top of the back of a yellow chair. There's nothing out there, he told her. Marilyn's breathing was so loud, so labored, that it hurt him to hear it. He could feel her heart straining.

There's nothing there, he said again, but Marilyn scratched at the window until he wondered if she could

From the Pages of *The Critic*

break it, her breathing became a high whine. Cory walked up to the window and, cupping his hands against the cold glass, looked out into the night. There in the crotch of a sycamore tree, just in the edge of the pale yellow light coming from the kitchen, sat a squirrel.

Cory wasn't sure if he had ever seen a squirrel at night; he wondered if there was something wrong with this one. It sat on its hind legs, tail curled in a question mark, holding its tiny front paws by its head as if lost and trying to remember the way.

The window fogged over with Cory's breath. Gramma, he said, there's a squirrel. And if it was there now, who was to say it wasn't always there? Ten times a day. He stepped back, now able to see only himself in the window, hearing the beginning of a college basketball game. Marilyn stood watch. Gramma, Cory said again as he heard the toilet flush. Come here.

A moment later Cory's grandmother came back into the kitchen, rubbing her hand across the back of her neck.

There's a squirrel in the tree, Cory told her.

No, she said, I'm too busy on Wednesdays. Besides, what do I want with his meetings? He's a sweet man, but honey. . . .

Gramma, Cory said loudly, trying to get through, Come look out the window. Marilyn did her part: she raised one paw and scratched frantically at the glass.

Oh, said Cory's grandmother, smiling, just look at my puppy. Then, confidentially: She thinks there's a squirrel out there. I haven't seen a squirrel out there in ten years.

There is, Cory said. There is a squirrel. Come look.

Just Good Reading

He put his hand on his grandmother's shoulder and felt the coarseness of her dress, the hardness of bone just beneath the skin.

You know, she said, reaching past him to the styrofoam sandwich containers, I save these. I wash them out good and save them. You could give these to people. You could use them.

I know, Cory said. He felt as if he and his grandmother were two sides of a broken zipper; every time he thought they were on track he looked down and saw the empty space between them. Look, he said, trying to get her to hear him. There really is a squirrel outside.

His grandmother satdown heavily, planting herself in her chair. She reached for her milkshake. Cory walked back to the window, where Marilyn was sitting still now but whining. When he put his hands against the glass the dog jumped down and barked twice, running into the other room. Cory looked out again, the cold like ice against the tip of his nose. The squirrel was gone.

Cory stood looking, holding his breath to keep the glass clear. He looked hard into the shadows, but he could see no sign that the squirrel had ever been there. Leaning forward, looking through one pane of the window, he felt like that drunk staring at the strip of negatives. He imagined that if he looked long enough he would see the black guy in the Cubs jacket getting up the nerve to go to another restaurant, bum another meal. He would see the man from Texas alone in the cab of his truck, looking down at his arm, feeling himself go numb, trying to think and coming up with nothing better than the phone number of his sister nearly three hundred miles away. He would see Mrs. Phillips' house at

From the Pages of *The Critic*

the end of the block, the dark television in a corner of the living room like a bet that hadn't paid off, and Mrs. Phillips, alone, sitting quietly, waiting for Wednesdays.

Cory stepped back and saw his grandmother, alone in her kitchen even as he stood beside her.

I have to leave now, he told her.

I'm not finished, she said. She held up the last bite of fish as if it were the last piece of a puzzle she refused to put into place.

I'm sorry, he said. I have to go back to the store. Then I'm going home.

I'm not finished, she said, not touching her food, sensing that a rule of her game was about to be broken.

I'm sorry, Cory said. I'm sorry I have to leave. I'm sorry you won't let me move in with you. I'm sorry you won't go with the Reverend on Wednesday.

Nobody has to bother themselves about me, his grandmother said, standing to say goodbye. She didn't look angry, or sad; she didn't look as if there were anything wrong at all. She said, I've got my puppy and my TV. I don't have time for all the things I have to do.

Cory bent down and kissed the rough skin of her cheek. She closed the door behind him without waving, looking back into her house.

The car didn't start on the first try, or the second. There were always things wrong with Cory's car, problems he couldn't afford to have fixed. The air conditioning had stopped working last spring. One high beam was burnt out. The handle for the window on the driver's side had fallen off, so he had to open the door to pay tolls. These were problems that Cory lived with.

Just Good Reading

The headphones swung upside down, both earpieces on firmly now, Cory heard the radio more clearly. The Blue Demons were off to an early lead; their fans were yelling, filling the Rosemont Horizon with sound that carried through the air to the pieces of plastic against his ears. Cory was a careful, observant driver, he watched the road as he listened, so he saw that he was coming up to a four-way stop at the intersection of two residential streets, he had already moved his foot to the brake when the little girl ran out from the sidewalk on the right. He pushed his foot to the floor, the car did not respond, and he hit her.

At first he thought she had stopped just in time, though her momentum had been too great: he felt the soft shock from the fender in the tips of his fingers, but she didn't fall. Instead she spun, almost gracefully, her back to him, as if some invisible wall separated them, shielding them from each other. Then, as the car passed her and she continued spinning, Cory looked out the passenger window and saw her falling away in the pool of a streetlight, her arms out like a tightrope walker's, her face a circle of blood, her chest flapping open in front of her.

The car continued through the intersection. Cory pumped the brake again and the car stopped immediately, throwing him forward against the steering wheel so hard he felt its imprint on his ribs. He was stopped on the wrong side of the street, his back to the intersection. He looked into the rearview mirror, saw no cars. He meant to back up, to get out and hold the little girl in his arms, but in his haste he forgot to change gears, and when he pressed the accelerator the car rushed forward

From the Pages of *The Critic*

into the darkness.

Now Cory knew he couldn't go back. Someone would have been there in the shadows, a mother or father, another child, a neighbor. He had left the scene of the accident. His heart hammered as if it were about to explode through his chest.

He would call an ambulance. And then the police, to turn himself in. As he thought this he was passing houses and gas stations and restaurants, all of them with telephones, but some automatic part of his mind had taken over, was driving to the grocery store. Then, stopped at a traffic light, he realized in a burst of bad logic that he couldn't go to the store: that's where he had told his grandmother he was going. She would be able to tell the police where they could find him. Sitting at the light, pressing the brake so hard that his knee hurt, as if pressing it harder now could make up for its failure a moment before, Cory realized that the little girl was dead, that if he called the police he would be locked in a cell for the rest of his life. He sat at the longest red light of his life, waiting for something to change. A man with a deep voice complained about nagging back pain. Cory reached into his beard, threw the headphones across the car, turned right on red and raced down the street.

It is less than a mile away, advertised by the light in the air like the light over a baseball field, like the beckoning palm leaves of a mirage in the desert. Cory hears the guttural pulse of the car's engine louder than it has ever been, and around it, beyond it, a silence so large that he feels lost. He reaches across the dark seat for the headphones, but his fingers find only cold vinyl. He concentrates on the road, certain that every car is a

Just Good Reading

police car, every person knows what he has done, his crime is written on his face.

Cory pulls into the mall parking lot, stops in a space on the outer edge, jumps out and runs for the nearest entrance. The lot is crowded, and as he passes couples and families he hides his face, staring down at himself, acknowledging his guilt. He reaches the mall door panting, out of breath, the cold air like knives in his lungs.

He pushes through socks and underwear, girdles and stockings and intimate apparel, and finds his way out of the store, into the middle of the mall. A cluster of six phones stands inside a circle of benches crowded with people. He picks up a receiver, pushes in a coin and, with shaking fingers, punches out a number he has memorized without trying.

A woman puts him on hold. Here in the mall the silence is filled with voices: not one or two particular voices but a storm of them, human voices hanging like clouds under the mall ceiling, voices like warm rain beating down. Cory looks into the faces of two old men talking, one of them with his hand wrapped over the top of a cane; an enormous woman holding a baby, surrounded by packages; a crowd of teenagers spilling over the furniture, covering it, making it their own. He knows he must try to tell them.

"Cory," says a voice more familiar to him than his own. "How are you tonight?"

Cory takes a deep breath, and when he speaks he feels his throat tighten, he feels the blood forcing its way through his body as if he has just been brought to life.

"Hello?" he says. "Am I on the air?"

TAKE A NUMBER, CAESAR

by Joel Wells

THE STORM of controversy surrounding the Administration's proposed radical reform and simplification of federal income tax laws (Form 1040 in its entirety would read: "How much money did you make last year? _____ Send it in.") is overshadowing an even more revolutionary development that will affect millions upon millions of Roman Catholics around the world next year.

Through carefully cultivated and highly reliable sources deep in the bowels of the Vatican, *The Critic* has learned that the Holy See, tired of being chronically in the red and furious over puling public pressure to sell off some of its art treasures, has moved to formulate a universal income tax to be levied on all Catholics who earn the equivalent of eight thousand U.S. dollars annually.

As an independent state, Vatican City is empowered to legislate such taxes as it will; it is not obliged to take into account the burden of taxation imposed upon Catholics by the sovereign states in which they happen to reside. The feeling is that too many Catholics, particularly those living in Europe and the United States, have fallen into the idolatry of consumerism and are shirking their duty to support both the local church and the Holy See.

Says one highly placed Curia official: "They whine

Just Good Reading

about the high cost of living, they say that mounting welfare and public medical taxes strip them of disposable income that they once gave to the Church. Some are brazen enough to suggest that the Pope cut his travel budget to the bone. Shirkers and hypocrites! On the rare occasions they go to Mass it is in their Mercedes and BMWs."

Traditionally, change comes slowly to the Church of Rome. Not so in this instance. The newly created secretariat for collecting the universal income tax—Vatican Revenue Service—hopes to be in full operation beginning in 1990.

Asked if there were plans for consultation or meetings with the bishops of the world, the same official scoffed: "Collegiality is for matters theological; this is a unilateral fiscal decision. If the matter were to be put to them, the bishops would become nattering nabobs of nationalism. We are simply taking something that has been voluntary—Peter's Pence—and making it obligatory."

Will the Peter's Pence collection now be abolished?

"Certainly not. One does not free the bird in the hand because others fly into the net."

What about Catholics who refuse to pay the new tax?

"They will be playing with fire. We here at VRS are not without teeth. Delinquents' names will be printed weekly in parish bulletins. Proof of parental tax payment will be a requirement for registration at any Catholic school or university, as well as for those individuals wishing to be married in the Church—or buried from the Church, for that matter."

Exact details are cloaked in secrecy. It is possible, nonetheless, to construct from our sources a very close

From the Pages of *The Critic*

approximation of the form that Catholics worldwide can expect to find in their mailboxes in the near future:

A.M.D.G.
VATICAN REVENUE SERVICE — Form X-XL
For reporting income in Church Year MCMXC

Christian Name _____		
Address _____		
Parish or Inst. _____		
Baptismal Certificate Number _____		

Filing Status (Check only one): ___ Deacon		
___ Virgin not a martyr ___ Martyr not a virgin		
___ Married ___ Clergy or Religious		
___ Celibate layperson ___ Layperson living in sin		

Check here if you wish $1 of your taxes to go toward the promotion of one or more of the following causes: (Names and addresses of those who do so check will be noted.)
___ Ordination of women ___ Married Clergy ___ Rethinking *Humanae vitae*

INCOME:			
I.	Total personal or family income, (wages, interest, Social Security, capital gains).	I	
Ia.	Inheritance, lotteries, bingo, coins found in the street.	Ia	
Ib.	Rents, royalties, and children's paper routes (before all taxes—federal, state, city, real estate—are deducted).	Ib	
II.	Total Income:	II	
SUBTRACTIONS:			
III.	Tuition paid for dependents in Catholic schools.	III	
IIIa.	Contributions to Parish and Special Collections. (Attach receipts or cancelled checks.)	IIIa	
IIIb.	Contribution to Peter's Pence. (We know, so don't try to inflate it.)	IIIb	
IV.	Total lines III-IIIb, multiply by a tithe and enter the result.	IV	
TAXABLE INCOME:			
V.	Subtract line IV from line II. This is your taxable income.	V	
PENALTIES AND ADDITIONS:			
VI.	If you fail to make your Easter Duty multiply the amount on line V by two.	VI	
CALCULATING YOUR TAX:			
VII.	Multiply the total of line V or Line VI, whichever is greater, by a tithe. This is the amount of tax due:	VII	

Remit the amount on line VII to the VRS by the Ides of March. Failure to do so will result in dire ecclesiastical sanctions. Certified checks or International Money Orders are to be made payable to: VRS, Vatican City. (Note: Payment in kind, e.g., pigs, sheep, chickens or native artifacts, is not acceptable.)

The VRS thanks you for your cooperation and asks that you commit its motto to memory: "The Lord loves a cheerful giver but He did not have to meet a payroll."

DEATH ROW:
Reflections on the Wall

by Michael W. Posey

THE average person has a crossed idea of prison. Most never go, or even get near one. The mystique that surrounds the place fascinates and frightens people. It's that fascination with the unknown that leads people to want to read about prison, and prisoners.

I spent twelve years in two prisons. I was twenty-one when I went in, and thirty-three when I got out. Much was revealed to me in those corridors of loneliness, as I walked through hell on earth. My life there was like the other lives . . . wasted. The vastness of the suffering is limited only by the degree of separation. The stark reality of prison is pure in its presentation, untarnished by the usual problems of the outside. The rent is paid. You get three meals a day; the cell you live in provides shelter; and you go about existing in a reasonably stable manner. Routine is routine . . . regimented, droning, oppressive sameness. All the other people become nondescript. Faces in a crowd.

Noise is the heartbeat of the prison. The blue denim-clad men the blood. The routine is the pulse, and the whole place breathes and moves like a huge stone and steel machine. Grinding monotony, endless noise, a cacophony of metal doors slamming, loudspeakers blaring, bells ringing, and men dying.

From the Pages of *The Critic*

At night there is a perceptible presence that haunts the prison existence. It's the Animal. Fear, hate, pain desolation, loneliness, all accumulate into one living, breathing being that consumes your mind in an insatiable orgy of crying and helpless screams.

No light enters the dark, grey corridors. The cellblocks stand like sentinels. Endless rows of bars, doors, and concrete floors that stretch to nowhere, and leave you breathless with fear. This is your Inferno. Your vision of hell. The hopeless men scream their impotent threats, and they are consumed piecemeal, by the Animal.

The Beast roams the corridors at night. You feel its awesome presence. You know fear in all its horror. But you must survive. You scream and rebel and it keeps coming. Finally, your mind is consumed along with your body and your soul. The Animal defecates, and out come the violated victims, insane and raging in agony. They kill and rape with psychotic impunity. There is no right only might. Death becomes the handmaiden. Life has no meaning.

Totally emasculated, we went about our wretched lives, hoping they would end. Death is peace. Death, the Angel of Mercy, has no power there. You don't fear it, you welcome it. The dead lay bleeding on concrete floors, their viscera exposed to the men who step over them. Their blood mixes with layers of wax on the floor, and has a color that is red beyond belief. No amount of death is seemingly enough to quench the thirst of the Animal. It seems to thrive on our bleeding, torn corpses.

If there is eternal Life, then prison is eternal Death. You die by inches. Your soul escapes into the abyss of

Just Good Reading

fear. You become an empty shell. No compassion, no real feelings. You simply play the game, and try to live another day.

Never having to face real life you forget life exists. It becomes so foreign to you. You are not able to find right or wrong. It becomes a meaningless exercise.

The guards are also victims. They get consumed as well. They are the Animal's trusted servants. They are the absolute losers. They go home at the end of their shifts. They have to live out there, and in the prison as well. I pitied them.

We were all slain by our social disabilities and tossed into the maelstrom that is prison. To become what? I used to think. Animals of a nature that you can only imagine. Consummate villains, it seemed. The epitome of all that is evil. Dead men, in more or less live bodies. No real compassion was allowed to surface. Any feeling shown was a fatal flaw in that hell. The sick minds caged there watched for moments of weakness. A tear, a smile, any change of expression would drive the psychotics into a frenzy of humiliation, or worse.

Life meant so little in prison that it became uncommon to have a common bond. The desolation I felt was typical. The need for human contact drove men to humiliating acts of degradation. These pitiful men sought any contact. I watched them performing sodomy on each other almost desperately. I never ceased to feel that sickness you feel when something obscene is played out in your sphere. But as the years slowly progressed my abhorrence changed to pity and, then, finally to acceptance.

Reality there, in that human cesspool, was only fleet-

From the Pages of *The Critic*

ing in appearance. The unnatural caging of men in a desperate condition only brought the abstractness of the prison to bear more heavily on all of us.

No amount of thought could bring escape from the grinding boredom. The mind stagnates under the constant assault of noise and stifling routine. You find release in daydreaming. Men in prison incessantly talk of how it was, "on the bricks." Women, cars, and crimes committed are the topics of much conversation. Fantasy lovers, fantasy crimes—on and on it went. We built fantastic reputations for prowess, all imagined. The necessity for an identity required that we manufacture our own personality. So we became what we thought we were, not what we were in actuality.

Most men in prison are there for petty crimes of little significance. A few dollars taken from a house. A few hundred from a gas station. No amount can be placed on a human life. Many men kill for no reason. Senseless murders of people in a small business, often callously killed for small amounts of money, even for nothing. The men who killed for thrill were the most dangerous. They often continued that behavior in the prison. They often killed with homemade weapons, in a frenzy of lust or psychotic despair.

We who survive to get out—it's so rare to survive mentally intact—and choose to stay out, often don't try to tell our stories. But the story needs to be told.

We put ourselves there. We were plagued by our inability to cope, in prison or out. Once released we felt alienated. Too soon we reverted to our old behavior patterns, unable to do anything else. The maw of the

Just Good Reading

Beast opens; we're swallowed into the oblivion of that House of Horrors; and we die, again and again.

The repeat offender has to return to prison. His obsession is mind-boggling. What man would continue behavior that guarantees him the Horror? you ask. A man whose mind has been bleached white of any ability to comprehend even his own mortality. A man who must have the regimented existence of penal servitude. A man who is absolutely polluted by the vileness of his own thoughts. He will surely die in that wretched existence.

The human spirit is indestructible, it appears. We managed to live there. We managed to normalize our lives to a great degree. Somehow the years go by, and we keep our lives together enough to survive. I often wondered how I managed to find a modicum of peace. I read books avidly. Books provided escape from utter loneliness. Many of us used the printed word to find that escape from ourselves and our environment. Nothing interfered with our routine too often. It was daily, grinding fear that fueled our cause. It often seemed almost poetic justice. We were put in a place to be punished, but also rehabilitated. It was up to them to strike the balance between punishment and rehabilitation. They usually failed miserably.

We came out of prison and began life again haunted by the demons of the past. We go through life seeking release from our mental devils. But even if we manage to do that the residue remains. Nothing ever really becomes normal again for us. We are absolutely degraded and it takes a long time to cope with that feeling of degradation.

Constantly being reminded of our inadequacies by

From the Pages of *The Critic*

authorities doesn't help our overall ability to cope "out here." We usually don't do well while in the grip of the Beast, whether he be allowed to kill in there, or out here. Fighting seems to help but actually it only puts off the eventuality of our demise. The will, the spirit are really our only defense against the desperate unreasonableness of our plight. It's true outside, as it is inside. If your will failed in there, it shortly fails out here. And to fail is to die.

I often wished for that pleasant envelope of death. The prospect wasn't frightening to me, as it might have been. As I have progressed "out here" over many years, the sounds fade; the loneliness lessens. Living seems a nice alternative to dying. Success is mine. Freedom is mine. Love is mine. All the feelings are there again. It feels good. I love to touch my wife. Just that feeling of closeness sustains my days. I write of fear—and I still have it—but it is slowly fading into a bad memory.

In the final analysis the experience was horrifying and purifying, good and bad. It taught, it extracted, it replaced and it left me empty. It helped fill my life with new meaning, and it removed the social disability I suffered with for so long. I have concluded it to be my greatest learning experience, and one that, God help me, I am thankful for. To have endured that decade-plus in the lair of the Animal, and to have survived with my faculties relatively intact is a miracle that isn't lost on me entirely. I realize that Grace of God every day that I live. I thank him for the ability to put my thoughts on paper, and I am thankful that he chose me to live. I would have missed so much otherwise. I would have never known real love, and the feeling of accomplish-

Just Good Reading

ment that I get when I finish a project, or just go to my job and make a few dollars. I support myself, and another human being, with the knowledge that my salvation was hard earned and terribly expensive for me, and my family. The pain they felt while I was locked away was acute, and they suffered knowing that their son, and brother, was fighting to live every day. I am so grateful now, but then I would have traded all my remaining days for the sweet victory of death. It seems ironic now, many years later, that I want to live and look forward to life's challenges. It is surely an indication that a Power Greater Than Myself exists in this universe. I feel awed by that Power, but am thankful that it exists. It has been very good to live. . . .

THE CLOAK OF FORTUNATUS

by Samuel Hazo

YOU left too soon so suddenly,
   and all your skill and wit
   and generous skullduggery went
   with you like a fire fading
   into smoke and back to air . . .
                  Just now
your letter, written on your last
live day, arrived.
               It took
   the vengeance from your exit
   since you talked about "the next
   roller coaster ride" and thanked me
   for my thanks.
                 "This, happily,
   seems to be my lot," you said
   with just the right degree
   of poise and peppery resilience.
Like any father, artist or perfectionist
   with more to do than time
   to do it, you did the best
   you could and left the rest
   to God and a martini.

Just Good Reading

"The cloak
of Fortunatus," you resumed, "keeps
one from being too annoyed
and too frustrated."
I checked
the reference and came up dry
and now prefer it unexplained.
But still it vexes me the way
it vexes me to say that no one's
life concludes as planned.
There's
always something left undone,
unthought, untold, and we depart
unfinished as the world,
which goes on being what
we tried or failed to make it
while we had the chance.
Like Peter Sarkis, who could still
thank God the same for life
and dying, we can go in gratitude
for what we had.
Or we can fight
like Helen Middleton, who had
her hand still fisted, even
in the coffin.
Or we can leave
like you with all sails full.
But still we're missed as you are
missed right now.
I'm glad
we took the time to make
the most of time.

From the Pages of *The Critic*

>>>>>>>I'm proud
>>>we worked where poetry and music
>>>danced and kissed.
>>>>>>>I'm grateful
>>>for the said and silent words
>>>and for the sung and unsung songs.
>I only wish these lines
>>had never to be written, Ed.
No matter what they say,
>>>they leave too much unsaid,
>>>and still my hand's a fist.

NEVER GAMBLE WITH A MAN NAMED DOC

by Joel Wells

I OWE my contact with the late Nelson Algren to Ensign Pulver, the totally amoral character in Thomas Heggen's novel *Mister Roberts*. It was Pulver's theory, raised through empirical experimentation to the level of an axiom, that a great many women remained virgins simply because no man had ever offered to relieve them of their burden. In other words, it never hurts to ask.

That became our working theory at *The Critic* in the 60s. We had little money to offer writers, artists and cartoonists, but these people still like to work and be published. Furthermore, they often turned out more good work than the top dollar magazines could use and hated to see it languish. What they want is a "respectable" place to publish in company with other good names. The trick is to get the first good name to appear in your magazine.

So we asked. We won some and we lost some, but if you could match the right book, say, with a reviewer's prime interest area, it was hard for them to resist. So we got a review of a feisty historical work out of Arnold Toynbee, and one on a theatrical opus from Brooks Atkinson. Painter Ivan Albright declined to illustrate a short story, however, on the reasonable grounds that it took him six to seven years to complete a work. But Ben

From the Pages of *The Critic*

Shahn could not resist embellishing a story by his favorite writer, Isaac B. Singer, with three full-page sketches.

And there was Nelson Algren, one of the country's great writers, living at 1958 Evergreen right here in Chicago. I didn't know that Algren was anything less than rich, or that he was feuding with most of the local press. I didn't even know if he would deign to review a book. I did know that he was supposed to be a no-nonsense man with something of a chip on his shoulder about being a prophet unappreciated in his own city.

Would he be willing to review *Tell Me How Long the Train's Been Gone* by James Baldwin? I sent him an issue of the magazine, added that his friend Mike Royko had once said a kind word about it, and crossed my fingers. Yes, he would, but Baldwin wouldn't like it: (he) "sounds like Tennessee Ernie Ford singing 'I Believe' while counting the house. . . . Dizzy Gillespie used to carry his trumpet around in a container of costly hand-tooled leather that he called 'my watermelon bag.' The beauty of his trumpet's sound justified his irony. But when Baldwin's hand-tooled prose is intended to sound most exquisite, all James is doing is sashaying around."

Surely Graham Greene's *Travels With My Aunt* would fare better: "By consciously contriving an entertainment out of literary observations and travel notes, while declining to feel any personal involvement himself, Mr. Greene leaves the reader reluctant to feel concern for people about whom the author himself cares nothing. . . . Yet one understands: the war against boredom must go on."

Bernadette Devlin's *The Price of My Soul* did: "A

Just Good Reading

beautiful book by a beautiful woman." But Algren really went all out for poet James Dickey's *Deliverance:*

> Had Mr. Dickey asked my advice about writing a novel, before going ahead on his own, I would have discouraged the whole idea.
> "Look, buddy," I would have been forced to caution him, "you may be greased lightning in the hundred-yard dash, but sustaining a poem is one thing and sustaining a novel quite another. As you'll find out for yourself when your breath starts coming short with 20,000 words behind you and 60,000 to go."
> It was therefore with the pleasant anticipation of watching a front-runner break down at the turn for home that I settled down with *Deliverance* in the early morning hours.
> The novel moved at an even pace—but an even pace isn't enough. Halfway through I thought irritably, "Doesn't he know that something has to happen?"—and was about to put the book down.
> "Two men stepped out of the woods, one of them trailing a shotgun by the barrel."
> When I looked up it was early light. I became aware that I'd drawn myself up into a defensive posture and was holding the book across my lap to protect myself from a murderous kick. . . . It was a shaky way to begin a new day.

In all, Algren would write a dozen book and film reviews for *The Critic*, an article and three reports on his journey to, and stay in Vietnam in 1969.

From time to time he invited me to lunch and to join

From the Pages of *The Critic*

him at several receptions and parties celebrating the publication of books by local authors.

After one of these affairs, Algren and his party of five, including me, were joined by a group of youngish ladies, four in number. It did not appear to be a chance encounter. A small grimace of consternation displayed itself on the face of one of the women. She took Algren aside and began a whispered conversation. She was a good whisperer; he was not.

"Not to worry," he said. "There's no need to call anyone. Mr. Wells here is a good family man who'll soon be heading home."

In person he was always genial, though he was given to making less than charitable remarks about some of the newspaper people who would turn up at these parties. He was also fond of delivering brief therapeutic maxims: "What you need most when you spend 150 billion dollars a year on defense is an enemy;" "It's not prudent to eat raw fish in a place with sliding doors;" "Never gamble with a man named Doc."

He followed this last piece of advice himself one Friday afternoon when he visited our Thomas More Association offices on Wabash Street. He came to record an audio cassette of his short story "Dark Came Early in that County." I introduced him to Dan Herr, president, publisher and columnist for *The Critic*.

"I've heard of you," Nelson told Dan.

Dan replied: "I've heard of you, too."

Nelson, abashed, said, "That was a dumb remark of mine."

In those days it was our custom to mark the close of the working week with one hand of showdown poker

Just Good Reading

for a dollar ante. When Nelson emerged from the recording module I invited him to join in. He feigned deep shock and the author of *A Walk on the Wild Side* and *The Man with the Golden Arm* actually appeared flustered. He took off in a hurry, leaving his sunglasses behind. The following Wednesday I got a letter from him:

> Thanks for the tour. Although your "editors" looked vaguely familiar to me, I couldn't place them until, when you suggested a fast game of blackjack with the house deck, they all snapped on their green eyeshades with a single motion. I've often wondered where all those dealers went when Brown & Koppel's closed down. Now I know.
> But I must admit that I never saw a finer front than "The Thomas More Association." Thomas More indeed! God help the poor Christian who wanders in *there* in search of *faith*.
> Thanks, too, for returning my shades; the value of which almost equals the cost of posting them.

Some time later, Simone de Beauvoir published *The Coming of Age*. Algren was convinced she had sold out their famous love affair by including some of his letters to her in *The Mandarins*. She was a woman who invaded her own privacy, he told his friend Joe Pintauro who, in his *Chicago Magazine* article on Algren, quotes him as saying, "I mean, she really destroyed that relationship. Love letters are private. I've been in whorehouses all over the world and the women there always

From the Pages of *The Critic*

close the door." He reviewed the book for another publication and sent a copy of it to me.

"I think that both Cyril Connolly and V. S. Pritchett take Mme. Driveleau too seriously," he wrote. "At any rate I'm enclosing my own reaction to her arrival at complete pomposity. My own title for the review was 'The Clothes of Others.'"

Early in January, 1969, Algren set out for Vietnam. He was under commission to write some articles for *Atlantic* but wondered if we would like to publish some "color" pieces and observations in the form of a diary or letters. He got hung up in military red tape, perhaps laid on even thicker than usual because of his reputation and known opposition to the war. At any rate he wrote saying that even though he had accreditation from *Atlantic* it was necessary to have a second accreditation in order to get an American Press Card. "Its value consists in that (1) it constitutes an airline ticket to anywhere American Army planes fly; (2) it entitles the bearer to eat in American army messes; (3) it entitles its bearer to shop in American PXs."

We sent him the necessary letters and he got the cards. He did not get the check we sent him for the first two of the brief color pieces he wrote for us, however.

"The five hundred dollars that didn't reach me would look very big right now. Can you send another edition of it? I would also suggest that you enclose the check in a piece of carbon paper without folding it, inky-side out. This is to make contents less revealing when held up to a strong light. Mail from the USA is inspected closely here, especially by Vietnamese helpers."

Just Good Reading

In another letter he reported that "Saigon seems less of a war-town than a boom-town. What war is being waged appears, locally, to be waged most fiercely by the Vietnamese police against the Vietnamese girls employed in the PXs. The Vietnamese M.P.s and police are much harder on their own women than are the American M.P.s. The American G.I. seems to feel protective of the Viet girls. Some of them are incredibly beautiful (the girls, not the G.I.s). I'll write you more fully after I've found out why the girls who ride behind their procurers on Hondas going 65 MPH should ride sidesaddle."

After his return from Vietnam, Algren wrote a few more reviews for us. In 1973 he pulled up stakes, bade a petulant goodbye to "Chicago, City on the Make," and moved to New Jersey to tilt at the windmill of rescuing Rubin "Hurricane" Carter from the cold hands of justice. After that, aside from a Christmas card, I never heard from him again.

In 1980 he moved to Sag Harbor, Long Island, where he died of a heart attack on May 9, 1981. He's buried there in Oakland Cemetery, about twenty-five yards from the road, in a pressed-wood composition coffin. He was 72.

If he could, I like to think that Nelson Algren would give us all one last maxim to cherish: "Never move to Sag Harbor unless you want to stay there."

ROME WASN'T FLOUNDERED IN A DAY

by William A. Herr

Incredible as it may seem, many people still believe that Rome was founded by Rhombus and Rhesus—a blunder which, among knowledgeable people, is roughly equivalent to ordering red wine with ice cream. Such errors, however, can be prevented: a quick review of Roman history could save you a great deal of embarrassment one of these days. After all, you never know when you might meet a Latin teacher.

THREE primitive tribes are especially important in Rome's early history: The Umbrians, so called because of their habit of taking umbrage (a mild narcotic); the Villanovans, who often behaved like college rowdies; and the Swiss Lake Dwellers, who built their homes on stilts by the shores of rivers, thus proving conclusively that mud is thicker than water.

These people wandered down from the north or up from the south (or, sometimes, sideways from the east or west) and settled near the mouth of the Tiber—which, fortunately, was closed at the time. The most enterprising of these people became Romans; the rest turned into Etruscans and became extinct. The early Romans borrowed much from the Greeks, who had the unfortunate habit of carrying gifts around with them.

Just Good Reading

An important cultural development of this period was the evolution of the Latin League, a professional baseball circuit. Rome's team, the Lions, played in the Colosseum. Other famous teams were the Adriatic Pirates, the Sicilian Straits and the Greek Gods. When the league expanded, in the fifth century A.D., the Mongol Hordes and the Gothic Cathedrals were added.

The Lions' most sensational player was a young outfielder named Venus, whom the Romans dubbed "the Fly-Trap" because of her fielding adroitness. These games generated intense excitement at Rome. When a scheduled contest was cancelled by Senatorial order, the poorer classes revolted and overthrew the government. It is the only instance on record in which a reign was called on account of a game.

Early in its history Rome was threatened by the Sabines and their agricultural neighbors, the Combines. After a long struggle the Romans conquered these trouble-makers and abducted the Sabine women. What they did with the Combines has not been recorded.

The most important men in Rome were the Consuls, who carried on diplomatic functions and cared for exiles. (An "exile" was what was left when a Roman governor finished ruling an island.) The most important of these men was the Consul Romanus ("Roamin' Consul"), who managed foreign affairs. Each important family put itself under the protection of one of these dignitaries; in return the family was expected to provide food and lodging for its benefactor. This was known as "keeping your own Consul."

Other well-known officials were the Censor, who

From the Pages of *The Critic*

burned incense at official functions; the Tribune, who was in charge of transmitting news; the Praetor, who conducted religious services; the Quaestor, who went around asking questions; the Dictator, who in time of danger composed messages for the Tribune to write down and deliver; the Cure-all, who was supposed to protect the public health; and the Aid-all, who dispensed government relief. Rome was also well acquainted with the Be-all and the End-all, who was usually the emperor.

Probably the greatest crisis in Roman history involved that great commercial city in North Africa, Cartilage. This city claimed to have been founded by travelers from Tyre, but the Romans, considering the settlement to have had illegitimate origins, referred to it as a "phony scion" colony.

The Cartilaginians were an industrious people, justly famed for their scientific and mechanical achievements and especially skilled in the manufacture of bone. This material was widely used by the Cartilaginian navy, which often operated with skeleton crews. Their greatest scientist was the noted biologist and geneticist Hannibal, who astounded the world by attempting to cross the Alps with elephants.

Despite their own reputation for great intelligence (whence the expression "a Roman knows"), the Romans were insanely jealous of these achievements. Urged on by the orator Horace, who suffered from a chronic sore throat, and Cato the Censor, who read dirty books and had a one-track mind (he was always at the Aquaduct, watching chariot races), they swiftly mobilized. Soon

Just Good Reading

after, they also began to prepare their army. Because of the haste of these preparations, the ensuing struggles have been called the Panic Wars.

This challenge did not especially frighten the Cartilaginians, who were busy having a Baal. Their confidence was justified: in addition to a splendid army and a well-supported navy (see above), they possessed a secret weapon—a motorized vehicle called the Hamilcar.

But even this was not enough. After a long campaign Rome defeated Cartilage and imposed an indemnity of 3,200 talents. Despite their industrial accomplishments, however, the Cartilaginians were not an especially talented people, and thus they found it impossible to meet this demand. Instead they proclaimed their undying hatred of Rome (which they referred to as "the Infernal City"), and again declared war.

This time the Roman armies were led by Publius Cornelius, who, despite a fondness for drink—his men called him "Old Scipio"—was a great military strategist. Cartilage offered heroic hesitance, but the Romans weren't interested: they persisted until they had achieved victory.

Julius Caesar first came into public notice by exploring Gaul, after which he reported that it was divided into three parts (and his critics immediately contended that he had all three). He also claimed that the Belgians were the strongest Gallic tribe, because they were the furthest from modern conveniences (such as bathing). While in Gaul he conquered a number of native tribes, including the daring Nervii and their flighty chief, Aviatrix. These victories earned Caesar a great deal of fame,

From the Pages of *The Critic*

which embarrassed him acutely. He kept insisting he was just an ordinary Gaius.

While Caesar was fighting in Gaul, Rome was being endangered by two ill-dispositioned men, Pompous and Sullen. Pompous, a general, was threatening to lead his troops into the city. Sullen, a physician, had poisoned hundreds with his infamous "prescription lists," which druggists could not read correctly—he kept writing them in Latin.

In this crisis Caesar proceeded to Rome and took over the government. Because of his somber nature (he was called "the gravest of all the Romans"), his enemies became legion. More important, his legions became enemies. He was finally assassinated by three men (Brutal, Cautious and Trepidous) in 44 B.C.

Like all good things (and most bad ones), Rome had to come to an end. This it proceeded to do in 476 A.D., with the help of several barbarian tribes. Chief among these were the Goths (some of whom were later ostracized and became Ostrogoths); the Visagoths, who were the only ones with passports; the Versagoths, who often recited poetry to themselves; and the Vandals, who carved their names on trees as they passed. The greatest barbarian leader was Attila the Hungarian, who called himself the Scourge of God. No one knows what God called Attila.

These individuals were allowed to penetrate Rome's borders chiefly because of the weakened state of the empire's defenses. The entire army, in fact, was usually off somewhere building roads instead of fighting, despite the fact that Roman citizens seldom used roads, prefer-

Just Good Reading

ring to travel on galleys, or floating kitchens. The Roman army maintained a special school for young men who desired to learn highway engineering. These youths were known as Roads' scholars.

These splendid roadways were a tremendous help to the barbarians, who used them to sweep into Rome—which at the time needed sweeping badly. The one-way street, unfortunately, had not yet been invented. Had it been, Romulus Augustulus might be alive today.

I PUT MY FOOT UPON THE CHAIR

by Arthur Roth

WHEN I was a young nipper growing up in County Tyrone, Ireland, some 35 years ago, the people had a great belief in cures. I don't mean the often-efficacious folk remedies such as moldly bread poultices for infected cuts, or fresh cow manure for bee stings. Moldy bread, of course, was an early if very weak forerunner of penicillin. And I imagine some form of bacteria in the manure helped neutralize the venom of a bee sting. But the people also believed in miraculous—some would say superstitious—cures. These cures were hedged about with all sorts of protocol, prohibitions and dire warnings and were, in all likelihood, tenacious hangovers from the druidical practices of pre-Christian Ireland. I once had occasion to take one of these cures but more about that later.

On thinking about cures it comes to me that most of them involved ailments that the body itself would soon cure anyway; such afflictions as ear aches, sprains, toothaches, sore throats, rashes, warts and shingles. I don't recall anyone having the cure for tuberculosis or cancer. All of which brings to mind my Uncle Packy's complaint that modern people were dying of far too many different ailments. In his day they all died of

Just Good Reading

either fever or the cramps, two clear cut symptoms that covered the whole range of fatal illnesses.

Only certain people had the cure for certain ailments, and I never heard of anyone having more than a single cure, with one possible exception. The seventh son of a seventh son was supposed to possess great curative powers in all ranges but I personally never knew any of those rare and exotic gentlemen. The gift of "having the cure" could be passed on, but only to someone younger of the opposite sex and, once passed, could no longer be employed by the donor. A grandaunt of mine, who was slowly dying, once tried to pass on to me the cure for ringworm and I remember the occasion vividly. She was propped up on pillows in her bedroom. Her small bedside table with its array of medicine bottles looked like a chess game in the middle stages. She seemed in remarkably fine fettle for a woman who was supposed to have "one foot in the grave and the other trembling after." She actually lingered for another three months. I was thirteen or so the afternoon I was prodded into her presence. At some point we were left alone and she leaned forward, caught me by the arm and whispered fiercely, "Will you take the cure for ringworm, I haven't passed it yet."

My natural awe at being in the presence of someone who was so near death that "she often heard the fluttering of wings" turned to terror when I heard her whispered request. In the first place I hadn't ringworm and in the second place I hadn't been aware that you could die from it and, much as I respected grandaunt Aggie, I had no desire to lift this burden from her aged body. If there was any passing to be done I'd rather she'd pass me by;

From the Pages of *The Critic*

if there was any dying to be done, let *her* get on with it. I was rescued by the reappearance of Aunt Margaret who called briskly to her mother, "Say goodbye to Arthur, he has to go home now." Grandaunt Aggie gave me such a malevolent glare that it put the heart crossways in me. In fact a few days after her funeral she appeared in one of my dreams, presenting me with what looked suspiciously like a huge and very alive ringworm. I fled screaming for the safety of consciousness and woke up to find the pillow and all the bedclothes kicked to the floor.

After I left the bedroom, Aunt Margaret gave me some lemonade and biscuits in the kitchen and I mentioned her mother's request. Aunt Margaret said not to pay any attention, her mother's mind sometimes wandered a wee bit and she obviously forgot that she had already passed on the cure to Mickey Pat Devlin in Tandaragee. I was to pay no mind to the matter. (No matter, never mind, as Bishop Berkely said.)

On another occasion I remember Uncle Packy having such a bad case of quinsy that he left the house at midnight to drive seven miles to someone who had the cure. For the next three days he wore a single strand of wool around his neck and at the end of the third day his sore throat was gone.

The wearing of some object on the body, be it a strand of wool around the throat, a black thread around an ankle, or a small purse-string bag suspended from the neck, was very much a part of these cures. Sometimes a prayer had to be repeated nightly by the afflicted person, sometimes not. Not infrequently the cure involved a prayer written on a small piece of paper that was

Just Good Reading

tightly folded and pinned to some interior garment like a shirt or undervest, with the admonition that the message was on no account to be read, and after three days—sometimes seven—the folded paper, still unread, was to be thrown on the fire and burned. Similarly, the small drawstring sacks were never to be opened. Sometimes these sacks contained a folded note and often what felt like small pebbles or other mysterious tiny objects.

It is my impression that the clergy, while condoning these practices, did not exactly approve of them, though one local priest was reputed to have a cure for alcoholism. I'm afraid this service was rarely availed of, to judge from the spirited consumption of alcoholic beverages in my home town.

I also remember a controversy once about a man who *mailed* his cure to relatives in Canada, it being held by certain people that cures wouldn't cure outside Ireland, by others that the physical presence of the curer was necessary to effect a cure, and by a third party that the cure wouldn't work anyway because the man was a Protestant. This last charge was patently false as the use of cures was not confined to Catholics. Many a Catholic went to a Protestant for a cure and vice versa. A local Protestant woman, for example, was famous for her cure of chilblains.

One cure for rheumatism mentioned by a historical writer involved the climbing of Croagh Patrick—a 2500 foot peak revered for its associations with Ireland's national saint—and passing a bell called the Blackbell of Saint Patrick three times clockwise around the body—in honor of the Father, Son and Holy Ghost. Passing anti-clockwise or to the left side is naturally taboo because

From the Pages of *The Critic*

the left (sinistral) side or direction is associated with the devil.

The time I had occasion to visit someone for a cure was one Sunday evening when I was nearly astray in the head with the pain of a toothache. I had suffered two full days with that throbbing tooth and couldn't look forward to any relief until the following Tuesday when the dentist, "Pincher" Sullivan, paid his weekly visit to our village and set up his temporary shop, appropriately enough, in the front parlor of our local butcher. I was only fourteen at the time and three of the older lads took pity on me. Biddy Logan, over on Murderers Row, had the cure for the toothache; they would take me to her. Biddy, of indeterminate age but determined alcoholic tendencies, was the widow of a retired British Army serviceman and lived in one of the town's narrow back lanes that was largely populated by a raffish working class lot.

There was one catch, the lads explained, it was customary to present Biddy with a couple of bottles of porter to take the edge off her ever-raging thirst. The pubs were all closed but one of the lads volunteered to slip in the back way of Tierney's and buy three bottles of Guinness stout. At that age I was a natural paranoid and suspected that neither Biddy nor I would ever lay eyes on that stout. Nevertheless, driven by that hot coal in my tooth, I turned my back and squeezed out one and ninepence from my hoard of pocket money. I was also a natural miser at the time.

In a couple of minutes the lads reappeared with the merchandise, and we all made our way down to Murderers Row and Biddy's front door. Biddy was fre-

Just Good Reading

quently bedeviled by young brats who would knock at her front door late at night. When Biddy answered she would be met by the shouted chant, "Biddy the Bottle is full to the throttle," then the whelps would run screaming down the lane. In fact, while waiting for Biddy to come to the door, we prudently flattened ourselves along the front wall of the house. Biddy was known to sometimes drench a caller with a pan full of dirty dishwater. After a certain amount of whispered entreaties Biddy finally opened up.

Once inside the smokey kitchen, the lads explained their errand of mercy and presented Biddy with the three bottles of stout. She promptly whisked them away into a cupboard. Then Biddy sat down on a stool, spread her hands to the fire and complained that giving the cure "took a lot out of a body." (The Guinness presumably put it back in.) Biddy, a skilled dramatist, knew the value of suspense and kept us waiting while my advocates, who also knew *their* roles, appealed to her compassion. "Sure the lad's in shocking pain." "Ah Biddy, can you not see the big jaw he has on him."

Biddy was finally coaxed into opening the ceremonies. I was sent into the scullery and warned, under penalty of having the cure "turn" and spread hellfire to the rest of my teeth, not to look into the kitchen. I stood in the dark scullery and listened to the whispering with intense curiosity. I thought I heard the cap of a bottle being pried off, but that left me none the wiser. Eventually I was commanded to come forth. Biddy stood in front of me and told me to close my eyes. I did so and felt a cord around my neck, followed by her fingers opening the top of my shirt. Something dropped inside

From the Pages of *The Critic*

and lay against my skin. I knew enough about cures to realize it was one of those cloth sacks containing tiny objects.

"Open yeer eyes," Biddy said. She made a few passes over my head with her right hand and muttered several phrases in a foreign language that, to my untutored ear, sounded like Latin or Greek. (The phrases may well have been a choice selection of obscenities in Punjabi or Tamil. Danny, Biddy's departed mate, had served time in India with the Connaught Rangers.) I was next given a litany of instructions. I was not to open the bag and look inside or the cure wouldn't work. I was to wear the bag until the third night and then burn it in the fire. In the interim I was not to remove the bag for any reason, even while washing my neck. I was to avoid touching the bag with my left hand. There were other strictures that memory no longer recalls.

Next came the dramatic climax of the cure. Biddy placed a three legged stool in front of me and told me to put my right foot up on the stool and repeat after her. I put my foot on the stool and balanced awkwardly on one leg, the stool being rather high for my chubby pre-adolescent limb. "I put my foot upon this chair," Biddy chanted and I repeated the phrase. "To keep my tooth from aching," said Biddy and I fervently echoed *that* line. "I take my foot down off this chair," Biddy said and I said it after her.

"Take your foot down," one of the lads whispered. I lowered my foot to the floor as Biddy intoned the last line, "To keep my ass from shaking."

"To keep my ass from shaking," I stupidly repeated before the enormity of my friends' treachery sank in. All

Just Good Reading

three of them were shaking with laughter, holding on to each other in the back of the kitchen.

I was still numbly rooted in the middle of the floor when Biddy flew into a no doubt pretended rage, snatched up a broom and began to belabor us. "Get out, get out, you brazen lumps, would you make mock of an old woman?"

Outside the house the three traitors staggered away, making the night hideous with their awful laughter. I stood in the lane, cured of my toothache by a hot and murderous hate that cried to the heavens for an awful bloodletting. As soon as I was in the privacy of my own house, I tore that sack from around my neck and opened it. Inside there were three bottle caps inscribed, "Guinness Extra Stout."

I was to visit Murderers Row on several later occasions, my role now changed to that of benefactor as I initiated some younger suffering lad into the mysteries of Biddy's toothache cure.

Alas poor Biddy is no more, passed on to her reward, presumably reunited with her Danny, and I fervently hope the pair of them are blissfully "full to the throttle." I hope too that, wherever she is, she has some angelic nymph or scowling imp standing in awe in front of her, one foot up on a stool as he repeats that opening line of her famous cure: "I put my foot upon this chair."

WHY I LIVE WHERE I LIVE
OR: HOW I MOVED TO THE COUNTRY
(OR, AS THE KIDS SAY, WHATEVER!)

by Margo Howard

ABOUT ten years ago, in a newspaper column, I stated my view of pastoral life. "The country," I wrote, "is where the birds fly around uncooked." Although technically correct, this is clearly a city-girl remark and I wish I could take it back.

This change of heart came about with a change of address. Having moved to the country, I now feel the zealotry one expects from the converted. There is simply nothing like having your own waterfall and a field full of lilies. (And this from someone whose idea of a garden used to be Anna's Flower Shop.)

Where we live is the northwest corner of Connecticut, in the Berkshires, abutting the Massachusetts and New York state borders. The terrain is alternately rolling hills and flatlands, with intermittent small mountains or large hills, depending on how one construes life. Our part of the state is rich in water, so that the mountain stream and various ponds on our land are not unusual. Thanks to an upper pond dam, we have a splendid waterfall.

I have come to regard all this water as a convenience for frogs, a great community of whom are in residence. They are gotten up in Army surplus colors—green and tan—and never fail to advise one another when I am ap-

Just Good Reading

proaching their turf. They do this with an urgent kind of chirp. Then they take a flying jump into the water and under the sludge. The larger ones occasionally stand their ground and offer, in greeting, a sound that is somewhere between a gulp and a ping.

The thing about living in the country is that there is always someplace to walk. When I lived in California, many areas were hanging over cliffs; when I lived in Chicago, there were plenty of sidewalks, but too many other people were using them. Because our Connecticut place has one-sixth the acreage of Monaco, it is always possible to take a walk without falling into something or bumping someone.

The land we have would probably classify us as gentlemen farmers. We have so far produced only one gentleman, however, and even that is debatable, seeing as how the young man is nineteen and given to lapses that make such a designation iffy. Unlike our farming neighbors, we have no animals, save for Alice The Dog. I do get great pleasure, though, from what I call my Budget Rent-A-Cows. They are a dairy herd belonging to Farmer Twing and they come, most days at four o'clock, to graze in our meadow. They come . . . they have *always* come. In fact, our first caller was Farmer Twing, asking if he might continue to use the meadow; he would repay us with liquid fertilizer. My husband said that would be fine. As for what we would *do* with the bartered substance we did not know, but neither did we wish to seem unneighborly. I always refer to this man, by the way, as "Farmer" Twing. More than one listener has suggested that this is an affectation. Maybe so, but when one has been raised on the corner of Lake Shore

From the Pages of *The Critic*

Drive where it becomes Michigan Avenue, surely a man in possession of a herd of cows can properly be referred to as "Farmer Twing."

People say that cows are dumb . . . so dumb that last fall, in Lakeville, a group of them walked *back into* a burning barn. Intelligence aside, they are good to look at and I find them calming.

As for Alice The Dog, she is not much smarter than the cows but she is terribly sweet and everyone likes her. Like most yellow Labs, her disposition is friendly, bordering on manic. She is the kind of dog George Carlin must have had in mind when he remarked, "If a burglar showed up—and this dog could talk—what she would say is, 'Wanna beer?'" Alice's only reason for barking, actually, is if another animal approaches. Human visitors receive neither yap nor yowl; it is wild turkeys and raccoons who merit a territorial whoop.

Though city folk have birds around, the supply seems more plentiful in the country. This is not altogether a blessing. I said to my husband, as a joke, one morning at six o'clock (when it is *not* my habit to rise), "Could you please turn off the birds?" It dawned on me (no pun intended) that there *is* no turning off the birds . . . that they are, for better or worse, a kind of God-given Muzak. Imagine my surprise, as they say in the old-fashioned stories, when I realized that a family of starlings had made a nest in the air-conditioning mounting in the front window of our bedroom. I became aware of this development when I heard a mad flapping of wings that sounded unusually close to me, then saw a slender twig being pushed through to "our" side of the window. The situation posed a moral dilemma. If the nest remained,

Just Good Reading

we could look forward to quadruplet starlings growing and chirping until they were old enough to fly off and set up housekeeping in someone else's air-conditioner. If it did not, we could look forward to pangs of guilt at the mere sight of a bird, a nest, or a blue egg. I finally decided to co-exist with the Westinghouse Starlings, though not from the finest of motives. I had an irrational fear that were I to dislodge said nest, all the birds in Connecticut would divebomb me whenever I left the house. I also had a nagging feeling that displacing a feathered family was not the correct way to behave towards nature. Anyway, the babies were born, and songbirds they're not. Living with their avian racket is like walking with cream of wheat in your shoe: it is not easy, but it is possible.

As for the people up here, they may have been painted by Norman Rockwell. Mr. Merriman, our mailman, also collects the trash. He has a wonderful sense of humor, as anyone can see by the pot of geraniums that serves as a hood ornament on his barn-red garbage truck. Tony, our United Parcel driver, always whistles his way up the walk, gives Alice a dog goody, then passes on the weather report. I will tell you a story about Tony, or maybe it's a story about living in a tiny town.

One day my husband was doing chores in the village. As is the custom up here on any nice day, car doors are unlocked and windows are down. Upon returning to his Jeep, my husband found a package in the passenger seat that had not been there before: Tony had simply saved himself a stop on our road. Familiarity (not the kind that breeds contempt, the kind that makes your car rec-

From the Pages of *The Critic*

ognizable) is a hallmark of rural life.

Another is acceptance. One of the neighbors on our road—a weekender—has a beautiful garden where I sometimes go to help myself to a bloom or two . . . only those, of course, that have just a day or two left of life. There was a decidedly homely touch to one of these outings when I noticed a little white note stapled to a stake in his delphinium bed: "Margo," it read, "Not these." Well, anyway, that should give you some idea of our "neighborhood."

Our larger neighborhood is known for the writers who live there: Arthur Miller, Philip Roth and Bill Styron. More newly arrived is what is called the sexual-industrial complex: Oscar de la Renta, Bill Blass and Geraldine Stutz. Meryl Streep is our newest famous person, and the shopkeepers are always glad to discuss her selections as a consumer.

Shopping in small communities is not the hassle it can be elsewhere. Charge accounts are a particular pleasure, allowing a person to pretend she lives in a pre-MasterCard era. The notation of goods charged is simply entered in a looseleaf notebook and no signature is required.

Celebrity residents or no, there is a welcome lack of Mercedes and Rolls Royces up here. I say that from no feeling of "Buy American," but from four years spent in L.A. I am thrilled to seldom see a gussied up automobile on these country roads and have, in fact, decided that real men drive pickups and Jeeps. (I have not made up my mind about the quiche.)

The pace in our neck of the woods is, predictably,

Just Good Reading

slower than in the city. Any city. Not many people here bother with an answering machine, and an answering service is an impossibility. In a pinch, the telephone operator at the White Hart Inn can take a message for the tree man or the game warden, but that's about it. Crime, as well, is suitably languid here. The last transgression I know about happened when a life-sized cardboard cut-out of a Hallmark halloween scene was defaced by someone who sketched in a naked lady over a ghost costume.

There is a warmth and personal connection one feels in the country that I believe is not possible in an urban setting. It is more than unlocked doors and zucchini waiting on the doorstep. It is a homemade banner in front of a house proclaiming, "IT'S A BOY!" and a wave and a smile from a driver, unknown, in the cab of a truck. There is a kindness and sense of community that, for whatever reason, seem unable to thrive in a city. Sheer size may be the variable, although I really think it's a connection to the land. There is something unutterably wonderful about healthy grass and low stone walls and wildflowers by the acre. And they don't call it quiet for nothing.

Sometimes I become fixated on the treeline at the curvy border of the back lawn and find myself waiting for Indians to appear. It's not that I think they are there, but that they *were* there, and somehow I can wish myself into their time. That back lawn, you should know, gives forth a bounteous harvest of fruit salad. We have apple and pear trees and jungly grapevines. For reasons I do not know, our grapes are at their tastiest after the first frost.

From the Pages of *The Critic*

Soon after our arrival there was a letter of welcome from someone who had lived in the house many years before. She wrote us all kinds of stuff about the property and its history. One piece of information was particularly interesting. "The soil," she wrote, "in the field by the access road will grow anything better than anywhere in the area." Well, of course! This is probably where Farmer Twing's liquid fertilizer was going . . . no doubt *had* gone for who knows how long. Anyway, on a day when you factor in the scent of woodsmoke and the sighting of a group of deer, the land tends to reinforce a feeling of gratitude to that Noted Clergyman who made us all. There is something almost otherworldly about the shadows and texture and smell of the countryside.

Things are not, however, all pineapple upside-down cake and Mason jars in the boonies. We did have a bit of go-round with the zoning board here . . . such as it is. When we applied for permits to rebuild the barn, it seems that the officials, five men good and true, were unwilling to agree that the barn was a garage. This was because it had not housed a passenger vehicle in eighteen years. This kind of thinking is always difficult to get back on the track, but we finally prevailed with the help of our architect (a former Selectman), contractor (a relative of a zoning board member) and a lawyer who graciously attended a zoning meeting on our behalf. Homey clout somehow seems less corrupt than big city shenanigans.

A barn, by the way, has got to be one of the best buildings devised by civilized man. The scale and flexibility offer limitless joys. My husband designed our

Just Good Reading

barn, conceptually, and named it "Hollywood." In it he put all the rooms that would not fit into a nineteenth-century farmhouse: a spa, gymnasium, exercise room, billiard room and 30 x 20 closet. He is probably the only "farmer" on our road who hits golf balls in his barn.

As for the main house—the farmhouse—it was built in 1800. Every door has hand-forged latches and hinges. There's not a doorknob in the place. And the center stairway has the traditional irregular step about two thirds of the way up; it is two inches higher than the others, its purpose being to send a burglar tripping and crashing down, in the dark, before he can get to the sleeping quarters. Family members, of course, drunk or sober, were in on the secret, so *they* never tripped, and they rested easy in terms of intruders—which there didn't seem to be any of, anyway, but better safe than sorry.

Our old house has a romantic history. It was once owned by a muralist of some note. His name was Ezra Winter, and people who know about art will tell you he won the Rome Prize. His studio, a freestanding building with a thirty-five foot ceiling and "walls" made of leaded-glass windows is like no other building I have seen. Next to it is a gigantic cactus garden . . . a commonplace, perhaps, in New Mexico, but eccentric in New England. As for the barn, Mr. Winter sometimes painted in there, as well as in the studio, and once in a while his colleague and neighbor, Norman Rockwell, painted in there with him. (Rockwell's own home was in Stockbridge, Mass., about thirty miles away.)

There is also lore about that barn that has to do with

From the Pages of *The Critic*

the second Mrs. Winter. It is said that she started a business there called "House of Herbs," after which she invented nail polish. The first achievement is verifiable, the second less so.

Having three daughters, Mr. Winter bought each a house on our road when they married. It is an odd footnote to his history that, owning so many buildings proximate to each other, he finally died in a tiny shack on a neighboring road. Legend has it that part of his artist's temperament was dark and depressed, making his final visit to the little shack not altogether surprising. It was there that he died by his own hand.

We did not, however, buy the place from the Winter estate. We bought it from a man named Don Thompson. The joke up here is that *everyone* has lived in this house, and I know for a fact that before Don Thompson there was Ollie Gignoux, Ed Dean, Mabel Hurlbutt, Scott Warner and someone whose name I forget.

Although I have not tried it, I hear there is a twelve-mile white-water canoeing run up here that is first class, along with some of the best sections of the Appalachian Trail. What I am more familiar with, however, are the 150 television stations we can now receive, thanks to the "dish." Satellite reception is an extraordinary capability to have, and though I basically live my life with maybe six of those channels, it is nice to know the others are there . . . just in case I ever want to see National Jewish Television, Meadows Racing Network, or Eternal World Television. Actually, TV in rural areas is given to extremes. Due to signal difficulties, there is either the feast of the dish or the famine of the unenhanced tube. Before

Just Good Reading

we went satellite, all we could get was ABC and two CBS's, the NBC fellow having defected to what he felt was a better affiliation.

I will admit that my nose gets a little out of joint when, in the weather forecasts from Hartford or New Haven, we are dismissed as "the northwest hills." I am not unaware that, to many people, the northwest hills, in particular, sound like Hicksville and that rural areas, in general, seem uninviting and unexciting. But I will tell you something: to live in the country is to be in on a secret. It is a place of peace, beauty, and wholeness. There is a validity to country life that I have found nowhere else. I do believe a man named William Cowper was right when he wrote, "God made the country and man made the town."

I couldn't agree more. Be it ever so humble, there's no place like sixty acres with a waterfall.

WEDDING NIGHT

by Bridget Kennedy

IT'S THE night of his wedding and less than five miles beyond the hotel he pulls sharply into a lay-by, switches off the engine and looks out into the dark, pissing rain. He calls her "Missus" and says he could never call her that before tonight. Finally, he reaches towards her in distraction, sensing her slump in the seat, only palpable in this dark. And the deep, inconsolable, unearthly sound of her crying to herself is so foreign, more than that, so separate from him, even now it catches him by surprise. He asks her to say something. Please. Just say anything. Is she afraid? Does she want to go back to the wedding party? And have one for the road?

Ha! Two years ago this night he was with the boys as usual in The Red Wheel dance at Burtonport. Twenty-seven years of age and still observing the ritual of the pillar. The stocking up with shorts and pints; the sally across the dim lounge to stand all night around the mirrored pillar to the left of the dance floor; chain-smoking, no dancing and absolutely anything interesting but the psychedelics, the throbbing music and the femaleness that surrounded them.

No, he was right. He wouldn't have seen her here before. He heard she was the only child of middle-aged

Just Good Reading

parents, Donegal born, spent most of her life abroad but was now a student in Queens. Home was less than six miles from Burtonport! She was totally unfamiliar with the parochial texture of his world. Not even remotely aware of the ritual of the pillar. And, unlike every other woman in the house that night, she hadn't grown up with his gaucheness, his unhappiness with language. None of those identifications. Then, as his aunt said, women weren't exactly beating on his door.

The others were more interested in her cousin, local, plump Rose Marie, full of promise. But, no, there was something else the others were aware of. Was it a kink, a contradiction in her. (And, looking back, damn them for backing off.) The big-boned, strong, stable frame, the open brown eyes, and her manner. Maybe like a character caught on stage in the wrong play. But if you read her like that it was also true, or so he had believed, that the play, the stage didn't matter to her. Indeed, what had attracted him to her in the first place was that inconsequentiality. Right then he felt elated, being on home ground, a host, an ambassador to her foreignness. And, naturally enough, challenged too, to display the fact that he belonged.

The pursuit was on, but there was no hurry. He was living easily enough at home (couldn't afford not to anyway), his mother a decent, open woman with five adult sons. He often worked 'til seven or eight at night for the cabinet maker of the town. A male world, the smell of wood and sap and resin. And for years, treasurer of the Deep Sea Angling Committee—drank with them most nights of the week.

In the beginning, the arrangement was offhand, feath-

From the Pages of *The Critic*

erlight, easy, he all the more attentive for that. Occasional weekends he'd go to Belfast and stay with her in student digs. A jaunt to Galway together, Dublin, Kilkenny. And that last summer was glorious. Glorious weather, glorious fishing, glorious late nights and she was always there. She said more than once she was looking for a three-piece-suit man with a Saab. Another time she took his hands in hers and shook her head at the rough outsize of them. These and a variety of other inadequacies made him all the more earnest.

He met her people only once before today. One September afternoon he drove her out to collect a dress she wanted to wear to a christening. She ran up to the house, leaving him to go in alone. He remembers vividly her father and uncle seated at a table in the darkened kitchen, a black labrador sleeping at their feet. In silence, they were counting out money. A thin, younger man with an ashplant in the corner. A clock and glasses on the table and the smell of linoleum, a dying fire, airless. The dog growled when he stepped forward, they turned and the picture dissolved.

Her father was broad, mountainy looking. He remembers being called "stranger" and "son." Introductions to the two men, would he have a drink, and where was her mother? Into the light of the front room, books, plants, a piano, photographs, clutter. And she came in from the garden, a slight figure in a cream dress, sunglasses, head to one side, touching her hair. A light voice telling no one in particular they'd heard all about this young man. Weren't they in the same class in Queens?

Then, where's the dress, Jesus, where's the dress? She

Just Good Reading

barely looked near them. Leave it, no, just forget it. Would she not stay for dinner and let them show more hospitality in this house? There's a girl for you. There's a handling. And they left.

She seemed to lose heart in the degree and spent more and more time in the town. She became part of his day. In his workshop making the men tea at the break. Or, night after night, sitting with him and his friends, quietly. Then, when his father finally died in the hospital, a tremendous help to his mother during the wake with his relations and all the visitors, up night and day. Afterwards, when his mother was down, she ran the house, cooked the meals and often stayed overnight in the spare room.

He met his friends less to stay in with her and watch TV or, if they went out, she preferred the company of married couples with children, setting up homes. Somehow, her friendship with her cousin had long since fallen apart, then she lived so far away from the Queens' students too. And felt she'd nothing in common with his brothers' girlfriends who giggled when they came in from the street. Sometimes they watched her silently, over with his mother at the knitting machine, head bent studying the patterns.

But to relate it all like this, marshalled, in a clear sequence, wasn't the way any of it happened. Because it happened almost imperceptibly, except for one episode. About six months before today they'd gone to his best friend's wedding. He felt giddy and raw at the loss, the end of an era, boys! He was the best man; brandy from breakfast on. Late afternoon she arrived at the church in

From the Pages of *The Critic*

a cream knitted dress and by the time the dance began the atmosphere was wild, excessive.

Late into the night he heard someone from the table asking when they were going to name the big day. My God, didn't they even go to mass together now? His brothers started slow clapping and he felt their women going quiet at the possible foretelling of their own futures. And she was getting to her feet, laughing, and taking photo after photo. Thickly, he understood that he had been led into something inextricable and permanent. Something that would always have to be nursed, but defended in public. Something deeply unequal. And then he was leaning across the table pointing a cigarette at her and telling her to get out of his fucking sight, woman. To leave him alone. Get out of here now and don't come back. As she ran out alone, he struggled to his feet, the boys moved in slow motion to catch him as he tried to mouth obscenities after her.

The following morning his house felt empty. He went downstairs, hair wet from a shower, a towel over his bare shoulder. And there she was in the kitchen, waiting for him at the window, looking blanched, lost, ill. Suddenly, the spaniel was wagging all over them on the couch and he was tucking her hair, again and again, behind her ear. He told her that she was special, different. But he could take care of her. She knew his father had left him some money. Would they get married?

Yes. He knows that the best thing right now is to leave her alone. The rain has stopped, he kisses her on the head and gets out of the car. Unties the bowtie, lights a

Just Good Reading

cigarette. Vaguely, he thinks of the words of his trade and their weight and sinew. Halving, bolting, cleating, cogging, housing, bracing, rib, lath, sill. And the job they'd have done last winter, restoring the church door blown loose in the big gale, and someone calling in the wind that she was unhinged, boys, unhinged. He stubs out the cigarette and turns back towards the car. They have a room booked for the night and miles still to drive.

A REMEMBRANCE OF WINE AND ROSES:
AN AMERICAN CATHOLIC EXPERIENCE 1950-1965

by John Deedy

NO ONE promised us a rose garden. But, in the 1950s, we didn't need promises. We had the assurances. It was a time of righteousness confirmed. The good war had been won. God was in his heaven (no feminist lingo then). Dwight David Eisenhower was in the White House. Edward R. Murrow and Walter Cronkite were on the tube evenings. And everything was upbeat for American Catholicism. The family that prayed together stayed together. Sex was discreet, not pervasive in the least. Everything was innocent by today's standards, even Hugh Hefner. Remember that early *Playboy* cartoon of the woman speaking from the bathroom on her wedding night: "Honey, I've got a confession to make. I dye my hair"? It was innocence that was pervasive in the 1950s. Bishops and priests were revered as oracles who could tell us anything (and often did)—from the altar, in the confessional, from the podium, at cocktail parties. We listened (most of us, anyway) because anything from Father's mouth was God's word. Somewhere, Wilfrid Sheed attributes a kindred Messiahship to sisters—the "Sister said" syndrome—but I'm not so sure it was the same thing. In any instance, ours was a rose garden and it was in full bloom through the mid-1960s. It was a great time to be a Catholic in the United States.

Just Good Reading

That was only thirty to thirty-five years ago but, looking back, the times seem a century removed from the 1990s. Ours is another world, another existence, certainly another Catholic existence, particularly compared to the 1950s. No one gets very nostalgic about the 1950s anymore. In fact, the impulse is to lampoon them. But I'm going to tell you, they weren't that bad. And of course the 1960s, until mid-decade, were deliriously exciting. In the early 1960s, we American Catholics were on the front page of *The New York Times* just about daily. What surer confirmation could there have been of religion's importance. Indeed, Catholicism's! We owned the present. The future—well, it was ours, wasn't it? We had Christ's word on that, or Father's anyway.

Everything was crystal clear. America was good, and democracy was steaming hot apple pie, with blue cheese yet. Our church had its Spellman and our government its Hoover, J. Edgar. It was all so reassuring. We knew the enemy was Communism and with Spellman and Hoover around the "cold war" couldn't be in better hands. Few of us thought to wonder, much less doubt. So, back in the early 1950s in Worcester, Massachusetts, when a monsignor of the diocese called one day and asked if I'd drop around to the local FBI Office because the boys would like to talk to me about a speaking engagement of mine coming up at a Unitarian church, I couldn't have been more flattered. Just think! To be able to do something for God and country at the one time! The agents had their eye on a couple of persons. They asked if, in the question period, I'd mark carefully what was asked and by whom, then report back. Which, by way of belated public confession, I did. I had little to of-

From the Pages of *The Critic*

fer and contributed nothing—except maybe to the paranoia that gripped us all. Later, in the 1970s, the FBI would have a different kind of interest in me because of certain involvements of mine as an editor and writer on the fringes of the peace movement. It was an interest which would not have flattered me in the 1950s, but it helped atone for that earlier indiscretion. We don't always get second chances in life.

But we were talking about the 1950s, and how sweet they were. Father Dan Lord was traveling from city to city and packing them in at his Summer Schools of Catholic Action. His hymns were pure saccharine, but oh how they were loved. One of the young ladies in our office eventually marched down the aisle to Dan Lord's "Lady in Blue, I Love You." (John Cogley used to wonder whimsically about the shock it would be for Catholics if, on arriving in heaven, that Lady appeared in brown.) I heard later that, when the Summer School of Catholic Action came to Chicago, priests would patrol the parking lots to guard against any action in the cars. We didn't have that problem back in New England. Culture gap, I guess.

However, as indicated earlier, there certainly was no communism gap. Louis Budenz was in our diocesan paper confirming "our" Christian, as opposed to "their" atheistic, politics. Gretta Palmer was supplementing Budenz's witness with her own, while Father James Gillis was adding Paulist blessings to the good life we had arrived at. We liked to think in our part of New England that ours was an "intellectual" anti-communism, not an emotional, knee-jerk anti-communism of the kind then being served up in columns of the national weekly that

Just Good Reading

visited Catholic homes from out in the midwest. But, of course, ours was just the other side of the one plug nickel. We presumptuously considered our postures confirmed after one of the most rabid anti-communist baiters on the other side of the nickel was pinched driving nude down a busy highway, with a young passenger in the car. Nothing like someone's else's grief to confirm one's own rectitude.

Sounds fictional, you say. Have it your way. But then, wasn't so much about the 1950s pure fiction, especially in American Catholicism?

The decade was unreal, when you reflect on it. Those seas of nuns in hotel ballrooms listening as priests told them what was best for them. Those phalanxes of priests assembling for summer retreats and listening as the bishop told them what was good for them. And the rest of us listening as Sister, Father, Bishop told us what was good for us. The bishop was getting the word, I suppose, from Rome, probably by way of osmosis. But the pope was peripheral to our existence. Who needed a pope when pontification was at arm's length and within earshot? The American church was full of popes in the 1950s.

We listened, heeded and obeyed and, curiously enough, the church flourished. So did country. Church and state were separate, but they were in a double ascendancy. It would be sharply downhill for both once we were a few years into the 1960s. John F. Kennedy would be assassinated in 1963. It wouldn't get better for the country for a long time after that. The church's turn would come after 1965. But for the time being, how

From the Pages of *The Critic*

beautiful the scene, and how wonderful the vantage point, at least mine.

I had a friend, deceased several years now, who quit his job at the old National Catholic Welfare Conference, what we now call the U.S. Catholic Conference, exclaiming, "It was better to see the show from the audience than from the wings." At first, I didn't get his point.

Me? I was out in the provinces at the time but still in the wings, sort of—first as a reporter for a daily newspaper, then as the editor of a diocesan newspaper. Two in fact. I liked my wings. It was for me a good place to be. I wasn't at the center of anything, but I was close enough to control central to be able to share the triumphs, channel the church newsbreaks, hype the causes and clobber the clods—with words, of course. I loved it, primarily because like most everyone else I was convinced the world belonged to the Christian "fellowship," and as Catholic Christians weren't we the best of the elite? We didn't have to delude ourselves about this. The Lord of the New Testament had said he would be with his people, his church, all days even to the end of the world. The 1950s didn't smack of Armageddon, not quite, or at least not all the time. Nonetheless, it was reassuring to know that God was on our side.

If communism dominated the political side of our Catholic brain, numbers did the other. The "official" Catholic census figures issued forth every May from P. J. Kenedy & Sons, and they documented the vitality of our American church. We grew as Catholics by the millions year by year. But then, anyone could make

Just Good Reading

babies, and Catholics held all the records. A more interesting statistic was the number of converts we were gaining. Converts topped the six-figure mark annually. If there was any leakage from the ranks, it was so infinitesimal as to need no accounting. If occasionally some prominent Catholic broke ranks and "defected," that person's loss would be more than offset by some flashy personage won over by Monsignor Fulton Sheen, like a Ford of Detroit.

Looking back, the remarkable thing about American Catholicism of the 1950s was its busyness. The years were full of meetings, conferences, conventions, and congresses. We were organizing with a frenzy, establishing a Catholic counterpart for almost everything which existed in the wider society. So we had our Catholic Boy Scouts, Catholic Girl Scouts, Catholic War Veterans, Catholic Association for International Peace, Ladies of Charity, and on and on. These coexisted or were piled onto old standby membership groups, like the Holy Name Society, the Women's Altar Society, Women's Guilds, St. Vincent de Paul Societies, and virtually countless fraternal and insurance organizations, from the Knights of Columbus and the Daughters of Isabella to the Catholic Order of Foresters.

Busyness, busyness, busyness. There were exciting new things happening on the liturgical front out in the midwest, and there were a few quiet but effective social movements, like Dorothy Day's Catholic Worker. But mostly it was a time of busyness. Busyness was the mark of the 1950s. The decade did not bustle with ideas, at least not in my corner of the rose garden. Ideas and challenging intellectual concepts belonged by and large

From the Pages of *The Critic*

to the thinkers and theologians of western Europe, France in particular: Congar, Chenu, de Lubac, Danielieu, Teilhard de Chardin. And they were just names to many of us. A counterpart to Europe's intellectualism we did not have here in the United States. Jacques Maritain, an imported scholar, was braving innovative thoughts at Princeton, and catching fire for it from an obnoxious order priest, a Dominican as I recall, whose name is lost to my memory. John Courtney Murray, the Jesuit, was judiciously probing the parameters of church and state in their American context, and for that was brought within sight of the cannons of the *American Ecclesiastical Review's* Father Joseph Fenton, a mercenary of the Holy Office's Cardinal Ottaviani. There were security people everywhere. The funny thing is that we lived with them and were not particularly appalled that they should exist. Oversight was a fact of life. It wouldn't be so to such an extent in the 1960s, but this was the 1950s still.

I was a diocesan editor beginning in 1951, directing a new paper (so much was new in those days) for an up-and-coming new bishop. The paper was *The Catholic Free Press* of Worcester and the bishop, John Wright. Wright would eventually lose favor with a lot of American Catholics, but in the 1950s he was the darling of the liberals and an exciting man to be around. For one thing, he had a mind. He read and he sensed the intellectual gap that existed between American Catholicism and European Catholicism, and wanted his paper, the *Free Press*, to be maybe not *Le Croix*, but better than most of what passed at the time for a diocesan newspaper. I don't know if we ever were, but we tried.

Just Good Reading

For Catholics who couldn't even spell "encyclical," we provided a course in the famous paper letters of history. It was a pro-labor period, so the labor encyclicals were musts. Our approach was shamefully middlebrow. We didn't run texts or lengthy, informed summaries of the documents. We ran Peter Maurin's "Easy Essays"—easy doses of what seemed then like strong medicine. For those who didn't read books and didn't suspect there might be such a thing as a Catholic literature, we serialized Myles Connolly's *Mr. Blue*, no rival to *Leaves of Grass or Moby Dick*, though a minor classic of a sort, And of course we ran endless articles, essays and letters on the theological novels of Graham Greene. Those were mostly 1940s books, the third in the trilogy, *The End of the Affair*, appearing in 1951, when the decade was just getting started. But the movie versions of all of Greene's theological novels were in the movie houses through much of the decade, so we expended all kinds of energy discussing the whiskey priest of *The Power and the Glory*, so drunk at his son's baptism that he could hardly stand, and so drunk too that he mistakenly gave his son a girl's name. Did Greene's book deserve the Holy Office's condemnation for its portrayal of the priest? And Scobie of *The Heart of the Matter*; was he saved or damned for that sacrilegious decision of his to take the host and thus hurt God rather than Helen, his lover, and Louise, his wife? And Sarah Miles of *The End of the Affair*; could anyone actually be led through adulterous love to divine love?

It was such fascinating stuff as this which preoccupied our 1950s—fascinating, but also frothy. Even Evelyn Waugh's reviews of Greene's books seem frothy in retro-

From the Pages of *The Critic*

spect. Should it ever have been necessary for Waugh to have to launch us into the 1950s with assurances that it really wasn't "the function of the Catholic writer to produce only advertising brochures setting out in attractive terms the advantages of church membership"? Waugh wrote that in 1948 in *Commonweal.* The comment rings so much of the obvious now, as to seem almost trite. Trite—but at the time it was a daring observation, which only an outspoken person like Waugh would have uttered. That's how regressed, how intellectually unsophisticated we were. Most of us were enthusiastic celebrators of our religious birthright, licking the frosting of ephemeral things like Greene's novels (tasty, but ultimately not substantive), and marking time until the parousia, the Second Coming, when everything would be ours.

Nonetheless, it was in the 1950s that the stage was set for change. The thinkers among us were beginning to raise questions and to wonder aloud if the church in the United States wasn't, in fact, anti-intellectual. John Tracy Ellis broached the topic of anti-intellectualism in *Thought* in 1953, charging that American Catholics were shamefully delinquent in upholding the intellectual traditions of the ancient and honorable universal church. Father John Cavanaugh, a former president of Notre Dame, picked up the theme in 1957 in a Communion-breakfast address in St. Louis, I think it was, demanding to know, "Where are the Catholic Salks, Oppenheimers, Einsteins?" The best answer came from Thomas F. O'Dea, a Harvard trained sociologist on the faculty of Columbia. He argued in *American Catholic Dilemma* that American Catholics were the victims of

Just Good Reading

authoritarianism, clericalism, moralism and defensiveness. The *American Catholic Dilemma* issued from Sheed & Ward in 1961 and, though O'Dea's thesis was intensely disputed in some quarters, by then the validity of his observations was pretty generally acknowledged.

Three people triggered three events which were to change our lives and rescue us, if not from our anti-intellectualism, then at least from certain certitudes that stultified. With those three people, those three events, the country would change, the church would change, and we would change.

First came the incident of December 1, 1955, when a Black woman named Rosa Parks declined to give up her seat on a Montgomery, Alabama, bus to a white passenger. With that refusal, the civil rights movement was launched in the United States. We Catholics were not a part of that movement in the beginning, and the leadership never even came close to belonging to us. Why should it have? In 1955, most of our churches in the South still practiced a form of apartheid. But the movement did force some soul-searching in the American Catholic Church in areas where heretofore there had been none. No less important, the civil rights movement projected us out of ourselves. So what if only three people showed up for Father Joe Pelletier's lecture on Our Lady of Fatima in the parish hall (I was there and did the counting). So what if the Holy Office didn't like Greene's portrayal of a whiskey priest. There suddenly were more important things to claim our attention—indeed, our moral commitments—and gradually we would be part of them.

From the Pages of *The Critic*

Second, what did the Republicans do but hoist themselves on their own petard. Having "endured" Franklin Delano Roosevelt into a fourth term, once in power themselves they decided to protect henceforth and hereafter against Democratic dynasties and passed legislation limiting presidential office to two elected terms. Dwight David Eisenhower thus had to step down after eight years. He probably would have anyway, given his health, but the Republicans had created a situation where there couldn't even be a thought of a third term, one which at some point in the term would likely have propelled another Republican, probably Richard Nixon, into office on Dwight's bad heart. The Nixon nightmare would come later. Instead, in 1960 we got a new President from the other party—and, what do you know, a President who was also a Catholic, first in the history of the land! John F. Kennedy was, however, a Choate-Harvard Catholic, a Catholic formed beyond the institution and responsive to it (non-responsive, really) in ways strange to the rest of us. Kennedy wasn't around very long, alas, but he would be around long enough for some of his institutional detachment as a Catholic to rub off on the rest of us. It was a good thing.

Third, there was the bombshell John XXIII dropped in an informal chat after celebrating a Mass for church unity January 25, 1959 at St. Paul's Outside the Roman Walls. In order to renew the church, to proclaim the truth, to contribute something to the well-being of the modern world, John announced that he intended to call an ecumenical council, a council of the universal church. Most of us didn't know what a council was, and so many of us expected so little from the council John

Just Good Reading

called—our bishops were conditioning us to expect little—that, in the beginning, we hardly took it seriously. For instance, few of us bothered to make arrangements to be in Rome for the Council's first session. It was only after Cardinals Lienart of Lille and Frings of Cologne submarined the Curia's plans for containment at the Council's first official meeting, October 13, 1962, that most Catholics suddenly realized that the Council would not be the pro-forma exercise the Curia wanted and our bishops expected. We American Catholics who were journalists realized we were on the wrong side of the ocean, a long way from the action. Our bishops had deluded us as, of course, they had deluded themselves. It would be different for the 1963, 1964, and 1965 sessions. We'd be there, as many of us as could. All eyes were on Rome for, obviously, the Council was going to give us a new church. And did it ever.

Those three happenings tumbling one upon the other launched us on speed courses in sociology, citizenship and ecclesiology. We learned fast, but also stumblingly. Don Thorman celebrated our emergence as Catholics—Catholics with both a purpose and, at last, a meaningful role to play within their church—in a 1962 book entitled *The Emerging Layman*. But even as we devoured his book, congratulated ourselves on our good fortune, and enthused about the new life Thorman laid out before us, it never occurred to us to wonder about the implicit sexism of the title. *Layman!* We were making progress, but we were lugging around yet a full load of male chauvinist attitudes. Some of this we would shed in time, no thanks to ourselves or our church, but rather to the

From the Pages of *The Critic*

"women's lib" movement which, in the process of rocking American society, shook our church and us as Catholics.

But that would come later. It was the now that was so beautiful and exciting, and how different these 1960s were from those 1950s. In the 1950s, we were so seemingly self-contained as Catholics; that was comforting. However, we were also smug, and that was debilitating, certainly intellectually. In the 1960s—well, we found ourselves really, although probably more by accident than by design. Our situation was different. The pilgrim-church analogy has been belabored, but it still fits us and those times for, in the 1960s, we were pilgrims almost in the literal sense. We were journeyers, searchers, people with a mission to discover ourselves and our church. It sounds pompous saying that now, but how else describe that trip? Our high carried through the Council years, 1962-1965. Every day, it seemed, brought a new discovery, a new insight, a new realization. The church was on the move, and we with it. The 1950s produced a New Look in fashions; the 1960s produced a New Look in religion. Roman Catholicism would be out front, the American church with it. As a group, we Catholics were all so heady by 1965 that even *Commonweal*, the Catholic grey lady of print, decided that it too wanted a New Look. It went to a new format, announcing solemnly that it had "redesigned" itself "to better express the contemporary nature of ideas, issues, and events" which the magazine sought to bring to its readers. Catholicism was entering a new phase, and no one wanted to be left behind, except maybe the reactionaries.

Just Good Reading

Then, all of a sudden, Roman Catholicism's New Look went out of kilter. What went wrong? I suppose part of the problem was that we all expected too much, and such change as we did get didn't measure up to expectations. Here we were thinking that we were an "emerged" people, but Rome and our bishops dribbled out change at so slow a pace as to make most of us feel almost infantile. It was the old paternalism bit with a vengeance. The vernacular Mass came to us in one, two, three uneasy steps, and in a translation so poor as to make the semiliterate blush. We assembled before Mass like preschoolers in day-care center to learn hymns that would physic a rat, as they say in Ohio. Suddenly it dawned on us that we laity, female and male, weren't so "emerged" after all—and indeed we wouldn't be until so many priests had shed the cloth that the church had to let the laity "emerge" in order for it to stay in business. So lay persons were brought into ministry, appointed to parish school boards, seated on marriage tribunals, consulted through parish councils, and the like. Bishops and priests would even start rendering financial statements to the faithful, as if ours was one big, happy and coresponsible family. But by then it was all too late. Too many had turned off. The magic was gone from the scene.

However, I don't blame clerical paternalism entirely for that. I expect the downturn would have come anyway. Once we were in on all the secrets, most of them seemed hardly worth knowing. It was a little like joining a fraternal organization and going through the degrees. Once you had finished them, you wondered what the big deal was all about. In sum, it seemed that a church demystified was suddenly a church without a lot of its

From the Pages of *The Critic*

old charisma. Whether that's good or bad is another question. What is clear is that the Catholic Church went through a radical demystification process after 1965, and we with it. That didn't make the church any less holy, catholic and apostolic, but many of us felt we had been left with a church that was a lot less mystical.

It didn't help the American church either for the war in Vietnam to heat up when it did. Certainly the war didn't help the image of the bishops. The American bishops had joined with the bishops of the world at Vatican II in condemning war in all its manifestations but, in the concrete, they could not bring themselves as a body to a condemnation of the war in Vietnam until the 1970s, when just about everyone, Richard Nixon included, was looking for a way out, any way out. One thinks back specifically to 1967 and 1968, and how few bishops could be persuaded to sign the nationally circulating "Negotiation Now" petition which encouraged Washington to begin peace talks and which, so far as Catholics were concerned, supported a peace position not far removed from that of Paul VI. It is easy enough to debunk petitions as a stunting exercise lacking any real impact or significance, but the "Negotiation Now" petition was different—at least different enough to place many nonsigners on the defensive. Bishop Wright, by now advanced from Worcester to Pittsburgh, felt pressured enough to issue a statement saying he wasn't signing because the petition didn't address the systematic murder by the Viet Cong of South Vietnam's intellectual and political leaders, and also because it didn't envision a reunited Vietnam. At the *Pittsburgh Catholic*, we ran Wright's demurrer under the headline "Bishop Hedges

Just Good Reading

Endorsement of Peace Group," and in the same issue published an editorial of our own unqualifiedly endorsing the petition. Our headline on Wright's statement was tendentious. I admit it now. But the church was becoming a tendentious place at that time.

Incidentally—no, not so incidentally—in St. Paul-Minneapolis, there was a reverse scenario to ours in Pittsburgh. Auxiliary Bishop Jim Shannon, later to marry and depart the scene, endorsed "Negotiation Now" in his column in the diocesan newspaper, *The Catholic Bulletin*, while on the page opposite, lay editor Bernie Casserly denounced Shannon's endorsement.

Two things can be said. Lay people could differ then with bishops on the bishops' own turf, and survive. It happened not all the time, but commonly enough. I'm not sure that same situation exists today—except of course with those in independent positions. Second, tendentious as the scene may have seemed at the moment, it was nothing compared to what it would become once Paul VI dropped the papal shoe *Humanae Vitae*. That did in the twentieth-century church.

I was at *Commonweal* at that time, and every day after lunch Jim O'Gara and I would take a walk down Park Avenue, turn around in the area where the old Madison Square Garden used to be, then head back to the office at 37th and Madison. A preoccupying topic was what was happening in the church. I mean, it was coming apart—or seemed to be. So many people seemed to be turning in their Roman collars, religious habits, rosaries, missals. "What do you think?" Jim would ask. "Could it be because of the Council?" O'Gara wasn't holding that it was, just asking a question which must

From the Pages of *The Critic*

have popped into just about everyone's mind at one time or another. Every instinct in me said the turmoil in the church couldn't be blamed on the Council, that things would actually be worse if there hadn't been a Council. But that was liberal lingo. For all the theorizing I did in conversation with Jim O'Gara, I don't think I ever really believed the Council was completely innocent of the evils that were befalling the modern church until I started to do this piece.

Those problems of skepticism and doubt, of repudiation, rejection and drainage were coming, every one of them, and for a thousand and one reasons. Perhaps the most obvious was that a more sophisticated Catholic had suddenly grown up in a foot-dragging, terribly archaic church. It was traumatic but, in the United States, the church and its people were conditioned for events of most upsetting kinds. Or should have been. Dysfunction had come to the church, but dysfunction of equal proportions had also come to much of secular society. We were a hardened people able to conceive of and deal with extraordinarily challenging adversities by the time the problems of church were thrust upon us. Or did we help manufacture them ourselves? Whatever, supposing we had been asked to cope with all or just some of these problems of church in the 1950s, during the time of our never-never land existence: Could we have? Could we have done as well? My feeling is that things would have been a lot worse.

So what about the 1950s, in retrospect? They were unreal. Maybe the 1960s were unreal too, but their unreality at least was rooted in inescapable realities. We'll see the 1960s again. We'll never again see the 1950s. R.I.P.

From the Pages of *The Critic*

The Queen gasped.

"You recognized me!"

Holmes smiled.

"I could not help noticing the little marks on your forehead, which can only be caused by a crown. Perhaps you have read my essay on 'Marks made by Hats'. You are not the Kaiser, therefore . . ."

They all gasped.

"Wow, you certainly have an incredible gift for deduction," said the Prime Minister. "But let us get on with the story. We are in great trouble, Mr. Holmes. The First Lord of the Admiralty has reported that the British Navy has vanished. If some German spy sneaks on us to the Kaiser, it could mean the end of civilization as we know it, or at least it could mean the German Navy coming and shooting our holidaymakers."

"Have *all* the ships gone?" said Holmes to the First Lord of the Admiralty, his keen eyes (Holme's eyes, I mean) looking out from under his keen eyebrows. "Even the Zeus class destroyers with twin fourteen-inch turrets?"

"Unfortunately they have all disappeared," said the First Lord. With one stride, and then another one, Holmes leapt forward and pulled the moustache, beard, spectacles, hat and false nose from his face.

"Gentlemen," said Holmes. "Otto von Krempel, the German spy!"

* * *

"But how did you know?" I asked Holmes later.

"Jolly easy," said Holmes. "Any chap knows that Zeus class destroyers have a sixteen-inch turret, also he spoke in a German accent. I am writing an essay on Ger-

Just Good Reading

man accents. They only have one, the Umlaut. I thought of that joke this morning."

"One thing more."

"Yes?"

"Who wrote that threatening letter to me?"

"Who do you think?" said Holmes, throwing a cushion at my head.

DEATH AT TEA TIME
Ernest Hemingway's first story
(14 years old)

HALEY went out into the school yard. The first leaves of autumn were falling and it was chilly. The teacher told Haley to get his coat on or he would freeze to death. Haley went and got his coat. Then he went out into the school yard. It was a school yard much like other school yards, or I suppose so as I have not seen other school yards yet. Even if I had I would say it was much like other school yards as I have just discovered the expression "much like" and I like it.

"Hello, Haley," said Andersen.

Andersen was a huge Swede, standing well over five feet. He had blood on his chin where he had tried to shave himself. His shoulders were much like big shoulders.

"Hello, Andersen."

"I am going hunting in the woods. Are you coming?"

Haley knew what he meant. They were going to look for rabbits. They had never caught one yet and Haley was glad inside himself because they said that when you

From the Pages of *The Critic*

cornered a rabbit it was much like a mountain lion and tried to bite you, only lower down, about the knees.

When they were in the woods, Andersen stopped and shivered.

"It is a funny feeling, hunting rabbits. It is like the feeling of the thing between a man and a woman."

"What is the thing between a man and a woman?"

"I am not sure. I thought you knew."

"No, I do not know. But I thought you knew."

"No."

They went on a way further and they watched the leaves fall from the trees and hit the ground, which is the way of leaves when they fall off the trees. Haley shivered and said it was cold. Andersen said nothing. Haley said it again. Andersen said that it was not too cold to hunt rabbits. Haley said he did not mean he was trying to get out of hunting rabbits, he only thought it was cold and that was all he thought.

"Look!" said Andersen. "A rabbit!"

"Where?" said Haley.

"Over there."

"I cannot see it."

"It has gone now. It does not matter. Perhaps it was not a rabbit at all. It is very cold."

"Shall we go back to school now?" said Haley.

They went back to school and did some more lessons and then Haley went home but he did not tell his parents of what had happened.

Just Good Reading

LORD ARTHUR WENTWORTH'S BLACKBOARD
Oscar Wilde's first play
(age fifteen)

THE SCENE is a richly decorated room, hung with damask curtains, rich brocade and the finest tapestries, but if you cannot get this your mother's dresses would do. There is a pale scent of incense and also the furniture is sumptuous. It is the Fifth Form at St. Topaz's School. A young man is seated at a desk, which is Arthur, who is the pupil. Standing by the gem-encrusted blackboard is a young man, which is Basil, who is the teacher. As the curtain rises, Arthur is lighting a slim, delicate cigarette.

Basil: You know it is against the school rules to smoke, Arthur.

Arthur: What is the point of rules if we do not break them?

Basil: You have just made an epigram. Do you know the derivation of the word "epigram"?

Arthur: Like most words in English, it comes from the classics. Without the help of the Romans and Greeks, Englishmen would be hard put to it to express their contempt for foreign languages.

Basil: I sometimes wonder who is giving this lesson—you or me. Now, where was I?

Arthur: You were trying to persuade me that a knowledge of Canadian wheat production will enrich my career as a poet and artist.

Basil: My dear boy, one does not have a *career* as a poet. Poetry is too important to work at. One must content one's self with devoting one's self to it.

From the Pages of *The Critic*

Arthur: Exactly. I shall write a play and with the proceeds withdraw to an exquisite house where I shall dedicate my life to a poem.

Basil: It is a charming thought. What will your play be about?

Arthur: It will be about two wonderful young men sitting in a classroom talking about art, poetry and Canadian wheat production. One must show the public one has taste and also has done one's lessons.

Basil: And how will the play end?

Arthur: Suddenly, without any warning at all.
(CURTAIN)

DR. EVIL
(Ian Fleming, 14½)

JAMES BOND strode into the hallway of Dr. Evil's house, wearing an immaculate school blazer which had been made for him by Jacob Schneider of Lucerne, which I think is in Switzerland, and asked the receptionist to tell Dr. Evil that James Bond had come to see him.

"Dr. Evil?" she said into the phone. "There is a boy called Bond to see you."

"Who is almost 17," said James.

"Who is only 17," she said. "Yes, sir. Will you take the lift to the third floor?"

When Bond left the lift at the third floor he found himself face to face with Dr. Evil, a squat, ugly, horrible little man who was uncannily like a certain schoolmaster.

Just Good Reading

"What can I do for you, Master Bond?" he said leering.

Bond felt in his pocket casually to check that his 2½ lb catapult, made of choice elm wood by a master craftsman in Bond Street, which is a very important street near Piccadilly, was loaded. He only used the very best conkers, imported from his aunt in Ireland, which was better than most aunts who only sent you book tokens.

"I think you know what I have come for," he said coolly, no, icily. "You have my replica authentic Japanese destroyer which fires real hara-kiri aeroplanes, which you confiscated for your own devilish ends, Sir."

The face of Dr. Evil went pale and he reached for his poison gun, but before he could pull it out Bond had pounced. At lightning speed he fastened the evil man in a half-Nelson, gave him a Chinese burn, did a quick knuckle-crusher and punched him in the nose. Dr. Evil sank lifeless to the ground, only he wasn't really dead. Like a flash, Bond entered the nearest room. There, on the bed, was the most fantastic blonde, really smashing, with no clothes on at all, if you know what I mean, like in books. There, on the table was his authentic Japanese destroyer.

"Who are you?" she gasped huskily, gazing at the handsome stranger.

"I am James Bond and I am 16¾," he said in as low a voice as possible. "I have just killed your friend Dr. Evil, but he will live."

He strode to the table and picked up the destroyer. Before he left the room he turned to the girl, well, woman, and said:

From the Pages of *The Critic*

"You will get cold lying around with no clothes on, anyway it looks silly, whatever they say in books. I would get a dressing gown on if I were you."

Moments later there came the distinctive sound of Bond's super three-speed-gear Raleigh as he pedalled away down the drive.

THE VERY, VERY LAST OF THE OLD BREED

by Richard Shaw

BARNABAS CRONIN had been a bishop too long and had sat through too many public meetings. He was overtired. The job of entertaining visiting prelates at this regional conference for some foolish social activist cause had shorn him of his nap earlier in the day. Now he sat on a podium with fifteen other dignitaries and stared sleepily at his reflection in the shiny dark table top. With his small, wire-rimmed glasses and a mouth puckered almost into a beak, he had been referred to for almost thirty years in his diocese as "the Owl." He was bored. His own coadjutor bishop had been talking for almost three quarters of an hour about a human rights commission which was going to end all the ills of the world.

"All the ills of the world," Cronin grunted to himself, ". . . one more cap feather for Alfred P. Coyle."

His forty-year-old coadjutor, with long silver gray hair brushed into a young executive style, silver cuff links glinting from a well tailored black suit and the promising smile of a man running for office, had the lightest of speaking styles. He was on a well-tuned wave length with the great number of professional people in front of him, and his presentation, interspliced with a contemporary sort of wit, won appreciative laughter in

From the Pages of *The Critic*

all the right places. Cronin loathed Alfred, and loathed him even more thoroughly because the man was a monster of his own making. He had ordained him from his own seminary, and because the lad had seemed bright and persistent—mostly persistent—he had sent him to study Canon Law. After that, he seemed always to be around, ready and eager to help his bishop. He had an instinctive flair for the machinations of diocesan politics. It made sense to assign the young man as vice chancellor. After that a pearly smile and a desk in the chancery were all the weapons he needed to control the domain he etched ever larger for himself. Cronin's dislike for Alfred had grown steadily, even before he discovered that his witty vice chancellor made a habit of embellishing his bishop's ordinary nickname 'Owl' into the more elaborate pun: "the man WHO. . . ."

Cronin had balked at the very idea of Vatican Two and he liked even less what was perpetrated when he went to Rome—bringing Coyle along with him for his recently learned knowledge of Church law. Once back home the bishop stonewalled against the changes—to little effect. He was still fighting the inclusion of Saint Joseph's name to the time honored list of Cletus, Clement, Chrysogonus and the other standards prayed to in the Mass, while his Seminarians, tuning poorly played guitars, choreographed ballerinas to body homilies in the sanctuary.

It just wasn't his kind of world anymore. He was so shaken by the negative response of Catholics to the Pope's birth control ban he went on the pill himself—Valium. Then when he was already over seventy, Paul called for clergy retirements at seventy-five. A funny

Just Good Reading

thing happened to Barnabas. He began to commiserate with and then began to fully understand the attitude of the birth control users. He had no plans to retire. Who was Pope Paul to tell him when to step down? Then one day he woke up to find that Alfred, who had made so many friends at the Council, was now his coadjutor with the right of succession. All the old man had to do was get out of the way and smiling, manipulating Alfred would be in the driver's seat. Barnabas began reading health magazines and sending away for high potency vitamins. Come hell or high water he was going to outlive Bishop Alfred P. Coyle.

The vitamins, however, were not working this evening. Having missed his nap he drowsed in and out of the speeches, pondering his own reflection in the table top. Finally he nodded off altogether, missing Coyle's finale and the whole of Archbishop Geary's remarks. He then added his own comment upon the conference by snoring heavily into his chest microphone until the college professor seated next to him reached over and unplugged it.

Awakened by a sharp burst of laughter, he stared angrily and owlishly into the yellow auditorium lights, wondering for a moment where he was. He cleared his throat as if to assert he had been attentive all the while, adjusted his lopsided pectoral cross and frowned to disagree with whatever had caused the laugh. Sister Mildred (formerly Immaculata) Harte was on her feet, her half curled white hair haloing a wrathful glare, her heavy fist pounding inadvertently on the shoulder of the man in front of her. Once a docile grade school nun, she had somehow gotten liberated during the previous de-

From the Pages of *The Critic*

cade, moved into the inner city and launched out on a crusade against her own background. She had long since discarded her veil, and judging from the bouldered sloops in her sweater, her bra as well. Now she was throwing verbal grenades as her contribution to the question and answer period.

"No, I mean it," she insisted, "the Church is a sexist organization. If you're setting this up as a permanent council, why aren't there any women on it?"

Coyle fielded the demand with a winning grin to assure her that, deep down, he was on her side.

"We have to be patient," he assured her, "dealing with gaps between what is ideally wanted and what is realistic for the present. If we are going to set up a working program centered in this city, at this time, we have to deal with certain limitations."

Cronin was facing the audience, not Coyle, but the momentary shift in everyone's glance from the speaker to himself made it evident that his coadjutor, with his usual innuendo of raised eyebrow and nod, had made it clear where the gap was. Cronin was accustomed to it. Alfred fed upon being liked. If there was a popular announcement to be made he had a way of beginning it: "I have been trying for a long while to establish. . . ." Restrictions or unhappy decisions—oftentimes decisions with which he had heartily concurred when with Cronin—were promulgated by him with a woeful, punished expression and an inference: "Unfortunately, the bishop feels. . . ." It was the great advantage of being second in command. Now he was jousting with the fiery Sister Mildred as if the two of them together were sparring a third party. All the more hypocritical, thought Cronin,

Just Good Reading

for no man was more of a woman hater than his coadjutor. Women were quicker to see through him than the priests in the diocese. He used his celibate status as a shield to keep any shrewd female at a distance, and nurtured a singular dislike for the crusading Mildred whom he once scored cynically as having "the worst case of penis envy since Joan of Arc."

Mildred finished her diatribe with her usual flag waving for the downtrodden and for women's rights.

"Women are making long overdue inroads in every other field of endeavor," she declared, "and yet, the Church preaching for two thousand years 'there is no difference between male and female' relegates women to a second class existence. You toss occasional crumbs— 'Let them read in Church; maybe they can take up the collection.' We're talking about full human equality throughout the hierarchy."

She sat down while the audience divided itself between groans and applause. It was the sort of performance that no one could top, and the meeting, thusly, was adjourned. Those on the podium being allowed to file out first, Cronin had to run the gauntlet of walking down the aisle where Mildred sat. He knew what was coming. As he shuffled past her row, face rigidly set forward, she waved broadly and called out:

"Hiya, Barney."

He stopped and turned to her. This was a regular routine; a great piece of entertainment for all within earshot. He glanced momentarily at the hefty breasts which stretched the yarn of her sweater at midriff and wanted to tell her that a wimple had always done wonders for her. But no one ever appreciated a target shooting the

From the Pages of *The Critic*

arrows back. He forced his pursed lips into a brittle smile and nodded with sarcastic gallantry:—"Hello Mildred"—then shuffled on his way to the exit, the hearty stamp of his cane being the only expression of anger.

The film report on the late news was merciless. A camera man had caught Cronin, head bowed almost to a right angle with his chest, and while the sound man tuned his snores to full volume the commentator offered:
"The Bishop, meanwhile, appeared to be deep in thought. . . ."

There were a few minutes of banter the next morning at breakfast. Then Coyle and the visiting Archbishop Geary moved into a rehearsed attack.
"Barney," the Archbishop said hesitantly, "you've got to make plans for when you're going to retire."
Cronin picked up the paper he had laid down, ignoring the picture of himself asleep, and giving it as much attention as he could, answered:
"I have a retirement plan."
"What?" Coyle blurted, too anxiously.
"Death," he snarled. "It will be automatic."
"What about the Pope's directives for stepping down?" Geary asked, doing his best to sound gentle.
Cronin snorted a small laugh and rustled the paper, turning pages: "Did you know that the Pope and I are the same age—to the week? Interesting, isn't it? . . ."
Coyle squinted and opened his mouth, but Cronin kept reading and talking:
". . . We have the same horoscope. Let's see. . . .

Just Good Reading

What does it say for Paul and me today.... Ah.... 'Be wary of accepting the advice of others. Trust your own judgment.' I should telegraph him to be wary."

The conversation was going nowhere. Geary cleared his throat.

"Barney," he said, his voice stronger than a moment before, "someone has got to be firm. As Metropolitan Bishop I am telling you that you are going to step down. If you insist on disobedience . . . well. . . . Every other bishop in my jurisdiction is ready to agree that this diocese is suffering from your inability to keep up with the times."

Coyle silently studied his fingernails. There was no need for him to add anything. Cronin slammed the paper down.

"I'll step aside when the Pope steps aside," he yelled. "If he made the rule let him keep it."

Then, trying to regain command he laughed, with effort:

"We'll go on a journey together—Paul and Barnabas. . . ."

"Barney," the Archbishop said, reaching for the paper, "look at that picture. What stronger evidence is needed. You're tired. Retire or it will be done for you."

Frustrated, Cronin tore his defiant glare from Geary to shoot a silent accusation at Coyle. The younger man smiled a smooth condolence and with a barely perceptible shrug, said:

"It's a whole new ballgame, bishop. And you're just not playing the game anymore."

"Game," he spat, groping for his cane as he pushed his chair back, "damn your game."

From the Pages of *The Critic*

He was out and he knew it. The fight at breakfast had been a final ultimatum. It had been a long time since he had driven his own car, but he took it and drove about for hours, bitterly talking to himself. He was the unjust victim of a world which had changed without asking his permission. New ballgame. He was mad at the Pope for all his retirement rules; mad at Geary who cared for nothing but that things look right; mad at Coyle who had scripted his ouster.

He was in the heart of the city, and barely noticed the storefront mission which served as Mildred Harte's headquarters. He probably wouldn't have given it a thought but that she was in front talking to a group of neighboring youngsters. Impulsively, he pulled the car over, staggered out, and limped over to her. She didn't see him until he was almost next to her and was so startled she addressed him properly:

"Bishop Cronin. . . ."

"Sister Immaculata," he returned, enjoying momentarily the advantage of shock.

She quickly regained her composure.

"Tell me you've swooped in to close this place down."

"Am I that great a tyrant?" he demanded.

"You put up a good show of it," she said, adding without ceremony, "Cup of coffee?"

He followed after her into the store, protesting:

"For whom am I a tyrant . . . my bathroom mirror? That's the only place where I've seen a positive response to anything I've said in the past fifteen years."

Seated at a table which the Salvation Army would

Just Good Reading

have rejected, Cronin pursued the subject as his hostess plunked a cracked white mug before him.

"Well, I won't be a tyrant over you much longer. I'm being forced out."

She stared at him a moment as if it were a joke. Then bluntly she said:

"I feel like saying hallelujah."

Somehow the remark was not offensive. They certainly knew each other well enough so that any other statement would have been phoney. Mildred was too honest for pretense.

"Do you suppose things will be that much better under Bishop Coyle?" he demanded.

"I think we'll see some strong direction," she decided.

"Hmph. . . . Strong direction," he coughed, "I'm a tyrant, but still, disapproving of most of your activities these past few years I've let you be. I only hope for your sake that the 'strong directions' in which Bishop Coyle pushes you are directions you want to head."

They sat in silence for a moment. Then, as long as bluntness was the order of the day he asked:

"Why haven't you done your community a favor and gone off altogether on your own?"

She flashed a grin of genuine amusement.

"They'd love that, wouldn't they?"

"You're not really a part of them anymore," he said.

"I'm their prophet," she countered, "a thorn for their flesh."

"My, how presumptuous," he clucked, so effectively she blushed.

"Well," she reasoned, "one has to say something. I don't want a religious community any more than they

From the Pages of *The Critic*

want me. But I want to be a representative of the Church. You wouldn't understand because a man doesn't have to join a religious order to serve. You have the priesthood. And you've done a good job of keeping it to yourselves."

He sat staring at her, his owlish characteristics becoming even more pronounced as they always did when he was deep in thought. He liked Mildred. She was as crazy as a bedbug, but she did a lot of good, and she was no crazier than a good number of his priests. A wild possibility had entered his head. Everyone agreed whenever it was discussed that it was only a matter of time. Some nut bishop would get a notion to go down in history.... And it would be valid. There was no arguing but that it would be valid. A whole new ball game, was it? They had all juggled his world apart; the Pope, the Council, the archbishop. What a shot back this would be. And what a present it would be for the orderly, woman-hating Coyle.

"Mildred," he cooed in a whisper, still half lost in his reflections, "How would you like.... How would you like to be the first Roman Catholic woman priest?"

THE ARROGANCE OF EVELYN WAUGH

by David Lodge

I MADE my first acquaintance with the novels of Evelyn Waugh at the rather precocious age of fifteen. They must have been the first "adult" modern novels that I read on emerging from that latency phase in individual culture when one reads mostly comic books. I remember the jaw of the art-master at my Catholic grammar school (it was run by De La Salle brothers, but he was a layman) drooping with surprise when I offered Evelyn Waugh as the name of my favorite author. "Do your *parents* know?" he asked. In fact it was my father who had first fired my enthusiasm for Waugh by passing me a Penguin edition (which, tattered and much repaired, I still possess) of *Decline and Fall*. His own interest in Waugh dated from some time in the thirties when the author had patronized a London nightclub where my father worked as a musician. By the end of my fifteenth year I was sufficiently hooked to beg, for my Christmas present, hard-bound copies, in the Chapman and Hall Uniform edition, of three of Waugh's novels, *Vile Bodies*, *Black Mischief* and *Put Out More Flags*. I had already read two of them, in library copies; but I wanted to possess them. It says much for the universality of Waugh's art, I feel, that these comedies of upper-class manners, which could scarcely have been more dis-

From the Pages of *The Critic*

tant from my personal experience and *milieu*, delighted and absorbed me through innumerable readings.

With the full onset of adolescence I came under the spell of Graham Greene's gloomily evocative imagination, in which sex and religion were so fascinatingly intertwined, but I did not abandon my allegiance to Evelyn Waugh—whose *Brideshead Revisited*, indeed, showed an obvious kinship in its handling of sin and grace, belief and unbelief, with the novels of Greene. It was a source of naive pride and encouragement to a young English Catholic with literary aspirations that at this time (late forties, early fifties) the two most highly regarded practicing English novelists were converts to my faith. As my literary education proceeded, and I went on to college, I made the "Catholic Novel" a special object of study, and in due course chapters on Greene and Waugh formed the climax to my Master's dissertation on "Catholic Fiction Since the Oxford Movement: Its Literary Form and Religious Content"—a seven-hundred-page monster of a thesis that (I understand) was one factor in causing the English School of the University of London, a year or two later, to impose a word limit on candidates for higher degrees.

In writing of both these novelists I found myself forced into a defensive posture, because a great deal of the academic criticism of their work was more or less hostile. There were many reasons for this: these two writers, it was alleged, were limited by their eccentric religious beliefs; they were propagandists; they were technically unenterprizing; they were too popular to be first class; they were not on the side of life; and if they had once shown promise, their achievement was now

Just Good Reading

definitely on the decline. This last emphasis was especially marked in discussion of Evelyn Waugh. Rebecca West and Edmund Wilson had started the trend by deploring *Brideshead Revisited*, its turning away from the dry, sophisticated comedy of the prewar comedies, to a self-indulgent romanticism in celebration of Roman Catholicism and the English aristocracy. Evelyn Waugh, it was suggested, had become snobbish, doctrinaire, and out of touch with the times: he had even, to a large extent, lost his sense of humor.

It was possible to deal with these criticisms in purely literary-critical terms, but the process was complicated by the fact that Evelyn Waugh himself seemed almost to go out of his way to give them credibility by his personal behavior. The photographs that appeared in the press of the author dressed in heavy squirearchal tweeds, posed, with a faintly menacing expression, beside the notices *"Entrée Interdite aux Promeneurs"* and "No Admittance on Business" that marked the frontiers of his country estate; his occasional testy contributions to the correspondence columns of the weekly reviews; his notorious eagerness to sue journalists on the slightest provocation; his well-advertised contempt for the Welfare State, the mass media, modern art and architecture; and his reputation for rudeness and arrogance in social intercourse—all this tended to create a public image of Evelyn Waugh as a kind of ogre—sinister or grotesque, according to the temperament of the beholder.

How truthful was this image? Was it a pose—and if so, what lay behind it? Or was it authentic—in which case, why did Evelyn Waugh's character develop in this way? These are the questions I have tried to answer—

From the Pages of *The Critic*

necessarily tentatively—in what follows. They do not affect the value of the novels. That is a matter for literary criticism, and for my own estimate I refer the reader to my short study *Evelyn Waugh* (Columbia University Press, 1971). But they are questions which anyone who has read and been provoked and stimulated by the fiction of Evelyn Waugh cannot fail to ask.

The obvious starting-point for any enquiry into the temperament and character of Evelyn Waugh in the last phase of his life is *The Ordeal of Gilbert Pinfold* (1957), because the "Portrait of the Artist in Middle Age" with which that book begins is very obviously a self-portrait. Mr. Pinfold, in his early fifties,"stood quite high," we are told, among contemporary novelists: so did Mr. Waugh, also, at this time, in his early fifties. In his youth Mr. Pinfold had traveled widely, and in World War II "had sustained in good heart, much discomfort and some danger;" now he lived in the country, some hundred miles from London, with his wife and a large family. All this was true of Captain Evelyn Waugh of Piers Court, Stinchcombe, Nr. Dursley, Gloucestershire. Mr. Pinfold had "never voted in a parliamentary election, maintaining an idiosyncratic toryism which was quite unrepresented in the political parties of his time and was regarded by his neighbors as being almost as sinister as socialism." Mr. Waugh's respect for hereditary privilege, and his corresponding distaste for the idea of an egalitarian society, had been very evident in *Brideshead Revisited* (1945). In his own person he referred to the Butler Education Act of 1944—one of the great pieces of progressive legislation in modern British

Just Good Reading

history—as machinery "for the free distribution of university degrees to the deserving poor"; and his response to the victory of the Labor Party in the General Election of 1945 was to write an article suggesting that Gloucestershire should be kept as a kind of game reserve in which the upper classes would be allowed to roam in their natural state for the instruction and edification of those seeking higher education. He made no excuses for the absence of working-class characters from the central stage of his own fiction. "I don't know them, and I'm not interested in them," he replied when questioned on this point by an interviewer. "No writer before the middle of the nineteenth century wrote about the working classes other than as grotesques or as pastel decorations. Then when they were given the vote certain writers started to suck up to them."

These quotations suggest that there was in Mr. Waugh's toryism, as in Mr. Pinfold's, a strong element of fantasy, of deliberately provocative role-playing, which made it equally inapplicable to the realm of practical politics. "I never heard him discuss politics seriously," his son Auberon has recorded. "He despised all English politicians since 1832 [date of the first Reform Bill], most particularly the Conservatives." Evelyn Waugh advertised the fact that he had never voted in a Parliamentary election, and when challenged on this point replied with inspired archaism that he did not presume to advise his Sovereign on her choice of Ministers.

Waugh's antiegalitarian attitudes, often inaccurately described as snobbishness, undoubtedly derived in part from a conscious or intuitive sense that his own art depended for its effectiveness on the existence of a finely

From the Pages of *The Critic*

graduated class-system and a delicately discriminated code of manners in which any disturbance or displacement was vividly expressive and often richly comic. When, in 1956, Nancy Mitford and Professor Harold Ross were amusing themselves and readers of *Encounter* magazine with a discussion of what was "U" (upper-class) and "Non-U" in English speech habits, Waugh deplored the crudity of this binary view of English society. "For there are no classes in England," he wrote in an open letter to Nancy Mitford. "There is only precedence. . . . There is a single line extending from Windsor [Royal palace] to Wormwood Scrubs [a prison] of individuals all justly and precisely graded (no one knows this order of progression: it is a Platonic idea)." In his last travel book, *Tourist in Africa* (1960), Waugh interestingly turned this theory upon the idea of *apartheid*. "*Apartheid* is the . . . spirit of egalitarianism literally cracked. Stable and fruitful societies have always been elaborately graded. The idea of a classless society is so unnatural to man that his reason, in practice, cannot bear the strain. Those Afrikaner youths claim equality with you, gentle reader. They regard themselves as being a cut above the bushman. So they accept one cleavage in the social order and fantastically choose pigmentation as the determining factor." In such ways Evelyn Waugh's "idiosyncratic toryism" could lead him to take up positions more characteristic of the left than of the right in British politics.

Mr. Pinfold was a Roman Catholic. "He had been received into the Church—'conversion' suggests an event more sudden and emotional than his calm accep-

Just Good Reading

tance of the propositions of his faith—in early manhood, at the time when many Englishmen were falling into Communism. Unlike them Mr. Pinfold remained steadfast. But he was reputed to be bigoted rather than pious. . . . And at the very time when the leaders of his Church were exhorting their people to emerge from the catacombs into the forum, to make their influence felt in democratic politics and to regard worship as a corporate act, Mr. Pinfold burrowed ever deeper into the rock." Evelyn Waugh was received into the Church "on firm intellectual conviction but with little emotion," to quote from his own account of the experience, *"Come Inside"* (1949). At the time—1930—he announced that the modern artist must make a brave and disjunctive choice between Rome and Moscow. His contempt for those writers, like W. H. Auden, Christopher Isherwood and Stephen Spender, who took the other path but subsequently doubled back, was expressed in the characters of Parsnip and Pimpernell, the left-wing poets who figure so ingloriously in *Put Out More Flags.* Apart from the biography *Edmund Campion* (1935) and occasional passing references in his travel books, Waugh's Catholicism did not make an overt appearance in his writing until *Brideshead Revisited* (1945); but he announced then that one of the things which would make his future books unpopular would be the attempt to represent "man in his relation to God." Certainly from that time on he adopted, both as a writer and as a private citizen, the posture of a militant and inflexible Catholic. He was apt to write to the weekly journals challenging the competence of their reviewers to pronounce on matters of Catholic belief and practice. He delighted in for-

From the Pages of *The Critic*

mulating propositions that were theologically sound but shocking to the secular humanist mind—for example, that he had no objection to the total destruction of the world providing that it came about by accident (i.e., without sin being committed). He liked to tease his non-Catholic friends in the same way—writing to Randolph Churchill, for instance, that "the best hope for the world is the remarkable increase of Cistercian vocations among the yanks." There was, however, no affectation in his distaste for *Aggiornamento* in the Church. The radical Catholic journalist Paul Johnson recalls that when he published in the *New Statesman* "an article called 'Rome Goes Left' prophesying upheaval, Waugh sent me a characteristically brief and sardonic postcard: 'I see your new vision of the Church: colored cardinals distributing contraceptives to the Faithful.'"

At the end of *Brideshead Revisited* the sanctuary lamp burning in the ugly little *art nouveau* chapel symbolizes a permanent and transcendant spiritual order that resigns the narrator to the passing of the aesthetic and social order represented by the house and family of Brideshead. The changes in the liturgy and the reformulation of doctrine initiated by Vatican II thus seemed to Evelyn Waugh to threaten the very foundations of the Church's historic role and of his own personal grounds for belief. In the Prefatory Note to the one-volume edition of his war-trilogy, *Sword of Honour* (1965) he observed caustically that the book was proving to be an obituary of the Roman Catholic Church as it had existed in England for centuries, and that "most of the rites and opinions here described are now obsolete." Waugh bitterly resented the introduction of a vernacular liturgy

Just Good Reading

and several of his own obituarists commented on the pleasantly appropriate circumstance that he died (on Easter Day) immediately after attending a Latin Mass said by an old Jesuit friend who was staying with the family.

To return to Mr. Pinfold:

> He had made no new friends in late years. Sometimes he thought he detected a slight coldness among his old cronies. . . . It sometimes occurred to Mr. Pinfold that he must be growing into a bore. His opinions were easily predictable. His strongest tastes were negative. He abhorred plastics, Picasso, sunbathing and jazz—everything, in fact, that had happened in his own lifetime. The tiny kindling of charity which came to him through religion sufficed only to temper his disgust and change it to boredom. There was a phrase in the thirties: 'It is later than you think,' which was designed to cause uneasiness. It was never later than Mr. Pinfold thought. At intervals during the day and night he would look at his watch and learn always with disappointment how little of his life was past, how much there was still ahead of him. He wished no one ill, but he looked at the world *sub specie aeternitatis* and he found it flat as a map; except when, rather often, personal annoyance intruded. Then he would come tumbling from his exalted point of observation. Shocked by a bad bottle of wine, an impertinent stranger, or a fault in syntax, his mind like a cinema camera trucked furiously forward to confront the offending object close-up with glaring lens; with

From the Pages of *The Critic*

the eyes of a drill-sergeant inspecting an awkward squad, bulging with wrath that was half-facetious, and with half-simulated incredulity; like a drill-sergeant he was absurd to many, but to some rather formidable.

We seem to be coming close to the heart of the matter here, which is why I have quoted this passage at such length. "He had made no new friends in late years." Waugh himself had remarked as early as 1946 that, "In the first ten years of adult life I made a large number of friends. Now on the average I make one new one a year and lose two." He lost friends, however, by quarreling with them rather than boring them. In his obituary Christopher Sykes recorded that "he spent a lot of time making amends to people whom he had hurt." But such breaches were not always reparable. As Frances Donaldson (who herself survived a period of estrangement from Evelyn Waugh) remarked in her memoir, his victims were "unable to believe that he could—uselessly and without apparent regret—impale the friendship of a lifetime upon one heartless sentence if he any longer cared for them."

The correspondence between himself and Evelyn Waugh which Randolph Churchill published in *Encounter* a few years ago is a fascinating illustration of how Waugh never hesitated to put a friendship in jeopardy by speaking his mind, scorning the little subterfuges, evasions and suppressions which, for most of us, oil the wheels of personal relations. Thus when Randolph Churchill asked him to sign first editions of his novels, some of which Waugh had already presented to him, the

Just Good Reading

latter replied sarcastically: "A handsome leather case has arrived with copies of books of mine for inscription. I am gratified that you should want a complete set for your own library. It is not clear why you require duplicates, unless you are going into trade. . . . I must point out that I gave you a copy of *Men at Arms* on publication. What happened to that? And why *two* more copies? Do you make frequent bonfires of fiction?" In a following, still more belligerent letter he wrote: "I should perpetrate a fraud if I inscribed to you personally books intended for the market. I have therefore signed dupliates in the title page as I do for charitable bazaars." Churchill wrote to explain that he wished to bequeath complete sets of Waugh's books to his two children, but the episode led to a certain estrangement. Appropriately enough, it was healed by a characteristic *bon mot* of Evelyn's. Randolph Churchill underwent surgery for the removal of a growth that happily turned out to be benign, and Evelyn Waugh was heard to remark that the medical profession had, with its customary incompetence, removed the only portion of Randolph that was not malignant. This witticism was reported to Churchill and so delighted him that it led to the reconciliation of the two men.

It was through Randolph Churchill that the British newspaper columnist Alan Brien had an encounter with Waugh which led him (Brien) to claim much later that he was the original of one of Mr. Pinfold's tormenting voices. Churchill had brought Brien to White's club, and chancing to meet Waugh there, introduced him to Brien. Brien admired Waugh's fiction, but was unable to get his attention until he revealed himself as the author of a re-

From the Pages of *The Critic*

cent newspaper profile somewhat critical of Waugh's life-style and social attitudes. Then, partly against his will, he was drawn into an increasingly combative interchange:

> Waugh directed all his remarks through Randolph as though through an interpreter. 'Who did you say this person was?' he asked. 'I knew the club had declined but I had not expected to be insulted here by someone so obviously lacking the equipment of a gentleman.' Randolph looked unhappy at the role of mediator. 'Really, Evelyn, you can't talk like that. Mr. Brien is a friend of mine and a guest.'
>
> 'I have had occasion to speak to you before about your taste in low companions,' remarked Waugh, with cold disdain, 'He is clearly out of place here.'
>
> 'I don't want to be a gentleman, thank you very much,' I spluttered nastily. 'What are your claims to that title, anyway? Birth and breeding? You were born in a flat over a dairy in the Finchley Road.'
>
> 'Your friend, as you call him, Randolph, continues to repeat his stupidities. I'm not at all ashamed of my upbringing, but kindly tell him my family had moved from what he describes as the flat over the dairy before my birth.'
>
> 'Tell him yourself,' said Randolph. 'I refuse to talk to either of you in this childish way.'

But the conversation continued in this way for some time. Brien figures in the scene very much as the "impertinent stranger" of the passage I just quoted from *Pinfold*, where the images of the cine-camera and the drill

Just Good Reading

sergeant, and the epithets "half-facetious" and "half-simulated" suggest that Mr. Pinfold-Waugh's manner in such confrontations was a conscious pose. But was the paranoia of the following postcard (sent, Randolph Churchill reported to Alan Brien, to Mrs. Ian Fleming) entirely affected? "Off to Ceylon for a sea voyage. All my friends in London appear to have turned against me. Even Randolph, my oldest friend, recently hired a Jew to attack me in White's." The question is not easy to answer because on that sea-voyage to Ceylon Evelyn Waugh had the experiences that he described in *The Ordeal of Gilbert Pinfold*. As Frances Donaldson's memoir makes clear, the novel follows the actuality very closely. Mr. Waugh, like Mr. Pinfold, was afflicted by—and for some time entirely taken in by—hallucinatory voices which enmeshed him in a fantastic web of intrigue and suspicion and accusation, displaced and distorted versions of his actual fears, phobias and guilts. The explanation of Mr. Pinfold-Waugh's medical advisers was that he had poisoned himself by the injudicious use of pain-killing and sleep-inducing drugs. Mr. Pinfold himself is skeptical of this positivistic diagnosis, but he does not offer an alternative one. Instead he accepts the gift of "fresh rich experience—perishable goods" and sits down to write it up. The novel ends with its own title page and first chapter heading, and this circular, tail-in-mouth shape epitomizes the way in which the book never quite delivers the personal revelation which it promises. "Mr. Pinfold," we are told on the first page, "gave nothing away" to inquiring research students; and Mr. Waugh gives nothing away to his readers, despite

From the Pages of *The Critic*

the highly confessional and remarkably candid character of this book.

The closest we get to an analysis of the relationship between role and reality in Mr. Pinfold-Waugh is immediately after the long passage last quoted:

> Prolonged prosperity had wrought the change. He had seen sensitive men make themselves a protective disguise against the rebuffs and injustices of manhood. Mr. Pinfold had suffered little in these ways; he had been tenderly reared and, as a writer, welcomed and overrewarded early. It was his modesty which needed protection and for this purpose, but without design, he gradually assumed the character of burlesque . . . the part for which he cast himself was a combination of eccentric don and testy colonel and he acted it strenuously . . . until it came to dominate his whole outward personality.

This seems clear enough, and it certainly expresses an important truth about Evelyn Waugh: namely, that the personality he projected in the later part of his life was a "protective disguise" which (as this passage hints and the story of Pinfold confirms) gradually acquired a slightly sinister autonomous life. But what was being protected and disguised in Mr. Waugh? Surely not something as mild and banal as "modesty?" Surely it was something darker, deeper and more vulnerable?

I believe it was, and that we may find a clue to its nature in these lines from Pinfold already quoted: "There was a

Just Good Reading

phrase in the thirties: 'It is later than you think,' which was designed to cause uneasiness. It was never later than Mr. Pinfold thought." In context, these lines point in two directions. We can refer them back to Mr. Pinfold's distaste for "everything . . . that had happened in his own lifetime," and infer the meaning: no one could possibly think that human civilization had reached a later stage of decadence than did Mr. Pinfold-Waugh. And this is a valid meaning. The "myth of decline," the idea that civilization is in a constant and accelerating state of decay is one that informs all Evelyn Waugh's work from his very first novel—significantly entitled *Decline and Fall*—and accounts for the inclusive and impartial irony of his comic imagination. For when culture is seen as a process of continual decline, no secular institution or value is invulnerable: the modern is ridiculed by contrasting it with the traditional, but attempts to maintain or restore the traditional in the face of change are also seen as ridiculous, and in any case the traditional itself also turns out to be, on close scrutiny, in some way false or compromised, already infected by decay. This is essentially the vision of T. S. Eliot's *The Waste Land* (from which Waugh took the title of *A Handful of Dust*) and it is one of the reasons why Waugh's work belongs to the history of modern literature rather than, like P. G. Wodehouse's novels, the history of modern entertainment.

So far, so good. But, "It was never later than Mr. Pinfold thought" also refers, in its context, to the slowness with which time passed for Mr. Pinfold himself, to his boredom with life and impatience for death. This note is struck so lightly and fleetingly that we scarcely realize

From the Pages of *The Critic*

its significance, but it is *very* significant for the interpretation of Mr. Waugh, if not of Mr. Pinfold.

"He was the only person I have ever known," Frances Donaldson records, "who seemed sincerely to long for death." "When Evelyn Waugh died suddenly . . ." Douglas Woodruff wrote in his obituary, "it was a merciful dispensation at the end. He had been unwell for a long time, much troubled by insomnia, and a great depression of spirits." It is something of a shock to realize that the man of whom these and similar things were said was only sixty-two when he died. One has the same reaction to Evelyn Waugh's presentation of himself in the last decade of his life. In his travel book *Tourist in Africa* he refers to himself as a "seedy old man" and the passage of his train through Paris calls forth the following sad reflection: "Paris at the cocktail hour. How gaily I used to jump into a taxi and visit the bars while the train crawled round the *ceinture.* Nowadays, hard of hearing and stiff in the joints, I sit glumly in my compartment." At the time of this trip, Evelyn Waugh was only fifty-six. It almost seems as if the myth of universal decline rebounded upon its author as a physical affliction, accelerating the ordinary processes of physical decay: if so, Evelyn Waugh nourished rather than resisted the visitation, exaggerating his slight deafness, for instance, by affecting an old-fashioned ear-trumpet, which he would sometimes put aside as a silent but crushing indication that he was bored.

And boredom, rather than aches and pains and deafness, was Evelyn Waugh's great affliction. Not the common-or-garden boredom generated by idleness or frustration, but a deep, permanent, almost metaphysical

Just Good Reading

boredom, something comparable to the existentialist *angst* or nihilistic sense of the void that he affected to despise in other modern writers. "From early manhood," Douglas Woodruff wrote, with a proper appreciation of this aspect of Waugh's character, "he had suffered from ennui, an affliction which ought to be classed among the major ills to which suffering humanity is exposed, something on a par with blindness or deafness." Woodruff recalled in this context an occasion "when he had ordered champagne in the afternoon at White's and when it came he gazed sadly at it and said: 'One thinks it will be enjoyable, and then when it comes, it isn't.'" What makes this little anecdote so poignant is, I think, that drinking champagne in the afternoon itself seems a last-ditch defence against boredom.

"He was joyous as a young man," Father Martin D'Arcy S.J., who received Evelyn Waugh into the Church, recalled after his death. "But he grew rather embittered." "Joyous" is a word made resonant by its rarity in modern English. Evelyn himself used it in a wry comment on a group of Anglican nuns with whom he found himself traveling in *Tourist in Africa:* "They did not seem notably joyous. But, who am I, of all people, to complain about that?"

One of the most vivid accounts of Evelyn Waugh in his youthful and joyous days is that of his friend of the twenties, Harold Acton, writing in 1948: "Though others assure me he has changed past all recognition, I still see him as a prancing faun, thinly disguised by conventional apparel. . . . So demure, yet so wild! A faun half-tamed by the Middle Ages, who would hide in some suburban retreat, and then burst upon the town with

From the Pages of *The Critic*

capricious caperings." Interestingly, Acton uses the same word, "embittered," as Fr. D'Arcy to describe his later character: "Evelyn had to set out on his travels again, embittered but not, as his writings prove, dispirited altogether. It was an arduous journey, for he had been wounded. His bitterness was a source of anxiety to his friends, for it made a most loveable person cantankerous. After many trials and errors his wound was healed by the Catholic Church." The event to which Acton refers here was the breakdown of Evelyn's first marriage (later dissolved by Rome) after only a year's duration; and certainly, if we are looking for a simple, single explanation of the pessimistic, melancholic strain in his character, we need look no further, so insistent is the theme of sexual betrayal in nearly every one of his novels. But some years before his marriage, Evelyn Waugh had felt sufficiently disillusioned to contemplate suicide. The story of that episode—of how he left his clothes and a suitable Greek quotation on a Welsh beach one summer night, and swam out to sea intent on drowning himself, only to be driven back by stinging jellyfish, is the carefully chosen conclusion to his volume of autobiography, *A Little Learning*. It suggests that there was always within Evelyn Waugh a bitter spring of negation and despair which experience was bound to expose, whatever his particular fortunes might be. His conversion to the Catholic faith ensured, perhaps, that this negative current in his character would never again be suicidal, but it grew stronger as the years passed, while the positive became weaker. It was, I believe, to insulate himself against this negativity, and to conceal it from the world's inquisitive gaze, that he

Just Good Reading

adopted the compound mask of testy colonel and eccentric don.

There is therefore, in contemplation, something of the archetypal tragic comedian about Evelyn Waugh: the despairing heart behind the comic mask. Certainly the slow draining away of joy from his own life never entirely subdued his ability to dispense the liberating joys of humor to others, in life and literature. "He was the funniest man of his generation," his son has written of him. "He scarcely opened his mouth but to say something extremely funny. His house and his life revolved around jokes." And his friend Christopher Sykes wrote on his death, "We never miss anyone so much as the friend who could make us laugh." Innumerable readers of Evelyn Waugh's novels will say Amen to that.

SEVEN FABLES FOR OUR TIMES

by Daniel Berrigan

IRENE

THERE was once a dove named Irene, who had learned in a Montessori school to say the word "peace." The method took; when Irene would sing out the word, it was evident that she was totally committed. Her beak would redden, her plumage stand up like cat's fur in a wind.

Then Irene took to smoking L & M's. This was a new phase in her peace work. She shortly was able, in a reasonably quiet room, to spell "peace" in smoke, in midair.

Various peace groups heard of the feat. Overtures were made. It was revealed that for a very modest stipend, or no stipend at all, Irene would spell "peace" in smoke at peace gatherings. And not long after, more deeply committed than ever, she came on a brilliant idea. She would train a whole team of sky girls to spell "peace" in smoke in the open air.

Once the idea was explored, it became clear that its horizons were unlimited. At one protest march, Irene and her girls, now a dazzling team of fifty, with fifty stand-ins, spelled "peace" in letters one hundred feet

Just Good Reading

high above Manhattan. The act all but eclipsed the parade itself.

Soon after, Irene and her girls suddenly disappeared. A few stragglers from her second team were still to be seen in Manhattan, scrounging in Central Park and City Hall Square. Rumors went thick and fast: Irene had been shot down, Irene had been subverted. Among Manhattan pigeons, a few, sharper of eye and leaner of hip than the others, took notes with transistor recorders. They pieced the rumors together and came on the truth. Irene and her girls could be found at a heavily guarded armory on the West Side. She was preparing a new show, under security wraps as tight as Billy Rose's. For a price, someone knew a way in, high up under the steel beams of the roof.

The price was paid. Two agents, posing as tourists, but fitted from foot to wing with electronic equipment, got through with their guide.

Inside, the air was heavy with a pall of smoke, noisy as a midtown athletic club. Irene's voice flowed high above all the rest; she was piercing and quick as a hawk, diving and swooping among her team. A final practice was about to start; the doves lined up. Irene shrieked a signal. From the floor, fifty white doves went up, very nearly vertical. They had been fitted with whistle devices in their tails, with beaks and spurs of steel. They screamed like skybolts, broke formation with blinding speed, then loosed a jet of smoke as white as their plumage. The message: "Bomb the hell out of Hanoi."

From the Pages of *The Critic*

DEATH AND THE BISHOP

ONCE, a Bishop was accosted in public by Death.

"My lord, would you have a minute to spare?"

The Bishop, who was a hearty man in public, thought he would.

"Would you by any chance have a smoke on you?" The Bishop who was a chain smoker, but not in public, handed one over.

"And Bishop," Death's skinny hand was now on my lord's coat, "could you spare the price of a cup of coffee?"

The Bishop thought he could, but less heartily. He strove to end the interview, and to pass on. His day was a busy one.

Death clung to him. "My lord, he whined, a poor man needs a coat. The winds are chill, even to an unbeliever."

This was pushing a bit hard. But they were in public, and a crowd was gathering. The Bishop, who was not beyond a gesture, had heard of St. Martin of Tours, though he had no ambitions in that direction. He took off his coat. Death put it on. The Bishop's hat as well. And his shoes. And his socks. And his ring. And Death went on his way, humming the Alleluia from Handel.

In the days that followed, Death had cause to marvel at his improved situation. People kissed his ring with fervor, his public relations warmed. Indeed a religious revival began to make itself felt.

And a small matter, heretofore thought unpleasant, took a visible turn for the better. Instead of violence and long wasting and absurd eventuality, Death adopted the paternal liturgy of a bishop. Men came to him willingly.

Just Good Reading

And a slight blow on the cheek, a gesture of confirmation, sufficed. Things ended satisfactorily for many. There was talk of a larger See, a more ample scope for this promising and adaptive person.

THE BOY AND THE TIGER

A YOUNG GOD once created for his pleasure, on the fourth day of the week, a tiger cub. On the fifth and sixth day, the boy was more than usually occupied. He returned home on Sunday to share his rest with his new pet.

The day was a delight. The two played and walked in the temperate weather of the garden. The cub was everything the god had hoped for—wisdom, insouciance, innocent and unawakened violence. When in the course of their play the tiger scratched the god's arm, both stopped and smiled and the tiger licked the blood away.

However, the second week went less well. The cub grew restive. He took to moping in corners, began to scratch himself, and turned away from vegetables. And one morning when the boy awoke, he found the tiger had wet the floor thoroughly, set up a sign nearby reading, "Freedom now," and disappeared. He was gone for three days. He finally lurched in again, with a wicked gleam in his eye and liquor on his breath. He slept all that day and his dreams must have been pleasant ones, for he snickered and belched in his sleep.

The god went to his father, in tears. But the father

From the Pages of *The Critic*

was in no mood to dispense sympathy. "You wanted a tiger, you made a tiger, now live with him. Or if you can't, turn him into a rug or a humming bird. I have my own troubles. The gardeners are on strike, and a snake from somewhere is organizing a union."

To cage the beast was to violate their agreement. The tiger knew it and took advantage of it. One night he got into the chicken coops and disposed of five prize Rhode Island reds. Then he sat in the garden for two hours, roaring at the moon. The other animals were terrified. Many of them fled for good. The others began to mutter about violence in the street and arming themselves.

The boy did his best. He took to reading the tiger long passages from the Sermon on the Mount. He pointed with modesty to his own record of nonviolence, and read passages from a handbook he was composing. He recited from memory the Chinese and Hindu poets, with special emphasis on the Zen ideal of the tiger who changed his stripes.

All this took a long time, and endless virtue. Finally the boy's patience seemed to be winning. The tiger grew more thoughtful. He wept frequently and asked for the sacrament. He was also growing older; his sleek coat faded, his teeth fell out. Then one morning, when the boy brought out the tiger's breakfast, he found no tiger at all, but a newborn lamb lying on an old tiger's skin. The boy gathered the lamb in his arms. Now at last he understood.

But he did not understand. A few days after, the lamb also disappeared.

In a remote field, sick at heart after a long search, the

Just Good Reading

boy came on his pet, reduced to fleece, tail and hooves. Nearby was a message in the old tigerish hand, written in lamb's blood.

"Dear friend," it said, "sorry. Consult Spinoza, volume three, question four: 'On the Persistence of Evil in the World. . . .'"

THE STATUE

ONCE in a remote Indian town, after many years of faithful service, a guru attained first place in the temple priesthood. He had passed exhausting years devoted to training young monks, to copying texts and supervising festival arrangements. Now his duties were radically reduced and honorific and, in truth, only a somewhat boring routine remained to him.

It came down to this. Once a week, he cut and shined the toenails of the great image in the inner sanctum. Armed with a silver-mounted brush, a golden scissors as long as his arm, and a quantity of bee's wax, he would enter the triple court, pass through the damask curtain, and stand at length before the enormous feet of the god.

Feet, shins, ankles, to be exact. The trunk and head of the statue had been lost; it had toppled in some former aeon; not a trace of the upper members remained. But from knees to instep, the stone colossus stood, the chief treasure of the people, their god among men. The enormous broken knees, covered with a trace of drapery, jutted through the open roof, cubits above the head of priest and people.

It is not superfluous, surely, to record that the priest

From the Pages of *The Critic*

was witness to a weekly miracle which never ceased to move his heart. The toenails of the god, that is, grew; they grew approximately an inch each week. And though the broken image was of stone, it was undeniable that the toenails were of some other substance, entirely mysterious and beautiful, their surface glittering like mica, their depths milky as mother of pearl.

The nail clippings he carefully gathered up week by week, and distributed to the faithful.

In one half hour, the stint was finished. He had clipped the nails and filed the edges, spread a coating of wax on the toes, rubbed them with a chamois cloth until they glowed like black phosphor. He turned and started out of the holies, his silver box of clippings under his arm, his tools in hand.

A familiar sense of depression welled up in him as he traversed the three courts. The temple silence, inviolate while he served the god, stood unbroken.

What the hell, he thought to himself with a sigh, back to the plateau of the middle forties. A glorified shoe shine with retirement benefits. That god! One half-hour of work a week; and I don't even know if he exists. Who does know? Who ever heard of a god from the knees down?

Clearly, a crisis of faith was brewing. He could see less and less reason, he said to himself with growing conviction, to play wet nurse to a heap of dry bones.

Yet his depression remained inventive. Like a mariner in a gale, he kept a weather eye out in all directions for any change that might bring him advantage: for a new sky, or a new tack in the wind.

He was even inclined to pray at times, as the temple

Just Good Reading

manual urged upon believers afflicted with acedia. Nothing happened for better or worse. But since his hopes were not high, he was not greatly cast down.

Why indeed this trouble of mind? He wished he could know; sometimes he sensed obscurely that the wish was father to the act—that he *did* know, that the truth was pushing and nudging at his shoulder with a finger of stone, a lost finger of a lost arm of a lost body.... Was he not universally respected, had he not come into possession of a sinecure many coveted and none but he could claim? Yes, yes, yes. The finger jabbed, a tic in his very soul. Yes, but he was dying, petrifying, in the service of a dead god.

One night he slept, and while he slept, a dream came to him. He stood on the pedestal of his new honor; and while he stood, he happened to glance down. Out of a curtained embrasure, a man no larger than an insect scuttled up to his feet, took an enormous ritual scissors, and began to cut his toenails. The priest stood there, invisible, remote, bathed in a kind of obscene stupefaction. Suddenly, a cry of triumph or despair from his servitor drew his attention once more. The little man held before his eyes like a trophy, a great bleeding toe; his own, the toe of Goliath or Holofernes. Then as he cried aloud in anguish and rage and realization, he heard the little man at his feet yell: "Wake up! Wake up!"

He awakened, bolt upright, bathed in sweat. His little son was shaking him by the shoulders.

From the Pages of *The Critic*

ALAS!

THERE was once a man afflicted with hemorrhoids. And he would fain have them shrunken. One day, in a subway, providence raised his eyes to an ad. It read: "Preparation H Shrinks Hemorrhoids."

The man lost no time. He tore his eyes from the evangel of hope, he hurried to buy, and to begin treatment.

Alas, in the onset of his joy, he read the instructions wrong.

Yet the fault had its compensation. Now his head is down to manageable size; his hats cost him less, as do his ideas. And if his trouble remains, he thinks about it less.

THE SHOES THAT FAILED

ONCE there was an elephant. He was unique only in this: Whether he walked or stood, he leaned to the left. Not far to the left, since his center of gravity was a matter of tons, and could not be seriously tampered with. But visibly off center, whether by fault or triumph in nature men were not agreed.

When he was led out for peace marches he leaned to the left, and was cheered for it.

But when a political party hired him for its convention, matters were different. He was booed and hissed, elements of the right cried "Traitor" and called for his removal.

His owners were no ideologists. But they could smell a good thing, and this animal smelled sweet indeed. So

Just Good Reading

they made for him a pair of interchangeable elevator shoes, colored grey to match his complexion. He would wear them on his short side, fore and aft, on conservative occasions, and on his long side, to introduce a note of danger, for movements of the left. The option was tried. He was led out, teetering like a drunken calliope, to protest a foreign landing by our troops. But in the midst of the consequent uproar, the beast fell, and that was that. It cost an enormous sum to hoist him upright. The elephant emerged shaken in his psyche, and more determined to be himself.

Shortly thereafter however, animal symbols fell from favor altogether. Instead, the war parties paraded with phalanxes of paper canons, which discharged war bonds into the air. The peace lovers devised cornucopias that disgorged drum majorettes chanting the beatitudes.

Galled and disheartened, the animal was sold—his flesh for rendering, his tusks, hooves and tail for whatever they would bring. He metamorphosed into history, mingling with the absurd options which time pretends to clarify. In vain! He became boots for the military, ivory for leisurely hours of chess, chemical agents, aphrodisiacs, vitamins and floor wax and buttons. After the mockeries of time, his real life was under way.

THE FIRST DAYS OF THE SCIENCE OF PRENATAL COMMUNICATION

THERE was once a child who even before birth caused his parents profound trouble of mind. It had been a peaceable, normal pregnancy, but in the seventh month

From the Pages of *The Critic*

the mother began to have sobering thoughts. She heard the child's heartbeat as a kind of high irregular beep. At first, she comforted herself with the thought that any offspring of hers was bound to be highly strung. After all, she said to herself, we're space people; daddy's work at the Rand Corporation is bound to show.

But she gradually grew aware that some strange pattern was emerging. The beeps were audible only from nine to five during the day. Moreover they repeated themselves according to an intricate pattern of long and short. She took the beeps down on paper, and went to her husband.

He was instantly excited. I'm certain it's a message, he exulted. I'll take it to our code people.

The Rand team confirmed it beyond any doubt. In ten hours they had broken the code. Under secrecy, the parents were handed a transcription. The child was saying get me an outside line, or failing that, get me out of here.

The code team, in fact the whole corporation, was delighted beyond measure. They set up an intricate cybernetic complex, involving extrasensory perception, and began to talk of a new science, prenatal communication.

Messages were now passing regularly between the world and the unborn child. In the week that followed, four were transcribed. They included an inquiry relating to moon photos taken by the Russians, a request in slightly cooler tones that his mother control her Martini intake, a marked expression of dislike for the family dog, and a complaint against an acrimonious family quarrel which, he said, had interrupted his reflections. If his father could not keep his voice down, his mother must.

Just Good Reading

All proceeded more or less on schedule, toward the day of birth. Except that by now, public interest was in a fever. It was agreed that the birth would occur in a specially prepared room at Rand. In order to include the world in this unprecedented moment, the President of the United States would exchange greetings with the parents and the newborn child, via Telstar. Moreover, several universities had offered doctoral scholarships to the child, to be pursued at its own pace and discretion. The child (by now it was apparent that it was a boy) conveyed its satisfaction with these arrangements.

So the child matured. One day toward the end of the ninth month, it asked to have read to it Blake's *Jerusalem*, and the *Letters of Madame Blavatsky*. That same evening, the mother felt a peculiar lassitude come over her, a floating lightness of spirit. All her fears vanished. She sat alone on a balcony of the apartment overlooking the East River, where the tugs and steamers rode the twilight waters, scattering the stars in their wake.

She slept, and her dream was terrible, Her waking landscape was unchanged. But the air was charged with malignancy and woe. Her child rode through the night astride a horse. Once, then a second time, a third, and yet a fourth, he crossed her vision. The horse he rode was alight with a devouring apocalyptic blaze.

War, he trumpeted, war over the world. A second time he passed. Famine, they shrieked, child, and horse together. A third vision; the terrible cry was Plague, Plague! Then a fourth—. But the mother rose in her chair and fell like a stone to the floor.

A few hours later, the child was born dead.

FOR WHOM THE NOVELIST WRITES

by Edwin O'Connor

I WANT to talk about a kind of relationship which exists between the men and women who write novels, and the men, women, and children who read them. You will have noticed that I did not mention "children" when I spoke of writers—this is not an oversight. The truth seems to be that children are not normally great novel-writers, except of course in France. In that extraordinary country the child-novelist is a common fact of life. Nowhere is the difference between our two cultures more clearly marked than here. At the very hour when the American teen-ager is at home, industriously putting a fine edge on his switch-blade, his French opposite number is just as industriously reading the reviews of his third novel. When the French speak of a juvenile delinquent, they do not mean some youngster who beats up old gentlemen in public parks; they mean, instead, one who uses a past participle badly.

In this country, however, we are confined to chronologically older novelists, and it is about them and their public that I propose to discuss. This public is most important to the novel, and there are those who say it is quite as important as the novelist himself. Not many novelists really support this view. Still, the fact remains that while it is the novelist who brings the novel to life,

Just Good Reading

it is the public which keeps it there. If the public is too small, the novel will die; if it is smaller still, so will the novelist. This may not matter much to the public, but if you are the novelist, it matters very much to you.

In a sense, then, the public *belongs* to the novel: it is the tail-end of every novel, the completion of the process. This process is one we all know at least a little about. It begins with the writer: it begins when he gets an idea, or a series of ideas. He thinks about these ideas, they grow in his mind, his imagination; before he writes a word a whole world may have taken shape, sometimes in roughest outline, sometimes in astonishing detail —depending pretty much on what kind of novelist he is, how he works, what his writing habits are. Then the writing starts, and this may take a week or it may take several years—and there is no guarantee at all that the book which has taken the several years will be better than, or even as good as, the one which has taken the week. But finally the book is written, it goes to a publisher, and here it is either published or it is not published. If it *is* published, it goes to you. It goes to the public, and it is at this point that we become concerned with it.

A question of definition arises: just what is, what makes up, a writer's public? I suppose you can say it's made up of the people who read a writer's books. And yet, curiously enough, we hear of writers who are said to have enormous publics, and in reality they are very little read. Quality is no particular gauge here; this can happen to very bad writers as well as very good ones.

For example, some years ago a famous businessman wrote his autobiography. It was published; it was sold.

From the Pages of *The Critic*

It was in fact on top of the best-seller list for some months. Yet surely very few people sat down and read this book. Perhaps no one did, outside the author's immediate family. And me. I read it: I was sick at the time, it was given to me in the way that bad books are given to the hospitalized. No one wants them around the house, so they are given to those who are thought to be too sick to care. This is doubtful therapy, but it happens all the time, and it happened to me with this book. It was a terrible book and I read it with fascination. As a writer, I realized I was in the presence of a kind of classic: a monstrously bad book, which would nevertheless sell millions.

On the other hand, and to return to the novel, there was the case of *Dr. Zhivago*. When that novel was published in this country and swiftly became a success, it was widely assumed that Boris Pasternak had acquired a great American public overnight. This was not true. Virtually the same thing happened to this novel that happened to the bad autobiography: a great number of copies were sold, and very few were read. I think it's quite safe to say that a very small percentage of those who bought *Dr. Zhivago* actually read it—or even read more than a few pages of it. In contrast to the autobiography, though, this was a genuine loss, for *Dr. Zhivago* is a marvelous book, and yet, like many best-sellers, it was bought for reasons that really had very little to do with the quality of the book itself. So it is entirely possible for a writer to become well-known, even famous— for one of many reasons—and still remain comparatively unread.

But even if we assume that the public we're speaking

Just Good Reading

of *is* a reading public, it is of course a mistake to speak of it as if it were *one* public: a great, single, undiversified mass. It isn't; for every novel there are several publics; they range enormously in taste and in intelligence and in sheer size. The novelist knows this. He knows that when his book is published it will be placed before a great public which is in fact a layer cake of smaller publics. Each layer will respond to him—assuming, that is, that it responds at all—in its own peculiar way, from its own distinct point of view, and with its own separate demands. The writer is fully aware of this, and he is aware, too, that not all of these responses will be of equal value to him.

There is, for example, the response of a very small public, made up, usually, of no more than a handful of people. These are the writer's colleagues, and not just his colleagues, but particular colleagues. Some of them he may know well, some he may know slightly, some he may not know personally at all. But all are among those very few writers for whom the novelist has a special feeling, for whose work he has a particular admiration, and for whose good opinion he cares a great deal. If, when he publishes a book, one or two of these respond with appreciation, perhaps even with enthusiasm, then this gives the novelist a kind of pleasure, a kind of reward which he will get from no one else.

Such a public is, of course, a professional one: its few members are all likely to be working writers. They are insiders, so to speak: they know what the novelist is trying to do, they appreciate the way in which he is trying to do it. But there is another public which is also professional, and is quite different. It is much larger, for one

From the Pages of *The Critic*

thing; it is also infinitely more uneven. This is the public which consists of those critics and reviewers who write about fiction for newspapers and magazines. In a way, this is a strange reading public. In the first place, its members are *paid* to read. They are not paid much—and in the newspapers, this is at least half the trouble—but they are paid: this makes them professionals. And they do not read for themselves. That is, while some of them may read the books for their own pleasure and instruction, their job is specifically to read them for someone else: to pass on their findings, in print, to others. They serve as a kind of bridge between the novelist and the general reader. From time to time there have been those who have questioned the structural soundness of this bridge.

I would say, speaking mildly, that this is not an age distinguished for its critics. Book reviewing in the magazines is apt to be on a higher level than that in the daily or Sunday papers, but this is a faint compliment. Generally speaking, the magazines have their old reliable workhorses who over the course of the years have become familiar, but not necessarily trustworthy—and certainly not inspiring! There are the specialists, who often write with brilliance about their particular hobby horse, but care nothing or less than nothing for the rest of the merry-go-round. There are the poets who, resting up between poems, write about poems, or about novels as if they were poems. There is Leslie Fiedler, who writes about Leslie Fiedler. There are the old Marxists, for whom everything of value in life came to an end when one day the armies of the Soviet Union invaded Finland;

Just Good Reading

they write about everything, but they write in the cold, disappointed prose of ghosts. And there are the professors, perpetually engaged in the most pleasing of academic pursuits: the slaughter of one's colleagues: "It is, however, surprising that so eminent an authority in the field of the novel as Professor Harold Stringtoe should have failed, in his own first novel, to advance beyond the primitive technique of the picaresque. . . ."

All this and more—in the magazines. In the newspapers, the situation is even more disappointing. In the last few years, I think I have seen the book pages—or half-pages, or quarter-pages or columns—of most of the newspapers in this country; with very few exceptions, they are unimpressive. And to say this is to be kind. The pages themselves are physically unattractive; one would think their primary aim was to repel readers at a glance. Quantitatively, the book pages of these papers are bad; qualitatively, they are worse. Quite frequently, the reviews in the smaller papers are faintly disguised steals from reviews which have previously appeared in larger papers; quite frequently, too, they consist largely of quotes from the information sheets supplied by the publishers—scarcely non-partisan material. In some papers very long books are reviewed in a very short sentence; other papers, with a taste for the concise, do not feel the need even for that. A phrase will do: ". . . riproaring farce," or ". . . a corking tale of derring-do."

This sort of thing goes on everywhere and all the time. And the fault is not the reviewers'; it is those who employ them who are to blame. The average newspaper publisher looks upon the book page with no enthusiasm. He knows that in some mysterious way that he

From the Pages of *The Critic*

does not quite understand, it has worked its way into his paper; he does not quite dare to get rid of it altogether: it is thought to have a certain "prestige" value; but he also knows that it does not pay its way in terms of dollars and cents. Accordingly he is unwilling to spend money on it, he gives it the worst space available, his reviewers are given nothing for their efforts but the books they review—and sometimes even the courtesy of a signature on the review is denied—and the final slipshod page serves as nothing but the perfect mirror of the publisher's distaste for the whole enterprise.

The novelist is wise if he pays very little attention to any of this. He is even wiser if he decides, quite early in his career, not to reply in print to his critics. Sometimes this is not easy. No one likes to be attacked, and the first impulse is to retaliate. But my own feeling is that this serves very little purpose. If a novelist feels the need to justify himself, he can do it much more thoroughly through his own books than he can through the limited confines of the correspondence columns of a magazine or newspaper.

Not all writers would agree to this. I know of two or three who are celebrated for the swiftness of their reaction to any critical attention; their names are old familiar friends to the man in charge of the Letters to the Editor: "Dear Sir: In his curious account of my book, *Ashes in My Mouth*, your reviewer, Seymour Mandelman, makes the statement that it is '. . . a thoroughly inexpert job from beginning to end.' I'm afraid a careful reading of his review must raise certain questions as to Mr. Mandelman's own astonishing lack of *expertise*...."

And so forth. Letters of this kind run pretty much to a

Just Good Reading

pattern. They are intended to serve as withering rebuttal, and their main fault is that they really don't wither much of anything. The Seymour Mandelmans of this world do not obligingly dry up and blow away—they write letters back. They *always* write back. And these letters, it appears, must be answered in turn or else—so the novelist feels—he will suffer public humiliation. And so the correspondence continues until at last a halt is called, not by either of the feuding parties, but by a weary editor.

All this wastes time and produces little, but as I say, there are a few novelists who seem to take pleasure in it—who seem, indeed, to find it necessary. I think this is true—that it is necessary, I mean—but I think it's true only because these novelists are not primarily novelists at all. That is, they write novels, but they're not really interested in those novels as such; what they *are* interested in is in having those novels—and themselves—written about and discussed. There is an odd reversal here: what is important is not the novel, but what comes after the novel—the letters, the articles, the protests, the denials, the heated speeches at the cocktail parties. The novel itself is merely the springboard from which one leaps into the stimulating pool of literary controversy. Which is a way to do things, admittedly, but I'm not so sure that it produces very good novels. Or very good novelists.

In my opinion, the novelist is best off when he leaves the critics alone. There are few critics, only a few, whom he can read with profit—for me, they are men like Edmund Wilson or Alfred Kazin; other writers have their own favorites. But for the most part, the writer can

From the Pages of *The Critic*

afford to ignore the rest. If they write about him, he may read them; indeed, he *will* read them—in my experience, most writers read what is written about them: the novelist who scorns to read his notices is pretty much a creature of legend. And in reading them he may be amused or annoyed or pleased or outraged, but he is not likely to be influenced one way or the other. This is not because he is above improvement or superior to correction; it is simply that he knows, quite early in the game, that the great majority of critics will tell him nothing about his own work that he does not already know.

But the public made up of critics and reviewers has at least one thing in common with that other public we spoke of earlier: that one which consists of the few colleagues whom the novelist values most highly. They are both specialized publics, and they are both small. By far the greater part of the novelist's readers belong, of course, to what is usually meant when "The Public" is spoken of: that large public which has as its distinguishing component what Dr. Johnson called "the common reader." The common reader of today is not quite what he was in Dr. Johnson's day, for the readers of books are now stratified into layers and categories which would have been unthinkable in that less complex age. Yet he exists, and he is important, for it is he, in fact, who buys, rents, borrows and persumably reads the novelist's books—on the simplest level possible, it is he who pays the bills. As I say, this is a simple level; it is a level on which the novelist often thinks. He may not be the canniest fellow in the world, this novelist, but he knows that when he goes into his tailor's for the delivery

Just Good Reading

of a suit, if the tailor says, "Eighty-nine fifty, with the alterations," and if he answers "Did you see what they said about me in the last *Kenyon Review?*" an interesting stalemate will result.

For some novelists there are a great many common readers; for others, not so many; for still others, very few. Yet, in whatever numbers, they exist; the novelist knows this, and is grateful for them. And if, suddenly or slowly, their numbers start to grow, to expand, the novelist does not become less grateful. There is, I think, some misunderstanding on this point; there is occasionally a willingness to credit novelists with a greater fastidiousness than perhaps they possess. There exists a persistent suspicion that any novelist worth his salt becomes uncomfortable and possibly even angry if his public threatens to increase.

This has not been my experience. I know many novelists, and some are fairly rarefied figures. I have not noticed that as their sales increase, they grow more resentful. Their first reaction may be one of pleased surprise; the second is usually a quick telephone call to the publisher to ask for more advertising, so that their sales may increase still further.

The truth is that most novelists like to reach as many people as they can; they are not remotely interested in any voluntary restriction of their audience. This is not to say that they will change themselves in order to secure more readers, a greater audience. Any move made in that direction is inevitably perilous. The air of history is filled with the moans of writers who have deliberately set out to placate a public—who have, to put it less nicely, sold themselves and their talent down the river.

From the Pages of *The Critic*

No, pandering to a public is cheap, is wrong, and is dangerous. But if the writer continues to write as well as he knows how, he certainly wishes to be read by as many people as can read and understand him. It is not his goal to write in isolation or comparative isolation; he wants as large a public as it is possible for him to have, and still remain himself.

To suppose anything else is to be hopelessly romantic. For example, let us take a book such as *The Magic Mountain*. Let us take another book, such as *The Carpetbaggers*. Obviously these two books were written on very different levels; obviously one is literature, and the other . . . well, it is not literature. Yet I think Thomas Mann, if he were alive today, would be neither outraged nor insulted if he found that a few of the readers of *The Carpetbaggers* had bought *The Magic Mountain* and were reading it; he would not for a moment consider that he had lost stature as a novelist. A writer can be supremely confident of his own abilities, and still be pleased when he learns that more and more people are finding his work of interest.

Of course, if in gaining this larger and quite different public, he should happen to lose his original one, then that's something else again. To continue with the somewhat unlikely example of Thomas Mann, if he had awakened one morning to discover that all the old admirers of *The Magic Mountain* no longer read him, and that he was now enjoyed by the followers of Harold Robbins . . . well then, he would have had to ask himself some rather pointed questions, the answers to which might not have been comforting.

In general, we can say that the novelist wants to reach

Just Good Reading

as large a public as he legitimately can. We can also say that the novelist of today has certain advantages and disadvantages, in relation to that public, that his predecessors did not have. On the plus side, he has enormous potential readership. There is now near universal literacy; in his wilder moments, today's novelist can almost persuade himself that if nearly everyone can read, perhaps nearly everyone will read *him*. In more lucid moments, today's novelist realizes that despite this, he will never, no matter what he may do, confront and captivate his public as did his predecessors of one-hundred years ago.

The nineteenth century was the Novelist's Century in a way in which the twentieth century never comes close to being. One-hundred years ago novels formed the great popular entertainment. They were read then as they had never been read before, and as they would never be read again. One reason is an obvious one: in this age lived the greatest novelists. It was the century of Tolstoy and Dostoevski and Turgenev; of Flaubert and Balzac; of Jane Austen, of Thackeray, and of Dickens. This is not a bad reason for a century's being called the Century of the Novel.

But it was more than the novelist; it was the public as well. For the public of that time did not read novels; they devoured them. A book was often spoken of in the same terms as food, and consumed as gluttonously. All classes did this, even those who could not read—for the novels of Dickens were read aloud to groups of illiterates. The novel was Everyman's meat, and Everyman ate heartily. And along with that went a sense of *belong-*

From the Pages of *The Critic*

ing to the novel in a way approached by no reader of today.

This was mainly because novels were rarely produced in those days as they are now—as complete books. They came out in parts, and as each part appeared on the stands, the public would seize it, read it and then respond by making their feelings known to the author. They were not at all shy about this; they knew what they wanted, and they wrote to the author, demanding to get it.

Dickens, for example, brought out most of his novels in monthly installments. When the January installment of *Nicholas Nickleby* or *Little Dorrit* appeared, there were many other installments which remained to be written. This gave the public plenty of room to move. It was a more emotional age than our own, and the readers responded emotionally and directly. They wept, cheered, stormed, applauded or cursed, all according to whether or not the slowly developing turns of plot pleased them. And if they protested in sufficient numbers, even the most eminent of novelists sometimes gave in. Dickens did; so did Thackeray. They knew their relationship to their public, and every once in a while, they heeded its suggestions.

I don't recommend this as the approved procedure for the writing of novels, but the fact is that it was done, and done by some of the greatest novelists of all time. The dangers of such a practice can easily be seen, and indeed even then these novelists were sometimes severely criticized for it, but the point is that the public of that time, both because of their tremendous appetite for

Just Good Reading

novels, and because of their involvement with those novels as they were actually being written, could be much closer to the novelist, and could exert far greater pressures on him, than any public before or since.

Certainly no novelist of today has anything like this rapport with his public. Is this a loss? In a way, yes. It is at least a flattering thing for a writer to have visible, tangible and almost limitless evidence that he is directly affecting a great many people, that he is—if only for a short while—deeply penetrating their lives. On the other hand, this involves certain obligations; a public, so aroused, may penetrate right back. Response is fine; every writer wants it, and yet, in order to work, he also wants a certain privacy. Speaking as one who writes novels, and who has at least the normal concern about his public, I can assure you that while readers may not react in quite the vigorous, unbuttoned fashion of a hundred years ago, they are not shy, nor are they silent.

Nor would the writer want them to be. Still, there are limits, and I can remember thinking, only a month or two after *The Last Hurrah* came out, that for me those limits had been just about reached. It was at this time I discovered what I had no need to discover until then: that an unlisted telephone number can be man's best friend.

I am, fortunately for me, a writer whose books happen to be fairly widely read. I am grateful for this. A great many of the people who read my books write and tell me that they do, and I am grateful for this, too. I am not so grateful that I answer these letters, however, and I don't answer them because the business of answering letters, in any kind of conscientious spirit at all, with

From the Pages of *The Critic*

anything more than perfunctory notes, can be an extremely consuming one, and the writer, if he is not careful, will find that he is writing more than ever before, but writing letters rather than books. Especially if many of those letters come, as they do, from students whose only object, as far as I can see, is to get the writer to do their homework for them.

I think a novelist has certain obligations to his public. I think, too, that those obligations should never be allowed to interfere with his work at hand. Because, in the end, what must matter to him most is none of the public we have talked about so far today, but still another one which has up to now remained unmentioned. This is a public which must always be obeyed, no matter what it demands. This is the only public which he can afford to placate, which he can—and indeed, must—set out from the very beginning to please. This is the most important public of all, and, strangely, it is also the smallest public of all. It is so small that it consists of just one person—and this is the novelist himself.

Egocentric as it may sound, the novelist knows that with his own work, he comes first. We have been talking for some time now about the novelist and these separate publics, these different layers of the one great public, each of which responds to a writer's work in its own way, each of which brings to the writer its own kind of reward. But in the end, when a novelist has finished his book, if he can pick that book up, and if he can begin to read it, and continue to read it with the feeling that this is not so bad, that it might even be pretty good; if he can read it, not with *complete* satisfaction, of course—I

Just Good Reading

think no serious writer has ever felt that—but at least with the satisfaction that he has done as well as he can at this particular time, and that the book he has before him comes fairly close to being the book he had originally intended to write; if he can read with that feeling, I say, then he is pleased in a special way, and no matter what else may come to him from others as the result of this book—whether fame, or money, or appreciation—it is quite likely to be this special private pleasure, this special satisfaction which he feels alone, and which he can share with no one, which will be his greatest reward.

OH BABY

by Anthony L. Moore

A SEVEN-FOOT blond bombshell steps out of the passenger side of a rusty menagerie-blue Ford pickup truck. She moves with the skill and grace of a cat. Her shapely legs are outlined by her tight-fitting black denim jeans, as is her richly rounded tush. As she walks toward the truck stop's diner her black leather boots kick up little swirls of dust in the windless dry heat of the desert.

Her jeans, perfectly complimenting her feminine characteristics, seem to absorb the sunlight into an absolute void, even the light reflected off the fuel pumps she passes on her way across the gas station lot doesn't touch her swaying curves. The sun beats down and makes triangles on the back of her loose fitting black leather jacket. Arched, as if caught in an invisible rainbow, on the jacket in a fabric that was once white but is now light grey, are the letters D-O-N-N-A. Below that, in the same well-worn fabric, is the symbol of a giant rat with, as if underlining the meaning of the symbol, the word "rat" in silhouette beneath it.

She stops a moment to admire the rustic heat-beaten highway, the highway that she supposedly lives on day in and day out. Or the highway that she is supposed to believe that she lives on and was raised on. It is but an illusion of life, and for a time she can pretend to believe

Just Good Reading

it. One thing about belief, is that if a person can't believe in something, then he or she may pretend to believe, if only to temporarily convince themselves that they do.

"Hey you, . . . Donna." She turns her head slightly.

"Yea you, bitch." She turns completely around to face the scruffy, mutt-faced man seated sidesaddle on a Harley Davidson 394.

"Yur a big un', ain't ya." Donna slowly walks toward him. "So what ya got fo' me, honey? You know you look real good in them jeans." Donna stops three feet from him.

"If you think you can handle it we can go for a ride, so's you can see what a real . . ." Donna hits the man with such force that he is knocked off his bike and creates a shallow imprint when he lands.

"I know what a real man feels like. I ain't your 'honey.' I grew up real young. I don't take kindly to be called 'bitch.' And I didn't give you permission to call me by name," she says in a tone that resembles a tomcat being wrung out after a good scrub-board washing in somebody's creek.

With all the strength the denim-clad biker can muster he yells, "Bitch, you are dead!" Putting a thumb and forefinger to his mouth, he whistles, long and loud. Bikers pour out of and from behind the diner and swarm toward Donna.

"Remember this," she spits at him over the noise of the charging bikers, while raising, seemingly from nowhere, what appears to be a double-barrel, semi-automatic, repeating, fifty-round, sawed-off, laser-sighted, semi-recoilless rifle. Producing a clip from beneath her

From the Pages of *The Critic*

jacket, she slaps it into place, points the deadly weapon and pulls the trigger. The mouth of this monstrous creation explodes with all the furies of hell. All in the path of the projectiles go down in an explosion of blood and flesh. Leaking pulps are all that remain of the victims who would have tried to do worse to her.

Bikers scatter everywhere in failed attempts to escape the vengeance of Donna. Motorcycles start, but are blown apart by the murderous machine. None get further than twenty feet. The screams of pain and agony can hardly be heard above the double explosion the weapon produces each time Donna squeezes the trigger.

After what seems like hours of blood-letting, there are but two bikers left alive—the one who caused all the commotion and another pleading pitifully for his life, "Please . . . I'll do anything, just don't kill me."

He tries to get up and run, but his leg has been shot off. Standing over the fallen victim, Donna knows what is expected of her. She does it, without a word, without a flinch, without mercy. With a slow squeeze of the trigger, the man's expression quickly turns from horror to pain and agony, then to a look of peace. As she walks away, juices still seep out from the bikers' wounds. She walks over to the biker who was the cause of all this, and stands before him.

Two state troopers drive up to the truck stop and get out of their vehicle with a "hooo-leee-dammm!" and a "Geeehosafat."

Donna lifts the biker from the ground with her empty hand. He has also been shot in the leg—intentionally—but as planned, he will live. She stares him in the eye

Just Good Reading

and speaks to him slowly and distinctly: "You remember one thing, slime face. You don't mess with me, 'cause I wasn't raised to take crap from scum like you."

The state troopers approach and she drops the biker in front of them. Seeing the smoking weapon in her hand, and all the dead bodies, they are smart enough not to arrest the blonde bombshell named Donna. They don't even want to try.

Donna walks slowly to the diner, stepping over the dead, and stops as she enters the doorway. Sitting on a high window ledge next to her head is a jar of baby food, strained peas. She turns her head toward the bottle, then turns to look back over her shoulder seductively in the direction of the troopers. Her sexy snarl turns into a giggle, then a burst of laughter.

"Cut! Cut! Cut! Damn, doll, can't you do anything right! All you had to do was give an animal-like snarl with some sex-appeal and say your line!" a man's voice yells from the direction of the state troopers. "We're selling baby food here, dammit! You have to sell it, make the kids love you, want to grow up to be like you! They have to want to eat what you ate when you were a kid. How's a three-month-old baby supposed to love someone who can't even give a proper snarl! Now get it right!"

The crew sets up again. The dead rise. They are tired, sweaty and restless. They must once again get cleaned up to look like real bikers for yet another take in the TV advertising campaign for "Oh Baby" baby food.

THAT WAS NO ALBATROSS

by Nelson Algren

THE S.S. *Moon of the Orient*, which I boarded in San Francisco on November 14, 1969 (bound for Japan) turned out to be a water-borne nursing-home. I was the youngest passenger. The crew was of my own generation. Which partly explains why it took us seventy-two days to make the crossing. The crew wasn't altogether to blame. East of the West Hebrides we ran into a sixty-mile-an-hour headwind which would have backed us up clear to South Senility, Utah, had it not been for a tailwind of equal velocity. The captain maneuvered his craft sidewise but we were still in peril of being smashed in two until I advised him to try being becalmed. To show him what I meant, I went down to my cabin and lay becalmed. When I got up the sun was out, the seas were running smooth, and the captain was still running the vessel from an astrology handbook bought in Walgreen's.

"Guess weatha cwear up, guess choppy weatha, guess wain cwear the weatha," was all I could get out of *that* one. The only thing the captain didn't seem to be guessing about were the birds that kept following us. He kept going around the deck telling taxpaying Americans, "That bird are albatross." Who ever heard of an alba-

Just Good Reading

tross with a thirty-foot wingspread and *webbed* wings? Fortunately, most of the passengers died *en route.*

South of the Lower Northerlies we ran out of sailcloth. By good luck I'd brought along an extra roll of waxed paper just in case we ran out of paper napkins. When six more died, the waxed paper gave out. We let the arbatrosses have *them.*

Well, I *told* you they weren't albatrosses.

It wasn't the storm that did most of the passengers in. The majority of them died simply because they were that old when they came aboard. The trip was worthwhile, nonetheless, because I got to see Johnny Weismuller on Japanese TV, being warned by a baboon, in Japanese, of the approach of the Blackstone Rangers. I don't understand Japanified Baboonese myself, but I got the idea.

Tokyo isn't a city—it's an explosion. It's the most alive city I've ever seen. New York is poky by comparison. Twelve million people living elbow to elbow, yet maintaining individuality. They move faster than anybody—yet there seems no undue haste. *Control*—the traffic is controlled, the economic explosion is controlled; and the lives of individuals *look* controlled—I haven't been hit by a single panhandler; nobody has yet offered to act as a guide or a tout or to introduce me to his virgin sister. The only beggar I saw was a tall man draped in the black of a Buddhist priest and tinkling a bell for alms. I peeked under his hood—it was an American!

No tipping, no kissing, no handshaking, no hauling, mauling, yanking or back-slapping. It's part of a very big thing about personal dignity here—sustained even in milling throngs.

From the Pages of *The Critic*

An incidental benefit of the incredible crush on the Tokyo subway is that it immobilizes pickpockets. If he has his hands up when he gets in, he can't get them down to your wallet. If he has them down, he can't get them up. Passengers' pockets are thus automatically protected—but unnecessarily so: the Japanese don't steal. I mean that. They don't think in those terms. A Japanese bartender may shake you down outrageously for a drink, but he won't go after your poke directly.

At the racetrack they leave their binoculars beside their racing forms. That's part of the big thing about personal honor, I suspect. Also, everyone is working. Twelve million people—and there's a labor *shortage!*

Personal cleanliness is also striking. If you buy so much as a two-bit cellophane-wrapped sandwich out of a machine, there is a small, moist napkin for your hands enclosed. Immaculate people. And as courteous as they are tidy. By seven in the morning streets of even the poor sections are spick-and-span. I took a tour of what a Japanese friend here terms "a slum." *He* don't know what a slum is.

The intensity of Japanese interest in writing, painting and the arts gives me the idea that Tokyo is going to be, in a time not too far away, what Paris was in the 1880s —the center of the arts for every country. It has all the feel of Paris now. It is so *new*, so *fast* and so *joyous*—an enjoyers' city.

The wonderful knack the Japanese have is for forever experimenting, trying to do things new ways—originating—and yet keeping their ancient forms. For example, the office building opposite my window here looks more like a gigantic tree than a business building. It has a cen-

Just Good Reading

tral beam, like an eleven-story oak with a dark-green cast; and the offices cling to its trunk like foliage.

Trees, water and rocks—these are the ancient forms in which the Japanese enclose new feeling. I saw *Antony and Cleopatra*, in Japanese, in a theater that made me feel I was watching the play in between great sea-walls. The play itself was good for the first three hours. But by the time Antony had died and been resurrected three times, I felt it was time to go. It may *still* be going on. It was too slow and obvious for my own taste.

The impression the Japanese often give, of being cold, is misleading. They are a passionate people but with a controlled passion. On the stage they get wildly demonstrative; but not on the street. Except, of course, when it's political, as in Shinjuku recently when the Shinjuku students—as well as workers—battled police for five hours trying to stop trains carrying American fuel through the area.

I've always thought I could make it as a stand-up comic, and that suspicion is now confirmed. I don't even have to stand up here. All I have to do is sit down in a snack bar with a sign in English outside—COFFEE & HOT DOG—and ask for coffee and a hot dog. The place breaks up. Apparently the "coffee" part isn't hilarious. It's the "hot dog" business. I've mentioned hot dogs to countermen and vendors in Chicago, but they don't have the sense of humor of the Japanese. Curiously, if I say *"Hawta* dog," all I get is a hot dog, and no laughs at all. Sometimes I don't say *anything* and they break up. Marvelous sense of humor.

A pretty twenty-two-year-old Japanese girl asked me,

From the Pages of *The Critic*

"You like to play *patinko* wid me?" I'd like to play *anything* wid her. *Particularly patinko.*

Pachinko is the rage and there isn't a block that doesn't have at least one *Pachinko* parlor. It is played by feeding small steel balls into a kind of vertical pinball machine; and if a ball falls into an opening in the machine's center, lights go on and it returns a handful of steel balls. If the player is both skillful and lucky, he can redeem his winnings at a cashier's desk.

Yet the game doesn't seem to be played for the sake of winning money. "When there is no one to talk to, you talk to a *patinko* masrine," the Japanese girl told me.

An old man of the middle-class was sitting in front of the Shinjuku Station here for three days with a sign: *Please Talk To Me.* Milling multitudes passed him, yet no person spoke to the old man. On the third day a younger man sat down on the corner across from the old man. His sign read: *You say something first.* The old man went home.

"*Pachinko* is a monologue of the lonely," Suji Terayama assured me. "The life here is outwardly joyous and full of amusements. But people are not amused. How sad their private lives are can be seen when young men stand for hours feeding small steel balls into a machine."

Yet it seems to take very little to get Japanese people laughing. They break up at a touch. For example, my telephone rings and a male voice informs me: "I spreak no Engrish. I spreak only Japanese"—laughter.

"I speak only English," I assured the voice. "I can't speak Japanese."

277

Just Good Reading

This, it seems, is funny too.
Voice: "Hord line one morment prease."
I hord line.
Second male voice: "This man spreak no Engrish. He spreak onry Japanese."
"I can't speak Japanese. Only English."
This time they *both* break up.
Finally: "Srank you very much. Goodbye."
This happens several times a day. I'd like to get in on the joke too.

Prostitution is illegal here. It was outlawed in 1957. Then what are those mini-skirted lovelies doing smiling to me under a red lantern? If they're secretaries, they're working awfully late.

What the Japanese do with neon is to make a fairyland of this city at night: the signs don't pitch, like American ads, by hard-selling: *BUY!* They seduce your eyes in purple, chartreuse, violet, orange, chinese red, pale pale blue, silver and green—signs that move in squares, in circles, up, down and sidewise in an alphabet consisting of pictures rather than letters. English is the second language, but it's running a poor second. French is third, and not too far behind to catch up. The French seem to be better liked here than Americans. Well, they never blasted a Japanese city as a demonstration of military might, for one reason.

It would be one of the great ironies of history if, in return for the most deathly strike any people ever inflicted upon another, the East should return that explosion with a life-giving one: if the arts of the West should be drawn away from Paris, London, and New York to the great cities of the Orient. After witnessing the con-

From the Pages of *The Critic*

dition of the arts in Chicago, one can only hope something like that is happening.

These people are nothing if not logical—especially if you're caught jaywalking in the middle of Tokyo traffic. These little cars keep at sixty, and they don't stop when there's no red light. It's *Jump, mother*—and mother jumps. So you see, that stuff about "Day of Infamy" is all wrong—they were just going that way, that's all.

I'll modify my observation about no kissing—mothers kiss their babies. I can't help wondering if in the privacy of their homes husbands kiss their wives—or do they keep bowing.

This bowing isn't just politeness. It's part of conversation: discussion is punctuated by bowing. The woman's deep bow to the man as she is introduced, and his short bow in return, indicate, I take it, that his station is higher than her own. Which is still how it is in Japan.

My two Japanese friends—Terayama and the twenty-two-year-old girl, Keiko—are modern young people whose ways and dress and interests are Western. Yet, after we had spent a day together Keiko told me, "Mr. Terayama aparigize because he cannot do Lady-First."

After a minute, I got it: I'd been opening doors for her to go first, helping her on with her coat, all the customary American deferences of the man to the woman. But a young Japanese man, like Terayama, doesn't 'even *think* of such deference—and the Japanese girl doesn't expect it. "Mr. Terayama must not aparigize because he is Japanese man."

It's perfectly natural for a man to hit his wife or daughter, Keiko believes, "if she deserve." But it is *never* all right for a woman to strike a man. Which accounts,

Just Good Reading

in part, for the relative contentment of Japanese women, compared to the disatisfied, irritable, unresponsive and boring American female. They have better taste, too.

This is my second ocean-passage to the Orient. The first was aboard an American cargo-liner, in 1962, on which I was the only passenger. By visits to Singapore, Kowloon, Calcutta, Pusan and Madras I acquired much of the Wisdom of the Ancient East. All of which I inculcated in the Confucianism: *Never Play Lowball with the Crew of an American Cargo-liner; or: There's been a terrible accident between starboard and port.*

Startling as this concept may appear, I have already expanded it on my present tour: *Never eat in a place with sliding doors unless you're crazy about raw fish.*

MY LIFE WITH HILAIRE BELLOC
—I THINK

by Sylvia Haymon

YOU know the way people, as they get older, say they can't for the life of them tell you what they did last week, but can remember every last detail of their childhood as if it happened yesterday? I am sorry to say that of late I have noticed that my friends, which is to say my contemporaries, have taken to reminiscing like mad about their early years, from which I must deduce that I too am not as young as I like to pretend.

It worries me, those confident excursions into the dear, dead past. How can they be so sure they've got the record straight? Because, speaking for myself, while I can't remember with the best of them what I was up to a week ago come Monday, the key incidents of my own childhood don't seem to me all that crystal-clear either. Whenever I dream myself back there, everything goes like a bomb up to a point, then—wham! it's gone like the punch line of a joke. I find this very disturbing.

Take the Hilaire Belloc episode. It has been a big thing in my life, the way, as a child, I deliberately tripped up Hilaire Belloc. As a story to work round to, it has always seemed to me to have everything—a famous name, humor, suspense, tragedy, farce; plus the obvious, flattering implication that as early as the age of ten I was already a personality in my own right.

Just Good Reading

What happened was that Hilaire Belloc came to my school to give out the prizes. Lord knows why he came because right from the word go he looked as though he was loathing every second of it, a square, purplish lump of a man, who just sat squat like a coal bunker on the platform in the Assembly Hall glowering at the unhappy parents down below.

From time to time he rotated his bulk ponderously and glowered at us, the pupils, for a change. We were ranged in tiers behind him, with the Sixth Form up near the ceiling and my form the lowest, down at platform level. So there I was, all got up in my white school best, slightly to the rear and three yards to the left of Our Distinguished Guest.

When the time came for him to speak he made a rotten speech, not half as good as the Chairman of the Governors who had spoken first and understood about putting in the jokes. What made it worse was that our expectations had been aroused. For weeks we'd had it drummed into us that Hilaire Belloc was a Great Humorist, and we had our laughter ready and all systems go. When he didn't say a single thing to trigger it off it made us feel terrible, like wanting to hiccup, only you can't.

All he did was stand there and get angry—with English education, English government, the Church of England, and English womanhood, which came in for particularly rough handling. We quite understood that what it all amounted to was that he was angry with us for having, somehow, landed him in his present situation; and, naturally enough, we got angry back.

From the Pages of *The Critic*

When I say "we" I know I should say "I," because of course I can't vouch for the way everybody else was feeling. Still, I feel pretty safe saying "we." We watched him getting bigger and squarer and purpler all the time like some horrendous, apoplectic toad, and waited hopefully for him to go pop. It was interesting to watch and almost made up for the complete lack of jokes.

As it turned out he didn't go pop, though the headmistress and the Chairman of Governors nearly did by the time he had finished. After that he handed out the prizes, turning his nose up at the titles and shoving the books hard against the prize-winners' rib cages, as if he were trying to see how many he could crack.

I didn't get a prize. I just sat in that front row at the back of the platform and took it all in. And when at last it was all over and, with the headmistress leading the way, Hilaire Belloc stumped across the platform as if he couldn't get down from it fast enough, I stuck out a leg and tripped him up.

He fell heavily and, falling, grabbed at the nearest thing within reach, which happened to be the headmistress's long black taffeta evening skirt. It gave way with that almost human shriek taffeta lets out when you rip it. Or perhaps it was the headmistress, because the next minute there she was in her sequinned top and camiknicks streaking for the exit like a moujik with the wolves after him; and there was Hilaire Belloc, the skirt draped round his shoulders like the cloak in the Sandeman ad, rolling about the floor of the platform laughing, and growing so purple that one of the fathers in the front row got up onto the platform, thumped him on the

Just Good Reading

back, and poured him some water from the carafe (I remembered it was cut-glass, Jacobean design, with a slight chip in the lip) that always stood on the table at prize-givings.

It so happened that nobody had noticed me sticking my leg out, and as the two separate bits of drugget that were always put down on the platform on special occasions met just about where I had been sitting, the handyman who had laid them got his cards next day. I suppose I should have owned up to save him being sacked, but there it is, I didn't; after all, I was only ten. I didn't tell anyone, actually, but my best friend and a few dozen other girls under strict pledge of secrecy, and they all thought I was lying; so Hilaire Bellock had his revenge, in a way. Not until I grew up did I come to perceive what a watershed the incident had been in my life—the birth of me as an individual, the issuance of a card of identity, negative into positive, B.C. into A.D., and so on.

But lately, somehow, with all this ripe Old English autobiography simmering round me all the time, I'm beginning to wonder whether a card of identity isn't a season ticket valid for a specified period only, or even a cheap off-peak; whether I haven't polished my prize-giving story so long and lovingly over the years that I can't be sure any more whether the headmistress lost her skirt or only might have, and it isn't all some giveaway Freudian nastiness I'd do well to stay mum about.

As for that climactic, hypostatic leg, I couldn't swear any longer that it was there or that it wasn't there. There are times when I see it as clearly, etc., etc.—black patent

From the Pages of *The Critic*

anklestrap over white sock with a wavy rib pattern and a dirty mark on the instep where Marjorie Prince, the clumsy clot, stood on my foot in the way up the platform stairs. I really do see it.

At least, I think I see it. At least, I think I think I see it. At least.

THOUGHTS ON THE GOSPELS

by Abbie Jane Wells

I KEEP wishing that Jesus had kept notebooks during his 40 days in the wilderness and afterward—then maybe we would have more to go on as to what he thought or meant. We tend to think he saw things through our eyes and minds, and it is hard to try to see things through his eyes and mind. He said, "All I have done you shall do and more," and I am beginning to wonder if maybe we are supposed to start with 40 days in the wilderness, as he did, and go on from there, in our own way, thinking things through. I am trying to do my "40 days" now in my own way, and it may take me 40 years! It is certainly taking me a lot longer to think things through than it took Jesus, but then, it might have taken him longer if he had done it in the 20th century, for there are so many more things to think through now than there were in the first century—2000 years worth of more stuff, near-abouts.

* * *

I always wondered what might have happened to the robbed and beaten man after the Good Samaritan had left him. If the innkeeper was out to make an extra buck, he could have put the robbed and beaten man back out beside the highway to see if someone else would have pity and bring him back in to be cared for. He could run

From the Pages of *The Critic*

one wounded man through many times, getting paid every time someone brought him in, maybe using the same wounded man as long as he lasted.

You can see that the story requires an innkeeper who could be depended on to do what he was paid to do. And it requires a Good Samaritan with money in his pocket, too. What if he had been without funds? Then what would he have done for the wounded man; cared for him himself? Maybe that's why the priest and Levite didn't stop—not because they had no pity but because they had no money to pay an innkeeper to care for him.

* * *

I think one of the reasons so many people shy away from things is that it hurts when anyone suffers a loss. God must hurt all the time—and Jesus, too, and all the company of heaven. Why do people think heaven is peaceful, placid, non-involved with what goes on in the world? Man, when you are in heaven you see it all and feel it all, not just one spot of it. Heaven is where you will become *fully* aware of all that goes on in the world and I am not at all sure that I am going to be able to take that. I'm having problems enough with just the little bit I see and feel here on Earth. People are going to have an awful lot of adjustments to make when they get to heaven, for I doubt it's like most people think it is. Couldn't possibly be.

* * *

You know, the Prodigal Son story ends with the boy's return and the father's open-armed and open-hearted welcome. Everybody usually assumes, "And they all lived happily ever after"—no differences of opinions

Just Good Reading

between the two brothers ever marring the peace and tranquility of the father's house.

But I wonder if it was all that tranquil after young Bud returned? I'll bet it was more peaceful for the father *before* he returned, and for the elder brother, too—no fights or disagreements between the kids to have to mediate. Elder brother got all of Pa's attention while the young'un was gone, now he must share. And the prodigal had lots of adapting back into the ways of his father's household when he returned. (I doubt if the elder brother was much help there.) I am sure that the father was understanding of the fact that even though the prodigal wanted to come back, it would take him a while to get back into the groove. But I imagine it took the elder brother quite awhile before he adapted to not being the only son around to help Dad, the only son for the old man to call upon or talk to. Now there were two sons to be considered.

Well, for awhile at least, I'll bet it was anything but the "and they all lived happily ever after" routine, for there was an awful lot of adjusting for all of them to do. Not that Pa hadn't always considered the prodigal a son, even while he was gone, but the boy was now underfoot all the time, and even though the father's welcome was so spontaneously joyous, I'll bet it took him quite a spell to get used to the idea that Sonny Boy was right here at home, to be in on everything.

One of the problems is that so much theology about God the Father is done by men who are fathers in name only. I don't think you can know what being a father is really like until you become a father yourself. The feeling of being a father, or a mother, comes only with ex-

From the Pages of *The Critic*

perience. You just think you know what it's like and what it's all about until you become one, and then you find out all the nuances and inflections you missed.

That's why we get a different picture of God in the New Testament than in the Old—he was different. He was now a father in his own right, no longer just a proxy father but a father for real. And he learned a lot about fathers and children by becoming a father himself—the ultimate being when he found out how a father—or mother—feels when something bad happens to their child which they are unable to prevent.

* * *

Once a priest friend said something about John the Baptist's first recognition of Jesus—how he knew who Jesus was the minute he saw him in the desert, like he had had a vision or was told by God—and I said, "Of course he knew who Jesus was! He had always known. His mom, Elizabeth, had told him how he leapt in her womb when she saw Mary. In fact, he had probably heard that story many, many times—we all have a habit of talking forever after about our unusual and breath-taking experiences. Perhaps the first thing Elizabeth told her son John as soon as he was able to understand, and maybe even before that, was about the son of Mary and what had happened the moment she saw Mary.

And Mary told Jesus who his Father was as soon as he was old enough to know. He had to take Mary's word for it, as Joseph did—and as my son and his father have to take my word for who the father of my child is, for only I know what I did with every moment of my life, and I am the only one who knows if I was true to my

Just Good Reading

husband. They had to trust and believe me, without proof. So does every man—no way he can know for sure unless he keeps his wife under lock and key 24 hours a day, unless he trusts her to be faithful so that he has no reason to doubt when she says she is going to have a baby, and he knows he is the father without her proving he is or proving she is faithful, because he trusts her to be faithful.

And speaking of faith and trust—Paul had to have a lot to even let Ananias get near him, even to cure his blindness. For Ananias was one of those Paul had been persecuting and he might have had in mind to get rid of the persecutor for good by doing him in rather than returning his sight (or so Paul might have thought). A lot like George Wallace would have to have a hell of a lot of faith and trust (this is a pre-1976 thought) to let a black person he didn't know get near enough to lay hands on him even if he said he could make George walk again as good as new.

And I'll bet those who crucified Christ—involved in it in any way—steered clear of him during Resurrection days for fear of retaliation. Never could understand those "out to get those who crucified Christ" through their descendents. Christ had 40 days to do any retaliation and he did nothing, so why should his followers down through the ages try to finish something for him that he never started and wasn't about to start? His, "Father, forgive them" from the cross was all-inclusive, unconditional, and without them admitting guilt and begging for forgiveness . . . There were none left unpardoned on either side. He forgave Judas, too, and the dis-

From the Pages of *The Critic*

ciples for hiding out, and Peter for denying him during the trial and crucifixion.

Jesus did no retaliation after the Resurrection, but the crucifiers didn't know for sure that he wouldn't, so they must have kept a low profile. It is sad that Jesus' followers have tried to retaliate ever since—they don't see that retaliation wasn't something he ever thought of doing. And much blood has been shed down through the ages by people "doing for Jesus" what he doesn't want done.

* * *

That dream the wise men had, to return home by a different way—the Bible doesn't say it was a dream from God as was Joseph's dream to take the child and his mother to Egypt. Why does everyone assume that the wise men's dream was from God, too?

And have you ever looked at it from Herod's point of view? Here's a King who sees wise men bearing gifts, but not to him. That alone would make a King mighty mad, regardless of who the gifts were for. And then they promise to return and tell him what they found and where—and they don't. They go back on their word, and that, too, would make a King mighty mad. The wise men treated Herod the way nobody in their right mind would treat a King—shabbily.

Another thing. If Herod had really wanted to find the Babe, wouldn't he have sent one of his own men that he trusted to follow the wise men, so he could come back and tell him where they went, etc., rather than depend wholly on these strangers to be men of their word and come back?

Just Good Reading

Have you ever wondered what might have happened if the wise men had gone back to Herod, and the questions Herod would have asked about any King, newborn or not? Like: "How many soldiers does he have?" —"Well, there were two, and one of them was his mother." "How many servants?"—"Well, there were two, and one of them was his mother." "How many followers?"—"Well, there were two, and one of them was his mother." "What's his palace like? How well fortified?"—"Well, it's a stable, with no fortifications."

This is a threat? To any King?

Could be that if the wise men had gone back to Herod, things might have been different.

Besides, the shepherds went and were changed by what they saw. The wise men went and they were changed. Herod, who said he wanted to go, too, was prevented from going. Maybe this made him a changed man, too—a *more* violent man. 'Tis possible, had Herod seen the Babe, he might have been changed by what he saw, into a *less* violent, maybe even nonviolent, man.

And I wonder how the wise men felt when they heard about the slaughter of the innocents. Did they wonder among themselves, "Maybe if we had disregarded that dream and gone back maybe something we could have said to Herod would have simmered him down so he wouldn't have struck out so violently and blindly in a rage."

It always makes me mad when people don't do what they say they will do, unless they have made clear that maybe they won't. And I wonder if perhaps Herod was as mad at the wise men as he was at anyone—taking it out on the innocent babes as much because he couldn't

From the Pages of *The Critic*

get at the wise men as because he couldn't get to the Christ Child—as "Child Abuse" often is. Taking gifts to the King into whose country you come is the thing to do—always has been the thing to do; and keeping your word to the King has always been the thing to do, too. The wise men did neither. They weren't as "wise" as people think. You just don't do this sort of thing to a King, no way, no how.

I WISH I'D SAID THAT
A Mini-Anthology

Accumulated by Dan Herr

"Ain't no sense in worrying about things you got control over, 'cause if you got control over them, ain't no sense worrying. And there ain't no sense worrying about things you got no control over, 'cause if you got no control over them, ain't no sense in worrying about them."

Mickey Rivers

"Ernest Hemingway wrote boys' books for adults."

Paul Horgan

"Everybody is somebody."

J. Morgan Puett

"Our ignorance of history makes us libel our own times. People have always been like this."

Flaubert

"You gotta take the sour with the bitter."

Samuel Goldwyn

From the Pages of *The Critic*

"An artist is born kneeling; he fights to stand. A critic, by nature of the judgment seat, is born sitting."

Hortense Calisher

"If you can sell green toothpaste in this country, you can sell opera."

Sarah Caldwell

"Of course, America had often been discovered before Columbus, but it had always been hushed up."

Oscar Wilde

"The danger of the past was that men became slaves. The danger of the future is that men may become robots."

Erich Fromm

"It does not do to leave a dragon out of your calculations, if you live near him."

J. R. R. Tolkien

"Critics are like eunuchs in a harem, They're there every night, they see it done every night, they see how it should be done every night, but they can't do it themselves."

Brendan Behan

Just Good Reading

"My father used to say 'Superior people never make long visits.'"

Marianne Moore

"If you would be unloved and forgotten, be reasonable."

Kurt Vonnegut

"The optimist claims that we live in the best of all possible worlds; and the pessimist fears this is true."

James Branch Cabell

"God invented football so grown boys would have something to do between wars."

Dan Jenkins

"If you want to find the most efficient way of doing something, give the job to the laziest person in your organization."

John C. Tully

"A mouse is nature's way of telling you to get a cat."

Janice Hopkins Tanne

From the Pages of *The Critic*

"Why can we remember the tiniest detail that has happened to us and not remember how many times we have told it to the same person?"

Francois La Rochefoucauld

"Joy is the most infallible sign of the presence of God."

Teilhard de Chardin

"Only childhood is ours. The rest belongs to strangers."

Don DeLillo

"The acme of prose style is exemplified by that simple, graceful clause, 'Pay to the order of.'"

Robert Heinlein

"Yes, Mrs. Dehning was a woman whose rasping insensibility to gentle courtesy deserved the prejudice one cherished against her, but she was a woman, to do her justice, generous and honest, one whom one might like better the more one saw her less."

Gertrude Stein

Just Good Reading

"Let us pray: O Lord, give us a sense of humor with courage to manifest it forth, so that we may laugh to shame the pomps, the vanities, the sense of self-importance of the Big Fellows that the world sometimes sends among us, and who try to take our peace away. Amen."

Sean O'Casey

"There is such a thing as too much couth."

S. J. Perelman

"Show me a good loser and I'll show you a loser."

Bear Bryant

"The only way to keep your health is to eat what you don't want, drink what you don't like, and do what you'd rather not."

Mark Twain

"A liberal is somebody who will do the right thing for the wrong reasons so that he can feel good for eight minutes."

Mort Sahl

From the Pages of *The Critic*

"The teaching in the Gospels to turn the other cheek is not a miracle of holiness or the pinnacle of flexibility but the only practical way out of a situation in which appearance is the judge of reality."

Boris Pasternak

"The American people, taking one with another, constitute the most timorous, sniveling, poltroonish, ignominious mob of serfs and goose-steppers ever gathered under one flag in Christendom since the end of the Middle Ages."

H. L. Mencken

"Moderation should never be confused with indecisiveness. On the contrary, a lack of self-confidence in one's most basic commitments is often expressed in extremism. Only one who is sure of what he stands for can afford to be moderate."

Norman Lamm

"The first half of our lives is ruined by our parents and the second half by our children."

Clarence Darrow

Just Good Reading

"You can have too much champagne, but never enough."

         An Archbishop of Rheims

"The Irish are a fair people;—they never speak well of one another."

         Samuel Johnson

"Asking a working writer what he thinks about critics is like asking a lamp-post how it feels about dogs."

         Christopher Hampton

"Mugging is usually no more than begging by force."

         Geoff Dyer

"If you live long enough, people think you are brighter than you are."

         James Michener

"In a consumer society there are inevitably two kinds of slaves: the prisoners of addiction and the prisoners of envy."

         Ivan Illich

From the Pages of *The Critic*

"People sup together, play together, travel together, but they do not think together. Hardly any homes have any intellectual life whatsoever, let alone one that informs the vital interests of life."

Allan Bloom

"What the American public always wants is a tragedy with a happy ending."

William Dean Howells

"The only polite thing to do when engaged in sky diving . . . or any other dangerous sport is die. That's what everyone's waiting around for."

P. J. O'Rourke

"When you go places where people are sort of nobodies, and you have to think of what to say to them, it's so hard."

Andy Warhol

"Next to ingratitude, the most painful thing to bear is gratitude."

Henry Ward Beecher

Just Good Reading

"It's not the world that's got so much worse but the news coverage that's got so much better."

G. K. Chesterton

"All human life has its seasons, and no one's personal chaos can be permanent: winter, after all, does not last forever, does it? There is summer, too, and spring, though sometimes when branches stay dark and the earth cracks with ice, one thinks they will never come, that spring, that summer, but they do, and always."

Truman Capote

"Charity is not the art of repressing differences, but rather the art of finding creative compromises."

Andrew Greeley

"A child knows most of the game—it is only an attitude to it that he lacks."

Graham Greene

"Fear less, hope more; whine less, breathe more; talk less, say more; hate less, love more; and all good things are yours."

Anonymous

From the Pages of *The Critic*

"If you don't got the ball, you can't shoot the ball."

                                            Moses Malone

"All civilization is based on a proper observance of ceremonial."

                                    Ancient Chinese proverb

"Beware of converts; they carry stakes and faggots and matches."

                                              Joseph Epstein

"All cruel people describe themselves as paragons of frankness."

                                    Tennessee Williams

"Impropriety is the soul of wit."

                                    W. Somerset Maugham

"Idealism increases in direct proportion to one's distance from the problem."

                                    John Galsworthy

Just Good Reading

"People will sometimes forgive you the good you have done them, but seldom the harm they have done you."

W. Somerset Maugham

"When someone does us an evil turn we engrave his name in marble; but when someone does us a good turn we write the name in dust."

Saint Thomas More

"Being against men is like being against death. I don't see the point."

Margaret Drabble

"No one can hate like a close relative."

Dorothy Parker

"In heaven an angel is nobody in particular."

George Bernard Shaw

"I don't know the key to success, but the key to failure is trying to please everybody."

Bill Cosby

From the Pages of *The Critic*

"A merry story exchanged with a friend refreshes us much and without harm lightens our minds and restores our courage and soothes our stomachs."

Thomas More

"All happy families resemble one another, but each unhappy family is unhappy in its own way."

Leo Tolstoy

"He who hesitates is sometimes saved."

James Thurber

"Advertising is the revenge of business on culture."

Doug Lucie

"The Latin church, which I find myself admiring more and more despite its frequent, astounding imbecilities, has always kept clearly before it the fact that religion is not a syllogism but a poem."

H. L. Mencken

"Only the winners decide what were war crimes."

Garry Wills

Just Good Reading

"The Bible tells us to love our neighbors and also to love our enemies; probably because generally they are the same people."

G. K. Chesterton

"The greatest love is a mother's; then comes a dog's; then comes a sweetheart's."

Polish proverb

"As one becomes older the shadows lengthen and the solitude becomes harder to endure."

T. S. Eliot

"Tread softly because you tread on my dreams."

William Butler Yeats

"People come to you for advice, they don't want you to tell them what to do. They want you to find out what they've already decided to do and then agree with them."

Robert Campbell

"You don't have to deserve your mother's love. You have to deserve your father's. He's more particular."

Robert Frost

From the Pages of *The Critic*

"The second half of the 20th century is a complete flop."

>Isaac Bashevis Singer

"Never hold discussions with the monkey when the organ grinder is in the room."

>Winston Churchill

"Just when I thought there was no way to stop the Japanese from steadily widening their lead over American industry, I saw a headline in the paper that said 'JAPAN TO OPEN ITS DOORS TO AMERICAN LAWYERS.' That ought to do it."

>Calvin Trillin

"The only constant is change."

>Martha Graham

"An American Catholic is a Protestant who goes to Mass."

>Conor Cruise O'Brien

"When people give you their reasons for liking or disliking cats, it usually develops that cats themselves are rarely the issue."

>Stephanie Brush

Just Good Reading

"Our senses can grasp nothing that is extreme; too much noise deafens us; too much light blinds us; too far or too near prevents us from seeing."

Blaise Pascal

"Show me a hero and I will write you a tragedy."

F. Scott Fitzgerald

"Poetry is simply poor punctuation. A poem is a thought unworthy of a paragraph, random words tossed on the page, literary lint. Poems are Laura Ashley prints for the mind, unicorn dung."

Paul Rudnick

"The best thing about animals is that they don't talk much."

Thornton Wilder

"Television is called a medium because it is rare that it is well done."

Fred Allen

"A friend in need is a pest."

Joe E. Lewis

From the Pages of *The Critic*

"A fish rots from the head first—it starts at the top."

> Old Greek saying

"Oh what a tangled web we weave when first we practise to deceive!"

> Sir Walter Scott

"A sportsman is a man who, every now and then, has to go out and kill something."

> Stephen Leacock

"A hospital is no place to be sick."

> Clare Boothe Luce

"One starts to get young at the age of 60, and then it's too late."

> Picasso

"Nouveau riche is better than no riche at all."

> Imelda Marcos

"Freedom is nothing else but a chance to be better."

> Albert Camus

Just Good Reading

"Beware of the young doctor and the old barber."

Benjamin Franklin

"Fame is when you market your aura."

Andy Warhol

"Nobody will ever win the battle of the sexes. There's too much fraternization with the enemy."

Henry Kissinger

"Men commit the error of not knowing when to limit their hopes."

Niccolo Machiavelli

"Anybody who has survived childhood has enough information about life to last him the rest of his days."

Flannery O'Connor

"What beastly incidents our memories insist on cherishing, the ugly and the disgusting. The beautiful things we have to keep diaries to remember."

Eugene O'Neill

From the Pages of *The Critic*

"How old would you be if you didn't know how old you was?"

Satchel Paige

"It is undesirable to believe a proposition when there is no ground whatever for supposing it true."

Bertrand Russell

"The game of status seeking, organized around committees, is played in roughly the same fashion in Africa, in America and in the Soviet Union. Perhaps the aptitude for this committee game is part of our genetic inheritance, like the aptitude for speech and for music."

Freeman Dyson

"The art of teaching consists of tactful condescension."

Ralph McInerny

"First you are young; then you are middle-aged; then you are old; then you are wonderful."

Diana Cooper

Just Good Reading

"Writing is like prostitution. First you do it for the love of it, then you do it for a few friends, and finally you do it for money."

Moliere

"A cat has absolute emotional honesty: human beings, for one reason or another, may hide their feelings, but a cat does not."

Ernest Hemingway